—THREE VIEWS—
ON THE
RAPTURE
PRE; MID; OR POST-TRIBULATION?

Books in the Counterpoints Series

—THREE VIEWS—
ON THE
RAPTURE
PRE; MID; OR POST-TRIBULATION?

Gleason L. Archer Jr.

Paul D. Feinberg

Douglas J. Moo

Richard R. Reiter

Previously titled *The Rapture*

ZondervanPublishingHouse
Grand Rapids, Michigan

A Division of HarperCollins*Publishers*

Three Views on the Rapture
Copyright © 1984, 1996 by The Zondervan Corporation,
Grand Rapids, Michigan.

Previously titled *The Rapture*

Requests for information should be addressed to:

📖 ZondervanPublishingHouse
Grand Rapids, Michigan 49530

Library of Congress Cataloging-in-Publication Data

Three views on the Rapture : pre-, mid-, or post-Tribulation ? / Gleason L.
    Archer, Jr. . . . [et al.].
            p.   cm. — (Counterpoints)
        Rev. ed. of: The Rapture. c1984.
        Includes bibliographical references (p.   ) and indexes.
        ISBN: 0-310-21298-7
        1. Rapture (Christian eschatology)   2. Tribulation (Christian eschatology)
    I. Archer, Gleason Leonard, 1916–   . II. Rapture.   III. Series: Counter-
    points (Grand Rapids, Mich.)
    BT887.R37 1996
    236'.9—dc 20   96–22775
                                                                                      CIP

Edited by Ben Chapman
Designed by Louise Bauer

Printed in the United States of America

98 99 00 01 02 /❖ DH/ 10 9 8 7 6 5 4

CONTENTS

PREFACE

One of the chief obstacles in coming to decisions on theological issues is the lack of interaction among proponents of competing views. Books and articles advocating one position or another are available, but one is often left wondering whether strengths have been overstated and weaknesses ignored or underplayed. Moreover, many readers are unprepared to evaluate the sometimes technical evidence advanced in support of a view. All too often such arguments appear more compelling than they really are. Even when two excellent statements of alternative positions are available, points made in one statement may not be dealt with in the other.

Such is certainly the case with respect to the issue of the time of the Rapture in relation to the Tribulation. Many excellent treatments of this theological question from various viewpoints are available; but there is still room for a careful, "head-to-head" discussion in which the alternative positions are evaluated. The present volume is intended to fill that need.

The three major essays of this book are revised and expanded versions of papers presented at the January, 1981, meeting of the Ministerial Association of the Evangelical Free Church of America. The authors write as members of this denomination, as colleagues on the faculty of its seminary (Trinity Evangelical Divinity School), and as personal friends. We write with charity and respect for one another but with no less conviction with regard to our own views. We write with forthrightness in exposing what we perceive to be weaknesses in each other's arguments. For some, the advocacy of differing positions on the Rapture among colleagues on the same faculty may seem incongruous. All three of us are wholeheartedly devoted to upholding the clear truths of Scripture but we do not believe that the relative time of the Rapture is one of these "clear truths."

The responses to the major essays have been written independently. While this format makes some repetition inevitable, it also allows greater freedom and better enables the reader to discern the differences in the various positions. Without intending any slight to other eschatological positions, we write from the standpoint of a premillennial eschatology.

Evangelicals in America have frequently been divided over the issue of Rapture. It is our hope that these essays and responses will promote an atmosphere of unity and tolerance in which the issue can be honestly and reverently discussed. Above all we trust that we may all be encouraged to conform ourselves to the character and conduct of the One whose return we await.

1

A HISTORY OF THE DEVELOPMENT OF THE RAPTURE POSITIONS

Richard R. Reiter

Richard R. Reiter is Market Data Systems Manager, Nations-Banc–CRT, Chicago, Illinois. He holds degrees from Michigan State University (M.S.) and Trinity Evangelical Divinity School (M.Div.). He has taken additional graduate study at McCormick Theological Seminary, Regent College (Vancouver), the University of Chicago, and Wheaton College (Illinois). He is A.B.D., at New York University. Mr. Reiter is a member of the the Conference on Faith and History and the Evangelical Theological Society.

The basic confessions of Christianity testify to the biblical teaching that Jesus Christ will return to earth to judge the living and the dead. Beyond this base for unity Christians developed diverse views on the nature and time of Christ's return. This essay examines the debate about the Second Coming in recent American history. The focus is on American Evangelicals who agreed that Christ will return before the Millennium, but who differed on whether the Rapture of the church would be before, in the middle of, or after the Great Tribulation.

This study covers just over one hundred years—from 1878 to the present. Within this era I shall examine three shorter periods initiated by key transitional events. The first was the three decades from 1878 through 1909, when differences in prophetic interpretation and related matters raised controversy within the Niagara Bible Conference. Next, spanning the time from 1909 to 1952, the advocates of pretribulationism gained widespread popular support and built their base of scholarship. From 1952 to the present we have seen the resurgence of posttribulationism through the scholarly growth of that perspective and diverse challenges to the dominance of pretribulationism among American Evangelicals.

THE NIAGARA BIBLE CONFERENCE ERA:
1878–1909

The Niagara Bible Conference popularized premillennial doctrine in North America. A few pastors and evangelists met privately for a quiet week of Bible study and prayer in 1875. Within three years others responded to evidence of spiritual vitality; the annual summer conference became public. The leaders emphasized Christian renewal through practical Bible study based upon literal hermeneutics, premillennial interpretation of prophecy, and a strong sense that the end of the age was near. Sharing interdenominational camaraderie, they hoped to avoid controversy, overcome sectarian prejudices, and foster unity among premillennial believers.[1]

This era saw a shift in premillennial eschatology. From the 1790s to the mid 1870s most premillennialists advocated historicism, believing that some events in Daniel and most of the Revelation refer to the church age. Spearheaded by the Niagara Bible Conference, a growing number of premillennialists adopted the futurist view, persuaded that Daniel's seventieth week was in the future and was described fully in Revelation 6–19.[2] Although most of the Niagara leaders held the futurist view, they did not exclude historicists. Their fourteen-point doctrinal statement, adopted before the 1878 summer conference, urged believers to be ready for their Lord's return. Section 14 dealt with corporate eschatology, stating: "This personal and premillennial advent is the blessed hope set before us in the Gospel for which we should be constantly looking." Scripture proof texts included Luke 12:35–40 and 2 Thessalonians 2:3–8, but not 1 Thessalonians 4:13–17.[3] The statement was not specifically dispensational, for it did not set forth a two-stage return of Christ; rather it was a general premillennial statement that outlined a number of beliefs about the Second Coming and left room for all premillennialists.

Later in 1878 another significant statement appeared, which again showed the generally accepted view of Niagara participants. The first general American Bible and prophetic conference in New York City passed five resolutions that later prophetic conferences also adopted. Article 3 stated: "This second coming of the Lord is everywhere in the Scriptures represented as imminent, and may occur at any moment."[4] Many readers concluded that pretribulationism held by many Plymouth Brethren in Britain was adopted wholesale by the conference. The most influential promulgator of pretribulational dispensationalism was Irish Bible teacher John N. Darby.[5]

However, if articles 2 and 4 are brought to bear on the

interpretation of article 3, then a different, and I suggest a more plausible, conclusion follows. This conclusion is reinforced by evidence that Willis Lord, a historicist premillenarian, drafted the resolutions. Taken as a whole they associate the entire complex of apocalyptic events with the visible return of Christ to earth in power and glory. Article 2 used the terms "visible bodily return to this earth," "glorious Epiphany," and "this blessed hope" of the same event referred to in article 3. Article 4 listed prophetic events in a sequence that would not be drafted by an informed dispensationalist. It affirmed that

> only at and by His coming in power and glory will the prophecies concerning the progress of evil and the development of Antichrist, the times of the Gentiles, and the ingathering of Israel, the resurrection of the dead in Christ, and the transfiguration of His living saints, receive their fulfillment, and the period of millennial blessedness in [sic] its inauguration.[6]

Two stages of the Second Advent were not distinguished. And yet the term "dispensation" was used in article 2.

It seems best to recognize that North American dispensationalism was in its initial stage of development. Many premillennialists seemed to use its vocabulary without fully following its arguments or working out its implications. The point is a disputed one. Probably this statement about evangelist D. L. Moody applied to others:

> The most that can be said is that Moody adopted the concept of an any-moment return and some of its attendant vocabulary from the dispensationalists. But that he had a carefully thought-out and expressed dispensational distinction between a pretribulational rapture and a posttribulational coming cannot be demonstrated.[7]

References in the resolutions to "dispensation" could be to its Reformed theological usage.[8] Not every premillennialist used it in the same way as Darby's followers at that time.

Also, a man on the resolutions committee provided a rejoinder. For the record the conference unanimously passed all the resolutions as a "united testimony." After fifteen years, when differences over the Rapture were openly debated, Reformed Episcopalian minister B. B. Leacock revealed his dissent. He claimed that he never held the any-moment view because he believed a series of prophetic signs had to be fulfilled before the Second Advent. But at the 1878 conference he was drafted onto the committee to present the ready-made resolutions. He did not protest or resign due to the press of circumstances.[9] He illustrates the tension that always existed in the conference regarding the meaning of "imminent."

Among the Niagara participants there were three different definitions of "imminent." A. J. Gordon, pastor of Clarendon Street (Baptist) Church in Boston, represented the earlier historicist position. He affirmed: "the ever-imminent return of the Lord from heaven" promoted godliness because it fostered "the realization that He whose servants we are may appear at any moment to reckon with us."[10] However, Gordon believed the Bible taught a long period of apostasy separated the First and Second comings—a period concealed from believers in former ages but revealed to believers in modern times by the symbols and chronology of Daniel and Revelation. Therefore, he argued that only the final generation, which knew the long interval was drawing to a close, are justified on scriptural grounds in believing that Christ *could* come for them at any moment.[11] Second, some futurist premillenarians, defining "imminent" in the context of their debate with postmillennialism, believed the imminent return of Christ meant that the signs could be fulfilled and that He could return "within the lifetime of any individual generation of believers."[12] And finally, futurists holding to the pretribulationist view asserted that "imminent" required "the coming of Christ *for* his saints as possible any hour."[13]

When these three different definitions of "imminent" are compared to the 1878 prophetic conference resolutions, it appears that only Gordon, Lord, and other historicists could be completely consistent with that particular statement. But at that time the futurists were unaware of the built-in tensions that would eventually become the focus of their debate on the time of the Rapture. In this case the posttribulationists would modify the definition of imminent as possible at any moment and the pretribulationists would maintain that the Rapture to meet the Lord in the air, not the later glorious return of Christ to the earth, was the event that was possible any moment.[14]

A few years after the 1878 conference Robert Cameron, a Canadian Baptist pastor who joined the Niagara program committee, restudied the Rapture issue. He abandoned the pretribulational view for the posttribulational. Later at one of the conferences the constant reiteration of the idea that Christ might appear at any moment irritated him; he now believed that an extended series of prophesied events lay between the present time and the Rapture.

While at that conference in the early 1880s, Cameron urged Presbyterian theologian Nathaniel West, a charter member of the Niagara group and leading historical theologian among American premillennialists, to give the any-moment view his serious attention. West promised to do so but also declared, "If I find the Scriptures teach contrary to what is taught in this Conference, I will reverse myself and boldly defend the truth."[15] By this statement West acknowledged the any-moment view was dominant at Niagara.

Although there is evidence from an ecclesiastical dispute a few years later that West had the capacity for dogged determination and even intransigence,[16] Cameron has overstated the intensity of West's response to the Rapture issue at that time. First, Cameron recalled this watershed conversation about fifty years later, after a lengthy and often harsh dispute in which the majority of American premillennialists rejected the position he held with West. Also, the internal evidence from West's treatment of premillennial themes before 1892 portrays West as a champion of premillennialism as over against postmillennialism, not as an ardent defender of posttribulationism vis-à-vis the any-moment Rapture view.

For example, in his massive, scholarly work, *The Thousand Years in Both Testaments* (1889),[17] he introduced to American premillennialists the history of salvation, or *Heilsgeschichte,* perspective as developed by such noted German scholars as Franz Delitzsch of Erlangen and Leipzig and J. C. K. von Hofmann of Erlangen. West aimed to demonstrate "the organic and genetic character of revelation and of prophecy" or the "organic structure" of "sacred [salvation] history" as a result of literal interpretation. These key terms show his use of the *heilsgeschichte* approach, although he used and blended the terms of both covenant and dispensational theology with it.[18] The posttribulation view was thoroughly embedded in this variant of futurism; West did not make it a separate issue until three years later. This ponderous tome displayed West's erudition but did not precipitate any movement away from pretribulationism and dispensationalism. However, when he taught at Moody Bible Institute in 1891 he persuaded at least one student to adopt the posttribulation view.[19]

Yet it was West who ignited heated debate within premillennialism by his fusillade of fifteen articles of biblical exegesis and historical theology in *The Episcopal Recorder,* official organ of the Reformed Episcopal Church. From late 1892 to mid-1895 he vigorously attacked pretribulationism, labeling it the "any-moment theory."[20] To West the comprehensive view of the Old Testament prophets (especially "the prophet of universal history," Daniel), the Lord Jesus (especially in His Olivet Discourse), Paul (especially in the Thessalonian epistles), Peter, and John (especially in Revelation) was essentially the same. Comparing Jesus and Paul, West claimed that *"the same series of events and the same order must precede the same Parousia for the destruction of the Antichrist.* This makes the Gathering of the Elect, the Resurrection and the Rapture and the Judgment on the Antichrist at the same stage of the Parousia, without any appreciable interval between. Nothing is more certain."[21] West attempted to refute the pretribulationist notion that Paul's doctrine of the Rapture was a new revelation. He said Paul appealed to Jesus' Olivet teaching as *"a discourse of the Lord."* West's own interpretive key was the identity of terms in both passages.[22] This was his application of the commonly held principle that Scripture interprets Scripture.

In his article on "The Apostle Paul and the 'Any-Moment' Theory" he identified the central theological issue separating posttribulationists from pretribulationists. He argued that his opponents used *"a false a priori postulate,* the source of all their errors in eschatology, viz., that no man can daily watch for an event, . . . *if he knows any other event must precede it!"* Using this controlling premise pretribulationists removed the Olivet Discourse from the church and the church from the Tribulation.[23] Later on proponents of the any-moment Rapture would confirm his view of the issue's importance, but would reject his evaluation of the postulate. In addition West derided pretribulationism for snatching the church from the Tribulation, for Paul regarded suffering for the name of Christ "her highest honor on earth."[24]

The confrontation over doctrinal issues was aggravated by West's tone, which ranged from paternalistic to denunciatory. Since his research refuted the "any-moment" theory, his "devout, evangelical, brave and true" friends who "received it as true . . . without a thorough examination" should abandon it.[25] The entire series exuded criticism and irritation, a number of *ad hominem* arguments, and the label "errorists" for pretribulationists. A different attitude was appearing within the Niagara fellowship, which its leaders had avoided in their own publications up to that time.

Conference president James H. Brookes of St. Louis published a short reply to West early in 1894. In addition to defending pretribulationism he referred to the quarrel over the Rapture among British Plymouth Brethren more than fifty years before.[26] When West continued his cannonade, Brookes published an extended series, "The Imminency of the Second Advent," by George N. H. Peters, a Lutheran minister from Ohio.[27] Apparently both Brookes and Peters regretted this debate, yet Peters replied to West thoroughly and confidently. Duty led him to influence others "to remain faithful and firm in their scriptural belief and attitude of constant watchfulness, . . . that it may honor the precise and plain command given by the Saviour."[28] Since West used the language of constant expectancy several times, Peters concluded that West had conceded his point. The language of expectancy for Peters (but not for West) forbade the intervention of any future events between the present moment and the Rapture, a position he believed the early church fathers held.[29] Interposing events before the Lord's coming made "watching in the true Scriptural sense *a moral impossibility*."[30] Peters' main thrust drew from Article 2 of the New York conference resolutions and a parade of speakers at the 1878 and 1886 prophetic conclaves.

What he considered plain precepts of Scripture had precedence over theories of interpretation.[31]

Peters was not a pretribulational dispensationalist; on some points he was closer to West than to those with whom he agreed on the any-moment Rapture. For example, he appealed directly to the Gospels, especially to the Olivet Discourse, for his view of imminency. Furthermore, he cited Brookes to that effect.[32] In contrast to the view of most dispensationalists that the Olivet Discourse was not addressed to Christians, Peters argued that Christians must obey Christ's commands. Viewing the Rapture as a special favor to those who constantly watch, he espoused a "firstfruits" or partial-Rapture doctrine. Ironically, he agreed with West that the church was not entirely or necessarily exempt from the Tribulation, but for him the Rapture rewarded watchfulness. "We fear lest we suffer the loss of a blessed and glorious translation, and of a resultant honor and glory, and be compelled to pass through the last fearful tribulation of the Church."[33]

While Peters saw West's attack as violent, his reply often sounded a similar polemical note. Linking his opponent's view with the logic of recognized liberals, he emphasized that scholars cited by West gave only "human interpretations." He hoped the bitterness of West's tirade was a "momentary indiscretion," noting there is room for latitude of opinion in the interpretation of prophecy.[34]

Even before the Rapture issue was sharply drawn, some premillenarian leaders stated that controversy was not to characterize their relations with other professing Christians. In 1888 A. J. Gordon, editor of The Watchword, warned:

> Gospel fighting, when it is earnest, is about the most bitter of any. We believe we ought to "contend earnestly for the faith once delivered to the saints;" but in doing this, we should seek to be like the saints once delivered to the faith. Meekness and humility over possible defects and weaknesses in our own creed, should characterize all our assaults on what we consider the error in the creed of others.[35]

Gordon died in 1895. Later Our Hope, a new periodical, repeated his concern. There was "too much dogmatizing on these points" of whether the Rapture would occur before or after the Tribulation, "therefore we prefer to leave it for the day to reveal."[36]

James H. Brookes admitted in 1870 that premillennialists differed among themselves. They agreed on substantial matters, but needed more time "to arrive at entire harmony of opinions." Furthermore, as faithful churchmen they differed with denominational doctrine and polity only in "particulars of little consequence."[37] With the disagreement between West and Peters in mind, he announced a prophetic conference late in 1895, stressing that all premillenarians should come whatever their views on disputed matters. He exhorted them to focus on Christ, not their disagreements.[38] Brookes considered Christ-centered fellowship far more important than total agreement in details of prophetic interpretation. His death in 1897 silenced a second voice for moderation and unity.

As controversy disrupted Niagara's fellowship, D. L. Moody became concerned about divisions among Evangelicals that might affect their evangelistic work. Niagara conference leaders participated in his Northfield conferences as well. It appears that Moody became more vague about eschatological details in his later years while urging all believers to watch, wait, and above all, work.[39] His death in 1899 left an irreplaceable gap in Evangelicalism, and affected the Niagara Bible Conference. Forces of moderation and tolerance suffered losses of the first rank while those of polarization gained strength.

Although the death of A. J. Gordon removed the personal influence of the outstanding historicist among Niagara participants, an aspect of the historicist perspective became incorporated in the theology of leading futurists. In an article published in *The Truth,* W. J. Erdman, conference corresponding secretary and Presbyterian minister, emphasized that the stone in Daniel 2:34–35 could not have struck the image of the worldly kingdoms until certain historical events occurred. His three main points were aimed directly at postmillennialism, but had implications for the any-moment Rapture view. Implicitly the form of the image carried prophetic significance to the very end of the church age. Therefore, prophesied events existed between the time of the apostles and the end of Gentile world power.[40] Cameron, who had moved to Boston, succeeded Gordon as editor of *The Watchword.* In 1895 he cited nine points from Scripture that indicated a long delay before Christ's return. He opposed a liberal critic who had argued that Jesus and the apostles erroneously proclaimed a momentary Advent, but that the apostle Paul changed his mind on the immediate return in his later writings. Using guilt by association, Cameron linked the evangelical, any-moment position that Christ could have returned at any time within the apostolic era with the liberal view that Jesus and the apostles expected a momentary Advent. However, he himself affirmed that Christians may now expect the Lord within a short time. Cameron's ninth point resembled Erdman's article on Daniel. Also the seven churches in Revelation 2–3 represented the historical development of Christianity; so he too used a historicist argument to undermine the any-moment Rapture view.[41]

In 1896 C. I. Scofield, Congregational pastor and protégé of Brookes, said that specific events, such as the division of the Roman Empire into eastern and western kingdoms, fulfilled part of the prophecies of the fourth empire in Daniel 2 and 7. In order to understand unfulfilled prophecy relating to the ten kingdoms of the end times, one needed to examine the present dissolution of the divided empire into many separate realms.[42] He sensed no tension between the historicism expressed here and the any-moment Rapture doctrine, which he also held.

Niagara leaders convened occasional prophetic conferences to promote premillennialism among their denominations and build their own unity. The fourth was at Allegheny, Pennsylvania, late in 1895. Speakers now openly expressed diverse viewpoints on the time of the Rapture. Presbyterian missionary spokesman Arthur T. Pierson reiterated his basic definition given in 1886, "The imminence of the Lord's coming consists in two things: its certainty as a revealed fact and its uncertainty as to time." But he added a new application against posttribulationism: "The imminence of the Lord's coming is destroyed the moment you locate between the first and second coming . . . any period of time whatsoever that is a definite period, whether 10, 100, or 1,000 years. I cannot look for a thing as an imminent event which I know is not going to take place for 10 years to come, . . ."[43] On the other hand William G. Moorehead, president of the Presbyterian Xenia (Ohio) Seminary, represented posttribulationism expressed through covenant premillennialism. He expounded 2 Thessalonians 2:1–12, referred to the wheat and the tares being mixed until the end of the age, and argued that the personal Antichrist had his Parousia before the Parousia of Christ.[44]

The debate continued between 1895 and 1901, with newcomers Scofield and Arno C. Gaebelein, editor of *Our Hope,* taking a prominent part on the pretribulationist side. On the other hand Erdman, who became editorial manager of *Our Hope* in late 1897, tried to promote unity at Niagara even while he was shifting to posttribulational dispensationalism. Gaebelein published Erdman's change of view, "The Oral Teaching of St. Paul at Thessalonica." Erdman said "that no rapture nor advent could take place until certain events first came to pass." Gaebelein courteously admitted that Paul did not teach an "immediate coming," but that he "did teach that our attitude was to be one of constant joyful expectancy, consistent only with the *possibility* of that coming at any moment."[45] Gaebelein also resisted West's private attempt to convince him of posttribulationism. Both men were speaking at a conference to give the gospel to the Jews, sponsored by Brookes' church in St. Louis. Here is Gaebelein's story:

> I roomed with Dr. West, but it was a sleepless night; only towards five in the morning did I get some rest. Dr. West was a great scholar and a strong advocate of the premillennial coming of the Lord. But we differed on the church and the great tribulation.
>
> Unlike Brookes, Gordon, Parson, Needham[,] myself and others, Dr. West believed that the church would be on earth till the very end of that period of trouble. He tried hard to win me over to his side, and started about 11 P.M. with the ninth chapter of Daniel, verses 25–27. After we had gone over the Hebrew text and agreed on the correct translation, he attempted to build his argument on this prophecy, but failed to gain his point. Then we drifted to the second chapter of the second Epistle to the

Thessalonians and here we kept our vigil. West maintained
that the hindering power is human government; I said that
it was the Holy Spirit. It was a hot conflict that strengthened my belief in my view, which I believe is based on
Scripture. We were good friends.[46]

Gaebelein proved his friendship by publishing West's studies
on Daniel in 1897 and 1898.[47]

Pretribulationism emerged as the dominant view of the
Rapture within American premillennialism as a new generation of leaders rallied their followers to its particular interests.
In the late 1890s Gaebelein moved from his work of Jewish
evangelism into prophetic conference speaking among Christians. As he consolidated his position as sole editor of *Our
Hope,* he also departed from its ecumenical and tolerant attitude. By contrast, when founding editor Ernest F. Stroeter
reported on the 1894 Niagara conference he stressed the oneness of all in Christ, noting that "all separating differences
between believers appear in their true littleness and insignif-
icance."[48] The problem of maintaining fellowship grew more
acute as some premillennialists ceased to value the separating
differences as little and insignificant. This change of convictions for Gaebelein occurred in 1899 when he came to a new
understanding of "truth concerning the church" in Ephesians
and Colossians. By adopting the ecclesiology of exclusive
Plymouth Brethren, he began to regard denominational affiliation as a link to apostasy. Furthermore, he accepted the view
of many Brethren leaders that the pretribulation Rapture was
a critical part of Christian faith and practice.[49]

Rising controversy over the Rapture and withdrawal from
allegedly apostate churches—two "shoals" Niagara's founders
hoped to avoid—grounded the flagship of Bible conferences.
Extensive private correspondence by Erdman, private meetings Cameron promoted among leaders to resolve differences,
and a final irenic international prophetic conference in 1901,
which stressed premillennial unity, all failed to turn the tide.
Niagara's summer conference for 1901 was announced but
never held.[50]

Differences on the Rapture also contributed to increasing
editorial rivalry between Gaebelein and Cameron. The latter's

series, "To the Friends of Prophetic Truth," in 1902 widened the breach. He said the any-moment Rapture view came from the "fanatical utterances of the illuminati in Edward Irving's London church."[51] Gaebelein protested, challenging Cameron's added claim "that before Dr. Brookes and Dr. Gordon died, they had changed their minds and had come over to his side. . . . There was a most satisfactory result to this controversy. It added to the mailing lists of *Our Hope* hundreds of new subscribers, many of whom had followed the controversy in connection with the Niagara Conference."[52]

Some wealthy Plymouth Brethren enabled Gaebelein, Scofield, and other pretribulationists to start the Sea Cliff Bible Conference on Long Island in 1901. They reported: "We know that many of our readers who used to attend the Bible Conferences years ago at Niagara on the lake will be very much interested in this move." Gaebelein turned all his efforts to "the most important and vital doctrine . . . in the New Testament, the imminency of the coming of the Lord. . . . With His help we will make that blessed Hope very prominent. . . ." Of course posttribulationists were not invited to address Sea Cliff meetings, for "No one can continue to give out a true, scriptural, *edifying* testimony to the coming of the Lord who believes that certain events must come to pass before the Lord comes or that the church will pass through the tribulation."[53] Although Gaebelein alleged he was carrying on the original legacy of Niagara, I hesitate to accept his claim for two reasons. First, Sea Cliff was exclusively pretribulational and dispensationalist whereas Niagara was more broadly premillennial. Second, due to Gaebelein's conviction on apostate churches, Sea Cliff emphasized nondenominational connections in contrast to the interdenominational fellowship promoted by Niagara. As a relative latecomer to Niagara, perhaps Gaebelein failed to recognize these factors as significant differences. But with regard to being the successor of Niagara, Sea Cliff should be considered the stepchild rather than the intended heir.

The other major pretribulationist leader, Scofield, maintained ministry ties with most Niagara premillenarians during the first decade of the twentieth century. Three of the seven original consulting editors of the *Scofield Reference Bible* (1909) held to posttribulationism: William J. Erdman, William G. Moorehead, and Henry G. Weston. Erdman's son, Charles, who would later write the article "The Coming of Christ" in *The Fundamentals,* also met with Scofield and furnished valuable suggestions.[54] Of course only the pretribulation view appeared in the notes, for Scofield and the other contributing editors held it. At that time Scofield evidently felt the overall contributions of posttribulationist scholars far outweighed their disagreement over what he called on one occasion "a question of detail."[55] In private Bible study sessions and correspondence the posttribulationists were welcome collaborators. But in the public arena they often received different treatment, especially from Gaebelein. Nonetheless, the final product of the Niagara cooperation was the Scofield Reference Bible.

THE POPULARITY AND PREDOMINANCE OF PRETRIBULATIONISM: 1909–1952

Pretribulational dispensationalism advanced during this era because Gaebelein, Scofield, James M. Gray at Moody Bible Institute, Ruben A. Torrey at Bible Institute of Los Angeles, Harry A. Ironside at Moody Memorial Church, and Lewis Sperry Chafer at the Evangelical Theological College (later Dallas Theological Seminary)

> popularized its doctrines widely. The pretribulation rapture became the standard position of most Bible conferences and Bible institutes. Of greater influence than any other single factor was the *Scofield Reference Bible* (improved edition, 1917), which inculcated the eschatology of dispensationalism even while making its primary contribution as a popular defense of evangelicalism, when all else seemed to be falling before the flood of twentieth-century modernism.[56]

As a result, "soon the badge of North American evangelicalism was the Scofield Bible."[57]

By way of contrast, posttribulational theology in the generation after Niagara lacked the leadership, the institutional bases, and the extensive literature to match its premillennial counterpart. Furthermore, there was far less personal contact and interaction than existed within the fellowship of Niagara. Lastly, the strongest posttribulational critique of pretribulationism, *The Approaching Advent of Christ* (1937), by Presbyterian missionary Alexander Reese, a seminary student under William G. Moorehead, had a printing of only three thousand copies by a British publisher. Reese produced a scholarly treatise that had the same derogatory tone that he discerned and deplored among pretribulationist authors.[58]

As the adherents of pretribulationalism closed ranks and surged forward, various ones expressed contrasting attitudes toward the minority of premillennialists who differed on the time of the Rapture. Although W. J. Erdman was excluded from Sea Cliff and the large prophetic conferences held in 1914 and 1918, he did address the Montrose Bible Conference (at the summer home of evangelist R. A. Torrey in Pennsylvania) and the Erieside Bible Conference. In addition, Moody Bible Institute's magazine published at least one article by Erdman each year between 1908 and 1918. Editor Torrey remarked about his "Analysis of the Apocalypse," "Recently Dr. Gray has been using it with the Class in Revelation in Moody Bible Institute. . . . It is published for the benefit of a wider circle by permission of the esteemed author," who was also called "a great scholar."[59]

Yet the feelings of many were so aroused on the Rapture issue that after Henry W. Frost, Home Director of the China Inland Mission, expressed his posttribulational dispensationist views in an address to the Toronto Bible Training School, he wrote, "I began to wonder if I should have any friends left in that city. . . ." Cameron is probably correct to note that many holders of the any-moment Rapture view "were greatly offended."[60] We might wonder what reaction the school administration received from such supporting constituency, or how it might have affected the China Inland Mission.

As early as 1895 C. I. Scofield asserted that both posttribulationism and postmillennialism lacked urgency, and said they "come perilously near to saying, 'My Lord *delayeth* His coming.' " But when he addressed the Wilmington [Delaware] Bible Conference in 1913 he called posttribulationism a deceiving and destructive opponent of the pretribulation Rapture.

> It seems to have been a prime object of Satan to confuse the minds of God's people about that Blessed Hope, anything to turn their eyes away from expecting him. Well, our Lord said it would be so. . . . I don't think that the enemy of the Blessed Hope is now so much postmillennialism, but it is rather posttribulationism.[61]

Perhaps such diatribe helps explain why Cameron replied in kind. He commended W. J. Erdman's *The Return of Christ,* an irenical posttribulationist book published in 1913. Cameron added the comments of a Jewish evangelist:

> I am glad to know there are some who are opposing this *Secret Rapture fly-away-from-tribulation theory.* It seems to me to be only a trick of the Devil to fool God's people so that they will not be on the firing line for God. Wherever I am I smite that God dishonoring Doctrine.[62]

Each side in this heated exchange obviously felt that, as the guardian of prophetic truth, it was being sinned against rather than sinning itself. Perhaps the heavier weight fell on the posttribulationists, who were a minority within a minority. The combination of apostasy in the churches at large and the added offense posttribulationism had for many Evangelicals turning fundamentalist made it "increasingly difficult each year to find new subscribers enough to take the place of those whose earthly work is done."[63] *Watchword and Truth* had to come to grips with its loss of subscribers and influence. Cameron reminded his supporters: "We have no agents, we are connected with no organization, we have no circle of Bible Conferences to which we can appeal."[64]

By way of contrast, in the broader theological context represented in *The Fundamentals,* published between 1910 and 1915, posttribulational premillenialism was considered part of the mainstream of conservative orthodoxy. Charles R. Erdman penned the article on "The Coming of Christ." In his discussion he defended premillennialism over against postmillennialism rather than arguing for the posttribulation Rapture as opposed to the pretribulation position. He defined *imminent* as "possible any generation."[65]

A prophecy conference held in 1914 showed the growing strength of pretribulationist forces. Schools like Moody Bible Institute, the conference host, carried on the educational ministry of those who held to dispensational theology. Unlike the former generation, few premillenarians either attended or taught in seminaries. But more than pretribulationists were included in the published appendix of premillennial advocates. Again in 1918 only pretribulationists were on the platform of the New York Prophetic Conference. Yet W. B. Riley, Northern Baptist pastor and later fundamentalist spokesman, hoped his address would effect harmony among his "beloved brethren" who "differed slightly" with him over "the time element in our Lord's return." Their prolific, polemical literature was a continuing reminder of premillennial dissenters from pretribulationism. Reminders of those former days were present also in the reprinted 1878 conference resolutions, which were published alongside the exclusively pretribulational statements of the current conferences, and in the sessions on "How I became a Premillennialist," which showed Niagara was the headwaters of American dispensational and futurist premillennialism.[66]

Part of the spirit of Niagara rekindled three years after Cameron moved to the Pacific Northwest in October, 1912. In addition to his own articles supporting posttribulationism, he published numerous ones by W. J. Erdman and his son Fred Erdman, Moorehead, West, Robert Brown, and C. L. Heskett.[67] Heskett, an evangelist from Eugene, Oregon, expounded a unique variety of dispensational posttribulationism. "The question of the imminence of the advent is one . . . of dispensation. To ignore this feature of it is to ignore the truth and therefore, its rightful application." Unlike Cameron, he believed the return of Christ was possible any time in the days of the apostles because "the conditions were favorable to the further fulfillment of prophecy pertaining thereto. . . ." But since those conditions have not been present for the past 1,850 years, the Advent has not been imminent during that time. Yet in the future, and he thought the near future, "when the prophetic word will find its fulfillment in the events prevenient to the advent of Christ . . . then the imminence of the advent will loom up as never before." He concluded: "Thus, the Scriptures teach the imminency of the advent of Christ, and, as we shall see later on, they teach its nonimminency, without involving in the least way any contradiction. Both are questions of dispensational interpretation."[68]

Cameron generally commended Brookes, Gordon, and Scofield as well as other any-moment Rapture holders. "As to these brethren, we have always aimed at the utmost courtesy and kindness. Let *that* be remembered, but with what seems to us plainly contrary to the teaching of Scripture, we have frankly exposed the error without any thought except loyalty to the truth."[69] In the next issue Cameron reported that the Jubilee Conference of the China Inland Mission had both pretribulationists and posttribulationists as Bible teachers and that they served together on the council of the mission. And two issues later he announced that M. A. Matthews, ex-moderator of the Presbyterian General Assembly and pastor of the First Presbyterian Church of Seattle (which was then the largest Presbyterian church in the world) had become joint editor of *Watchword and Truth*. Cameron reminded his subscribers that Baptist pastor Gordon founded and edited *The Watchword* and Presbyterian minister Brookes founded and edited *The Truth* until they died and the magazines joined under his editorship. Cameron noted, "The Presbyterian and Baptist elements, originally mingling with the testimony maintained, come back into the magazine. . . . Although the circulation is not large, numerically, yet it is broad and extended. . . ."[70] Two other elements mingled also, for Matthews was a pretribulationist who published his view of the Rapture in *Watchword and Truth* after he became joint editor. Matthews was a leader of the emerging fundamentalist movement. For both Cameron and Matthews faithfulness to the Scriptures, creedal fidelity, and the promotion of missions to the ends of the earth were more important than the distinctives of ecclesiastical affiliation or the Rapture issue. Matthews wrote:

There are Godly men who differ from me on the question of the Church's relationship to the Tribulation. The honored, scholarly editor of "Watchword and Truth," Dr. Cameron, perhaps holds a slightly different view, but that does not interfere with our relationship and friendship. He is broad enough and big enough to recognize that others who believe in the great fundamental truth of the pre-millennial coming of Christ are entitled to their views on the successive events of His coming.[71]

With the entrance of the United States into World War I multitudes not only caught influenza—they caught "Armageddon fever."[72] Cameron agreed with Emma Dyer of Chicago, "who made the Moody Institute a possibility in the beginning," that writers on the Lord's Coming should avoid date-setting and other kinds of speculation. Dyer said, "There should be a flood of literature on this subject, simple enough and brief enough for beginners." Cameron replied, "Right you are, my friend! Dr. Gordon used to say he was sure the devil hated the doctrine of the Lord's Coming by the cranks he sent to preach it."[73] Yet what may be regarded as a quirk by some may be turned to good purpose by others. Pastor and radio evangelist Charles E. Fuller's ". . . ultimate purpose in stressing biblical prophecy throughout half a century of preaching was to show people how relevant the Bible is to what is happening today and thereby to awaken them to their need of turning to Christ without delay."[74] As the record shows, Fuller had commendable success. Yet the same emphasis on the details of prophecy, from any view of the Rapture, had led some people to pursue novelty—an unhealthy fascination with the details of apocalyptic Scriptures and speculation on current events. Such unbridled curiosity has been deemed escapist, potentially fatalistic, and even pathological. No school of prophecy seems immune from this cruel, ironic twist of the Bible's "purifying hope."[75]

Those concerned with the missionary task were not caught up in speculative matters. In *The Fundamentals* Charles R. Erdman asserted that the coming of Christ would be hastened by the completion of worldwide evangelization; that concern was common to all premillennialists. In 1917 representatives of several independent mission boards, popularly known as faith missions, met to form the Interdenominational Foreign Mission Association of North America. They agreed that one of their four doctrinal distinctives, in which they differed from other agencies, was their adherence to the belief that the return of Christ was premillennial. In 1922 the term *premillennial* was deleted from the article on the Second Coming. The doctrinal statement read and still reads, "We believe that the return of Christ is imminent, and that it will be visible and personal." Since Henry W. Frost of the China Inland Mission and Roland V. Bingham, General Director of the Sudan Interior Mission expressed posttribulationist views, it appears that the undefined term *imminent* could be understood in the sense of "possible within any generation" as well as "possible at any moment."[76]

While pretribulationism gained a broader base of popular support, it also received exegetical and theological development after 1930 from a new generation of scholars. They were trained in recently-established seminaries doctrinally committed to dispensationalism. For example, Charles L. Feinberg and John F. Walvoord, students under and colleagues of Chafer at Dallas Theological Seminary, promoted a change in exegetical argumentation about key theological terms for the Second Coming. Prior to the mid 1940s, pretribulationists generally viewed the Greek words *parousia* ("coming"), *epiphaneia* ("appearing"), and *apokalupsis* ("revelation") as technical terms specifying distinct phases of the return. They interpreted *parousia* as Christ's appearance in the sky including the Rapture of the church to meet Him in the air (1 Thess. 4:16–17). By contrast *epiphaneia* and *apokalupsis* referred to the return of Christ to earth with His saints following the Great Tribulation (2 Thess. 2:8; 1 Peter 1:7).[77] But Feinberg in 1936 and Walvoord in 1944 refused to justify the distinction between the Rapture and the return to earth on the basis of technical terms. Instead, they concluded that a comparative study of the Scriptures showed that the distinction could be maintained on the basis of numerous contextual clues. Although these men now agreed with posttribulationists that the three Greek words are not technical terms in the sense indicated above, they continued to support the two stages of the Advent based on the nature of the church (contrasted with Israel) and other exegetical and theological considerations.[78] Niagara leaders George C. and Elizabeth A. Needham suggested to fellow pretribulationists around 1900 that the two stages were not distinguished by technical Greek terms, but most did not agree until the detailed exegetical work by Feinberg and Walvoord.[79]

Seminary-trained scholars brought changes in the way dispensationalists interpreted the Bible. When concluding his study of the Day of the Lord, Philadelphia College of Bible professor Clarence E. Mason urged "more free discussion and a willingness to consider the possibility of greater flexibility in terminology [in addition to] a renewed emphasis upon the principles of interpretation rather than upon arbitrary words and pat phrases."[80]

A different view on the time of the Rapture emerged in 1941 when Norman B. Harrison published *The End: Rethinking the Revelation.* He believed the Rapture of the church would occur midway through the seven-year period known as Daniel's seventieth week. As a result, the church will not be on earth when God pours out His wrath during the three and one-half years before Christ returns to earth. While other premillennialists call his position midtribulationism, he did not use that term. Noting that the apostle John designated the first half of the seven-year period, when the church is present, "sweet" and the second half, when the church is absent, "bitter" (Rev. 10:9–10), he identified the second half of the week as both the Great Tribulation and the time of God's wrath. On his own definition, Harrison thought that pretribulation and mid-week distinguished his view.[81]

Harrison's view raises a more general question. Should the Rapture be defined by its relation to the Tribulation, the length of which is keenly debated among premillennialists, or by the seventieth week of Daniel, which futurists generally agree to be seven years? The title of this book assumes the former, more common, usage. But the essay by Gleason L. Archer adopts the latter view. Put another way, do those who are called midtribulationists by others have the right or the opportunity to label the issue with their own terms? If so, they may follow the suggestion of Donald Meresco to adopt terms which relate the seventieth week of Daniel and use *"preweek rapture, midweek rapture,* and *postweek rapture"* in place of pretribulation, midtribulation, and posttribulation Rapture.[82]

While pretribulationists generally came to accept the exegetical changes of Feinberg and Walvoord but reject those of Harrison, the historical record provides an example that was rejected by many but still continues to have the support of a significant minority of dispensationalists. In his series "Rethinking the Rapture" in *Our Hope,* editor E. Schuyler English concluded that *apostasia* in 2 Thessalonians 2:3 meant "departure" or "withdrawal" rather than the more common translations of "falling away" or "rebellion." English based his case on lexical possibilities and contextual considerations to solve a theological problem. He also published replies by conservative scholars—some agreed but many disagreed.[83] Allan A. MacRae, president of Faith Theological Seminary in Philadelphia at that time, felt that the interpretation solved a serious problem for pretribulational interpretation. Kenneth S. Wuest of Moody Bible Institute approved it, yet most pretribulationists rejected it.[84] Probably none recalled that J. S. Mabie, connected with the earlier Bible conference movement, suggested "a most original answer" to the interpretation of *apostasia* at the Annual Conference on the Lord's Coming, Los Angeles, in November, 1895. It was the Rapture of the church set forth in 1 Thessalonians 4:14–18.[85]

In addition to conferences, schools, and scholars, some new associations of churches or denominations as well as mission agencies incorporated premillennial views into their doctrinal statements. In some cases these were explicitly pretribulational. Where it was a requirement for fellowship, leadership, or membership, these additions stood in contrast to their nineteenth-century predecessors. The earlier American premillennialists intended to expound their basic premillennial belief in opposition to postmillennialism. Many of the newer groups included the terms *personal, premillennial,* and *imminent* in their doctrinal standards. A case study will illustrate how people within these groups conscientiously differed on the meaning of the word *imminent*.

The Evangelical Free Church of America, with roots in nineteenth-century Scandinavian immigrant churches, adopted in 1950 a doctrinal statement that said: "We believe in the personal, and premillennial and imminent coming of our Lord Jesus Christ, and that this 'Blessed Hope' has a vital bearing on the personal life and service of the believer." According to a survey of pastors shortly after 1950, most were pretribulationists, a few were midtribulationists or posttribulationists, and over one-fifth did not express a definite view. The conclusion: "As with other matters where there has been honest difference of opinion, tolerance has been shown" on the Rapture issue. Although all were premillennialists, a degree of eschatological liberty was shown on the Rapture and tribulation. Many Free Church leaders and teachers were uneasy with Scofield's emphasis on the Jewish character of Jesus' teaching and the kingdom message.[86]

Earlier examples have shown that the clash of convictions sometimes led to harsh tones and vitriolic tracts. But during this period instances of regretable treatment of fellow premillenarians over the Rapture issue exceeded those of other times. For example, pastor Norman F. Douty, former president of a Bible institute and theological seminary, experienced severe curtailment of ministry opportunities and ostracism by some pretribulationists after he changed from the pretribulational view to the posttribulational. Lewis Sperry Chafer of Dallas Theological Seminary wrote a former student who had changed his view of the Rapture: "You will find yourself very shortly being avoided by all your classmates, by all the faculty and by all the alumni of the institution which has meant so much to you."[87] It is evident that those with minority positions were most aware of the sometimes severely uncharitable attitudes and actions toward themselves and others of a similar unpopular persuasion. Therefore they were the most likely to emphasize that differences of interpretation in what they regarded as eschatological details should not be made tests of orthodoxy or fellowship. In *The Great Tribulation Debate*, Douty concluded with a plea to pretribulationists:

Suppose we [who are not pretribulationists] are mistaken, does that reduce your responsibility for tolerance? . . . Consider how much we have in common. . . . I plead for moderation. . . . Have a care for your own good. Will your Lord and ours thank you in that Day for treating us as you have? . . . So then, brethren, think on these things. By so doing, you may save yourselves chagrin in the day of reckoning that draws on apace.[88]

THE RESURGENCE OF POSTTRIBULATIONISM: 1952 TO THE PRESENT

Since 1952 premillennial thinkers renewed their efforts to interact and to express their own distinctive views with scholarly depth. A key indicator of scholarly interest and influence was the lecture series George E. Ladd, then Assistant Professor of New Testament at the recently founded Fuller Theological Seminary, Pasadena, delivered at Western Conservative Baptist Theological Seminary, Portland, in 1952. Published later that year, *Crucial Questions About the Kingdom of God* had a preface by Wilbur M. Smith, English Bible professor at Fuller and preeminent evangelical bibliophile, that looked both backward and forward with keen insight:

I think that it is time for all . . . who love the Lord's appearing, and who believe that only in His second advent is there any hope for this world, to approach these subjects without dogmatic pride, without feeling that we ourselves have attained the last word, . . . If there is any body of people in this country prone to divide bitterly, it is the students of prophecy, who so quickly belabor others who do not agree with them in some points, as, for instance, the matter of whether the Church will go through the tribulation. . . . But if there is one body . . . who ought to be united in love for the Lord and His Word, it is this group. . . . I believe that Dr. Ladd's work is the first volume to appear in our country since the beginning of this century written by a thoroughly equipped scholar who knows the views of the principal New Testament scholars, . . . and who at the same time is a thorough-going premillennialist, a believer in a Messianic Kingdom and in the millennium to come. For this reason, his book assumes major importance.[89]

This volume initiated Ladd's attempt to mediate and integrate the literal interpretation of dispensationalism and the spiritual interpretation of amillennialism by focusing on the New Testament's interpretation of the Old Testament. He saw the kingdom as God's saving reign of "the age to come," which entered "this age" in Christ, is spiritually present and powerful in the church, and will be consummated at the Parousia, which inaugurates the Millennium.[90] His inductive study of the use of the Old Testament by the writers of the New Testament shifted the hermeneutical issue for premillennialists from strictly "literal" interpretation. Also his emphasis on the kingdom brought a new dimension to the previous focus on Israel and the church. Perhaps this renewed focus on ecclesiology hastened the publication of *The Greatness of the Kingdom* by Alva J. McClain, president of Grace Theological Seminary at Winona Lake. For many years McClain had studied and taught the postponed kingdom doctrine, which was standard among dispensationalists.[91]

The Basis of the Premillennial Faith by Charles Caldwell Ryrie in 1953 provided a dispensational counterpoint to Ladd's hermeneutical method. Through an inductive study of the terms *Israel* and *church,* Ryrie concluded that "the Church in its entirety is never designated Israel in Scripture." Also he believed that both natural Israel and spiritual Israel were contrasted with the church in the New Testament. This basic distinction substantiated dispensationalism and the pretribulation Rapture view as the most consistent expressions of premillennialism.[92] In keeping with the newer temperate mood, Ryrie said he didn't intend to add to the controversial literature on the subject. He averred that premillennialism did not stand or fall on one's view of the Tribulation. For him it was not the decisive issue.[93] The distinction between Israel and the church was more basic.

Additional evidence for the importance of the doctrine of the church came from the vigorous and capable presentation of pretribulationism carried on throughout the early 1950s by

John F. Walvoord, president of Dallas Theological Seminary, in *Bibliotheca Sacra*. Published in 1957 as *The Rapture Question,* the series of essays that preceded *The Blessed Hope* by Ladd in 1956 picked up and answered Ladd's criticisms along with those of earlier posttribulationists. Walvoord clearly established that "the rapture question is determined more by ecclesiology than eschatology" for the definition of "church" and "the doctrine of the church is . . . determinative in the question of whether the church will go through the tribulation."[94] In reply to posttribulationists who challenged him to cite a verse of Scripture that stated the church would escape the Tribulation, he acknowledged "that neither posttribulationism nor pretribulationism is an explicit teaching of Scripture. The Bible does not in so many words state either. Pretribulationism is based on the fact that it allows a harmony of the Scriptures relating to the second advent."[95] Here he countered the advocates of both positions who wanted explicit textual support for their position on the Rapture rather than reasoned theological argument. Although Walvoord changed the above statement in later editions of his book to read, "The fact is that posttribulationism is an interpretation of Scripture which pretribulationists believe is contradicted by many passages which imply otherwise," he did not think that arguing from inference destroyed his case for the logical coherence and comprehensive theological structure of pretribulational dispensationalism.[96]

Ladd focused on the Rapture issue in *The Blessed Hope* (1956). He agreed with Walvoord that the whole field of debate needed to move from unqualified claims that one's position was explicitly taught in Scripture to the view that one's perspective is a theological inference from the biblical text. But in addition to pointing out that pretribulationism is not directly taught by the Word of God, he urged: "nor is it an inference required by the Word, nor is it essential for the preservation of the highest spiritual values." As an unnecessary inference, pretribulationism was "an assumption in light of which the Scriptures are interpreted." But another inference, "that of a single coming of Christ to rapture the Church at the close of the tribulation has an equal if not stronger claim to support." Ladd did not think the claims were indeed equal, for he concluded that the location of the resurrection—placed at the return of Christ in glory (Rev. 20)—

> is more than an inference. Furthermore, . . . if we were left only to inference, our study has suggested that a single indivisible return of Christ, which requires a posttribulation view, is the inference which is more naturally suggested than that of two comings of Christ with a pretribulation rapture.

He applied the principle of parsimony to interpretation here.[97]

As mentioned above, Walvoord incorporated replies to Ladd in *The Rapture Question*. He also argued that the doctrine of imminency, defined as a Rapture that is possible at any moment, was "the central feature of pretribulationism."[98] He supported this not only from the nature of the church, but also from the nature of the Tribulation. And the latter focus was dominant in another scholarly work, published in 1956, *Kept From the Hour* by Gerald B. Stanton, a Dallas Theological Seminary graduate and professor at Talbot Theological Seminary (California). Like Walvoord and Ladd, Stanton urged "due restraint" and "Christian charity" in discussing the Rapture issue. He also countered posttribulationist assertions that pretribulationism led people into unjustified comfort and ease. Eschewing overly dogmatic attitudes as unwarranted, he also acknowledged the inferential nature of the theological debate. Using the right premises, though, "there are enough Scriptures to reach a positive conclusion. . . . The Church is expressly promised deliverance from the wrath of God. . . ." Stanton argued that the divine wrath is poured out during the entire time of the Tribulation.[99] A reviewer concurred: "Since one of the strongest arguments for the pretribulation rapture arises from the doctrine of the tribulation, the author has done well to consider this first so as to lay a foundation for later discussion."[100]

It appears that the writings of Ladd and other nonpretribulationist scholars resulted in increasing diversity among Evangelicals. At least many were open to diverse influences. For example, in the Evangelical Free Church of America more pastors came to hold midtribulation and posttribulation views than previously. Furthermore, their colleagues showed greater tolerance for these changes. A survey in 1958 showed that 87½ percent of the participating pastors and teachers believed in the two-phase return of Christ. (Recall that this would embrace midweek [midtribulation] views as well as pretribulational positions.) Yet somewhat fewer, 72½ percent, believed the pretribulation view was held by the apostolic church. Ninety-six percent answered that the phrase "imminent coming" in the statement of faith meant "at any moment" or something similar. Yet only 52 percent believed the midweek (midtribulation) view was excluded by the phrase, while 65 percent said the posttribulation view was so excluded.[101]

The nature of the Tribulation was certainly a key difference in several variations that appeared during this era. A distinctive position, known as imminent posttribulationism or, later, pasttribulationism, was developed by Old Testament scholar J. Barton Payne. In *The Imminent Appearing of Christ* (1962) he argued that the coming of Christ is a single unified event (i.e., posttribulational) and that it is imminent (i.e., possible any moment). "Both of these truths must be accepted at face value; and then, after having been conditioned by these matters of basic understanding, the student of the Word may proceed to work out the details of a more Biblically consistent eschatology."[102] Pretribulationists accept the second axiom while rejecting the first, whereas posttribulationists usually cling to the former and reject the latter. Payne said their common difficulty was their affirmation that Daniel's seventieth week is still future and that connected with it are prolonged future antecedents to Christ's return in power and glory. Therefore a historicist position on Daniel's seventieth week— which the others regard as the time of the Tribulation—is basic to Payne's approach. Although he claimed to stand in the tradition of A. J. Gordon's imminent posttribulationism, Payne believed that every generation of Christians could affirm "that the last times *could* be the historical present,"[103] a belief that Gordon did not share. When his massive *Encyclopedia of Biblical Prophecy* appeared in 1973, Payne's view of the

Second Coming was placed in the more comprehensive context of predictive prophecy as a whole.[104]

Another variation on the Rapture and Tribulation appeared in 1963 when J. Oliver Buswell, Jr., Dean of Covenant Theological Seminary in St. Louis, completed his *Systematic Theology of the Christian Religion*. Unlike most futurist premillenarians, who consider the Tribulation to be a three-and-one-half- or seven-year period immediately preceding Christ's return to earth, he believed it to be a three-and-one-half-day period "of most awful persecution for all Christians." This is his equivalent of the Great Tribulation. This will occur in the middle of Daniel's seventieth week after the Antichrist comes to power, and will be followed immediately by the Rapture of the church. For Buswell, "the correlation of data centering around the seventh trumpet [Rev. 11] as the trumpet of the rapture is so complete, so precise, and so unequivocable" that it constitutes his "bench mark" or interpretive key. The final three and one-half years will be filled with "the pouring out of the vials of God's wrath (a time which is commonly, but mistakenly, identified with 'the great tribulation')."[105]

In *Dispensationalism Today* (1965) Charles Caldwell Ryrie updated the debate about the Rapture by highlighting the salient features of dispensational (for him pretribulational) premillennialism. He pointed to consistent literal interpretation, the literal fulfillment of Old Testament prophecies, a clear distinction between Israel and the church, the pretribulation Rapture, and the millennial kingdom as integral parts of the system. He also acknowledged that formerly support for the pretribulation Rapture "was due to the emphasis of the early writers and teachers on the imminency of the return of the Lord; more lately it has been connected with the dispensational conception of the distinctiveness of the Church."[106]

Believing that "in the last spate of publications on the topic posttribulationism gained neither the volume of press nor the exegetical backing which was given to pretribulationism," Robert H. Gundry, Professor of Religious Studies at Westmont College (California), felt it appropriate for American Evangelicals "to reconsider the chronology of the rapture." In his exegetically oriented contribution to the debate,

The Church and the Tribulation (1973), Gundry clearly outlined his thesis in the opening pages. On the one hand he argued that posttribulationism had a direct exegetical base of scriptural statements on the return of Christ and the Resurrection, additional exegetical support of a more inferential nature, and the corroboration of the history of doctrine. On the other hand, he considered that pretribulationism rested on "insufficient evidence, *non sequitur* reasoning, and faulty exegesis." He was persuaded that the New Testament terminology of watchfulness justified an attitude of expectancy toward Christ's return, but not a belief in imminence. "By common consent imminence means that so far as we know no predicted event will *necessarily* precede the coming of Christ."[107] After exegeting the admonitions to watch he concluded: "If a delay in the Parousia of at least several years was compatible with expectancy in apostolic times, a delay for the several years of the tribulation is compatible with expectancy in current times."[108]

An early response to Gundry's challenge came from John A. Sproule, Chairman of the Department of New Testament and Greek at Grace Theological Seminary (Indiana). Noting that among young premillennialists a change of position from pretribulationism to posttribulationism "is becoming an increasingly recurrent thing," he warned: "If this trend is to be halted and in the right way (by sound exegetical and theological persuasion), then the time is long overdue for an equally scholarly defense (not the old shibboleths!) of pretribulationism."[109] Sproule located Gundry's basic error in the premise that most of Christ's teaching, especially the Olivet Discourse, applied directly to the church. Gundry's posttribulational view, with its distinctive elements, resulted from his approach to the Olivet Discourse. There Sproule critiqued Gundry's presuppositions, exegesis, and logic. Yet Sproule also thought Gundry effectively countered the view of Walvoord that imminency was the heart of pretribulationism. The heart of Sproule's alternative, with its hope of exegetical certitude, was openly set forth:

> If it can be established that (1) God's wrath embraces this entire seven-year period yet to come and (2) that the true church has been promised exemption from that wrath,

then pretribulationism will be essentially established. Once this proof is established then pretribs can rightly claim reasonable explanations of the many debatable passages (including those which seem to teach imminency) as support for their system.[110]

It appears Sproule will dig deeper into the area explored by Stanton in *Kept From the Hour.*

In *The Blessed Hope and the Tribulation* (1976) John F. Walvoord classified and critiqued four schools of posttribulational interpretation: classic (J. Barton Payne), semiclassic (Alexander Reese), futurist (George E. Ladd), and dispensational (Robert H. Gundry). He noted that in general pretribulationists criticize posttribulationists for great variety in their principles of interpretation. Posttribulationists tend to spiritualize prophecy and make "improper use of the inductive method of logic" in exegesis and theology.[111] Comparing it with pretribulationism, he pointed to unresolved posttribulational problems: the silence of Scripture in areas critical to posttribulationism, contrasting details between the Rapture and the second coming of Christ to earth, and inherent contradictions in interpretation.[112] Comprehensively,

> it becomes evident that pretribulationism is more than a dispute between those who place the rapture before and after the tribulation. It is actually the key to an eschatological system. It plays a determinative role in establishing principles of interpretation which, if carried through consistently, lead to the pretribulational interpretation.

Walvoord summarized the advantages of pretribulationism as consistency in logic, in literal interpretation, and in looking moment-by-moment for the Lord's return.[113]

Within the Evangelical Free Church of America the diversity of views on the Rapture was clearly expressed at the annual ministerial conference in January 1981 when three professors from Trinity Evangelical Divinity School presented their viewpoints. They have elaborated their presentations and replies in this book, so I shall give some historical background and reactions to set the scene.

From the replies made to questions from the floor at the

conference, it was evident that the professors believe the EFCA Statement of Faith is always under the norm of Scripture. Furthermore, they believe both thorough exegesis and on-going theological evaluations are part of their ethical commitment to the Lord of Scripture and to His church. I mention this because they gave different answers to the question, "Could Christ return today?"[114] Many Free Church people believe that originally the term *imminent* in their doctrinal standard meant that the Rapture of the church was "possible at any moment." In addition, it was considered exclusively pretribulational in both intent and meaning. Any other meaning removed "the blessed hope" of believers.[115] According to Arnold T. Olson, the first EFCA president (who drafted the statement) the word "tribulation" or "pretribulation" was not included because many thought the definition of "imminent" encompassed only the pretribulation view. Yet his feeling was

> that the omission was neither accidental nor intentional but providential. . . . Those nonessentials which divide believers are omitted. We call for the acceptance of the Bible as the inerrant Word of God. We recognize that within the framework of that faith there have been and are today differences between believers who are equally sincere, equally dedicated to what stands written, and equally determined to be true to that Word as they see it and equally concerned that brethren dwell together in unity.[116]

He also "conceded that one can hold to the post-tribulation view and still maintain belief in the imminency [possible any time] of the return of Christ provided he cannot determine just when the seven years of the tribulation begin."[117] This concession would allow also the variant of "imminent post-tribulationism" or "potentially pasttribulationism" proposed by J. Barton Payne, who used to teach at the Free Church seminary.[118]

Evangelicals who unite in a confessional statement do not always agree on the precise meaning of a doctrine. The EFCA illustrates that over the years a diversity of viewpoints has been represented within the bounds of its doctrinal standard. But some who disallow such diversity will charge those who affirm and embrace this latitude with creedal infidelity. One layman believed that the midweek and posttribulation views of Professors Archer and Moo compromised the doctrinal integrity of the EFCA. He did not consider their reasons to be valid, but felt that they were sowing the seeds of destruction for the future of the church because "all other doctrinal truths are subject to the same rationalizations." He admitted their "rationalizations . . . may relieve them of any ethical problem in signing the Free Church Statement of Faith," but he evidently did not consider their positions ethical.[119] However, in answer to such concerns at the ministerial conference, Dr. Moo put on public record that his posttribulationist view was made known to other Trinity faculty at the time of his hiring interview. Many of the laity may lack knowledge or approval of all that is taught in the divinity school, but in this case Moo's open discussion with the faculty who approved his appointment clears him of the allegation of ethical deceit. Even before the reorganization of Trinity in 1963 some seminary faculty members, such as J. Barton Payne, held a posttribulational Rapture view. Calvin B. Hanson is doubtless right that this "would have surprised the grass roots of the Free Church even more" than the insistence of TEDS dean Kenneth S. Kantzer that faculty not holding to the pretribulation Rapture would be recruited for the expanding school.[120] Whether Dr. Archer's midweek Rapture position is a variation of the more common pretribulation position or not is debatable.

David J. Hesselgrave, Professor of Missions at Trinity, expressed concern for the practical effects of the return of Christ in a letter in which he also noted the lack of any mention of missions in the papers presented by his colleagues.[121] While Scofield feared that posttribulationism "lacked urgency" and Ladd argued that "pretribulationism sacrifices one of the main motives for world-wide missions, viz., hastening the attainment of the Blessed Hope," it is evident to even a casual observer of evangelical missions that these fears or conclusions are not justified. Far more than one's view of the Rapture is involved in the commitment of all Evangelicals to worldwide evangelization.[122]

Evangelical groups with specific eschatological terms in their statements of faith face dilemmas when exegetical and theological work leads some members to conclusions that challenge their traditional formulations. Reactions may take at least two different directions. On the one hand, Dallas Theological Seminary elaborated its doctrinal statement to exclude virtually all but those who believe the Rapture is both pretribulational and possible any moment. On the other hand, the EFCA appears to be allowing latitude in the understanding of the term *imminent* for both the faculty of Trinity Evangelical Divinity School and ministerial candidates for ordination. This is in keeping with the ethos of the Free Church: "For believers only, but all believers."[123] These divergent attitudes and actions show that premillenarians lack consensus on what constitutes adherence to the spirit of watchfulness expected of believers and how the "blessed hope" is to affect their lives. One thing is certain: groups in the past have not noteably succeeded in remedying these multifaceted issues by confessional change alone. This historical observation should warn Evangelicals not to expect a quick and easy solution.

Summing up this era, historian Ian S. Rennie wrote, "In the post-World War II period, with the renewal of evangelical thought and life, eschatology has received a less disproportionate emphasis, there has been greater humility in regard to detail, and perhaps above all, there has been a new awareness of the oneness of the people of God in all ages."[124]

CONCLUSIONS

Two conclusions are evident from this survey. First, there is diversity among Evangelicals of premillennial persuasion on the issue of the time of the Rapture. Second, both the negative examples of fractured relationships and positive pleas for moderation from premillennialists support a call to unity that allows for diversity and promotes toleration.

A perceptive professor emphasized that God has limited our ability to understand scriptural prophecy; deep humility is needed to approach and unfold it. To conclude, we "should proceed in dependence upon God for illumination and with a profound respect and tolerance for other Christians of equal or greater gifts, and of integrity, who arrive at somewhat different results."[125]

2

THE CASE FOR THE PRETRIBULATION RAPTURE POSITION

Paul D. Feinberg

Paul D. Feinberg is Associate Professor of Biblical and Systematic Theology at Trinity Evangelical Divinity School in Deerfield, Illinois. He is a graduate of Talbot Theological Seminary (B.D., Th.M.) and Dallas Theological Seminary (Th.D.), and has received a Ph.D. degree in philosophy at the University of Chicago. Dr. Feinberg has contributed articles to *Baker's Dictionary of Christian Ethics* and the *Wycliffe Bible Encyclopedia* and has written a chapter in *Inerrancy*. He is an ordained minister in the Evangelical Free Church of America.

The time of the Rapture is neither the most important nor the most unimportant point of Christian theology. For some the Rapture question is a bellwether; its surrender marks the first step on the proverbial slippery slope that leads one to the rocks of liberalism. But such is neither logically nor actually the case. When one considers the whole spectrum of Christian theology, eschatology is only a small part of it. Moreover, the Rapture question constitutes only a small segment of eschatology. The contributors of this volume are in substantial agreement on matters of individual, or personal, eschatology and are all convinced of the same view with respect to the larger issues of premillennialism.

There are those who find the question of the Rapture insignificant and uninteresting; they pride themselves in being above the battle. But this is wrong. Theologically, no aspect of revealed truth is unimportant. The Rapture touches the extremely important issues of biblical interpretation, the relationship between the church and Israel, and the course of human history. Practically, the time of the Rapture is significant because we aspire to know the *whole* counsel of God. Furthermore, this matter touches the important issue of the nature of the Christian's hope and expectation. Am I to expect Christ's return at any moment? Or, is my hope the protection in and deliverance by God from a time of worldwide tribulation? Thus, the task before us is an important one.

SOME PRELIMINARY REMARKS

Before turning to the arguments for a pretribulation Rapture, it will be helpful to make some preliminary remarks.

On the Ecclesiological Backdrop

One often hears that the chief support or evidence for a pretribulation Rapture is dispensational ecclesiology. This is expressed in the writings of pretribulation authors[1] and critics.[2] One of the significant points argued by Robert H. Gundry in *The Church and the Tribulation* is his claim that there is no *necessary* or *logical* connection between dispensationalism and pretribulationism. His argument rests on the following considerations: (1) A central argument for the distinctiveness of the church is its mystery character. However, there are some mysteries that cross dispensational boundaries (e.g., the mystery of lawlessness, which is already operating but which will come to fulfillment in the Tribulation, and the mystery of the incarnation and earthly ministry of Jesus, which began before Pentecost but continues to the present). (2) There are Old Testament prophecies that mention or imply this age (e.g., the hiatus between the sixty-ninth and seventieth week of Dan. 9:24–27). (3) Not only do Old Testament prophecies predict this present age, but they are also applied to the church (e.g., most notably the application of the new covenant to the church). (4) The change from the old dispensation to the present one took place over a period of time (e.g., the events of the Book of Acts [Acts 3:12–21] show that the present dispensation took effect gradually). (5) While the distinctiveness of the church tends to emphasize its uniqueness and point toward a pretribulation Rapture, this is balanced by the biblical teaching of the essential unity of all believers (e.g., Abraham is said to be the father of *all* who believe, Rom. 4:11). (6) Finally, Gundry tries to describe what the Tribulation period would be like with both the church and Israel present as covenant people. His point is that there is nothing that is prima facie contradictory or beyond resolution (e.g., because Dan. 9:24–27 places Israel in the Tribulation, nothing prevents other biblical texts from putting the church in this same period).

I myself tend to think that Gundry is right. To put it in his words, "Posttribulation accords well with a scripturally measured dispensationalism. Conversely, a scripturally measured dispensationalism gives no advantage to pretribulationism."[3]

I would be more concerned than Gundry with the tensions that such a position would create. He suggests some problems. How would Israel and the church coexist since both have different regulations (law and gospel)? Would the Tribulation church be exclusively Gentile, or could some Jews be a part of it? Would each group preach a variation of the gospel, and so on? His response is that the mere existence of these questions does not preclude the possibility that such a state of affairs could exist. He cites as proof the Millennium and the eternal state where both Israel and the church will be present. There does seem to be an important difference between Gundry's proposed view of the Tribulation and these subsequent periods. In the Tribulation both groups will be in natural bodies, and will have members added to them. In the Millennium the Church will be complete and *glorified,* while in the eternal state all the redeemed will be glorified. But I would not want to press this point.

What Gundry does not say, but what should at least be noted is that dispensationalism has more often than not led to pretribulationism. Gundry's point, however, is a different one. It is that there is a certain logical independence between the two views. I think Gundry is right. If so, there is an interesting consequence that follows from Gundry's claim. It will not follow that an argument *for* dispensationalism will necessarily be an argument *for* pretribulationism. Conversely, an argument against dispensationalism will not necessarily be an argument *against* pretribulationism.

Presuppositions and Assumptions

There are two positions taken in this paper for which no argument is offered. First, it is assumed that following the return of Christ to the earth in power and great glory at the end of the Tribulation period, there will follow an earthly reign of Christ. One of the arguments advanced in favor of my position depends on such a reign. Second, there is presupposed a futuristic interpretation of Daniel 9:24–27 and the

Book of Revelation. This means that the return of Christ before the kingdom is preceded by a time of unprecedented tribulation. Daniel 9:27 gives the seven-year chronological framework, while Revelation 6–18 details the judgments that make up this period. The justification for not arguing these positions is that the Rapture question has mainly been an issue between premillennialists,[4] and also that most recent premillennialists have been futurists with regard to Daniel and Revelation.[5]

ARGUMENTS FOR A PRETRIBULATION RAPTURE

In my judgment there are at least four biblical arguments for a pretribulational structure of eschatology.

The Promise of Exemption From Divine Wrath

It might be wondered if there is anything that the participants of this debate agree upon. Surprisingly enough, I think there is. All agree that God has exempted the church from divine wrath. Consider these quotations from posttribulationists:

J. Barton Payne writes:

> They [some prophecies] do precede the appearing of Christ. Here we should include certain elements of the *wrath of God,* such as the great earthquake and the sun being darkened (Matt. 24:29, cf. the first four trumpets and bowls of God's wrath in Rev. 8 and 16:1–9). But as long as the *Lord protects* His people from these things (*and He does*: 1 Thess. 5:9; Rev. 7:1–3), and as long as they are restricted to events that last only a few minutes (and this is all they do: Luke 21:28), then such matters do not invalidate the Church's imminent hope [emphasis mine].[6]

George E. Ladd writes: "We have already pointed out that it is a clear teaching of Scripture that the *Church will never suffer the wrath of God.* At this point we are in agreement with pretribulationists."[7] Robert H. Gundry writes, "As now, the

Church will suffer persecution during the tribulation, *but no saint can suffer divine wrath*" [emphasis mine].[8]

J. Oliver Buswell, a representative of the midtribulation position, says: "*But the wrath of God is not for the Church. By the blood of Christ 'we shall be saved, through Him, from wrath' *" (Rom. 5:9) [emphasis mine].[9]

Similar claims can be found in the writings of pretribulationists. John F. Walvoord argues: "The *wrath of God* will be poured out upon the world during the great tribulation. Rev. 6:17 states, 'For the great day of their wrath is come; and who is able to stand?' . . . The only way one could be kept from that day of wrath would be to be delivered beforehand" [emphasis mine].[10] Leon Wood declares:

> The foregoing has emphasized that the purpose of the Tribulation is to bring judgment upon those deserving it. . . . However, the idea of the Church going through this same time of judgment does not follow this line of reasoning. For, although the members of Christ's body, the Church, are not spotless in themselves while here on earth, still the penalty for their sin has all been paid in Christ's finished work of redemption.[11]

Thus, there is at least this one point of agreement, the belief that *the true church is exempt from divine wrath.* However, before examining the Scripture texts that support this principle, let me make very clear what is meant by it.

First, this exemption from wrath does not mean that the church will never experience trial, persecution, or suffering. To use the terminology of the songwriter, the church has not been promised that she will be carried to the skies on flowery beds of ease. The world and Satan have never been friends of God and His church. The New Testament makes it clear that we should expect trial and suffering, particularly if we live righteously (e.g., John 16:33; Phil. 1:27; 1 Thess. 3:3; 1 Peter 4:12, 13). This promise, then, is not to result in softness. Rather, hardness in light of trials is enjoined everywhere in the New Testament. The Christian life is pictured as a battle (Eph. 6:10–20; 1 Tim. 6:12; 2 Tim. 2:3–4) and as an athletic contest requiring discipline and endurance (1 Cor. 9:24–27; Phil. 3:1–16; 2 Tim. 2:5).

Second, the ground for the exemption is not that Jesus Christ on the cross has borne our wrath so that we will not come into wrath. This view has been taken by some but Gundry is right in pointing out the inconsistency of this at least for a pretribulation position, when he says:

> Pre- and posttribulationists agree that a host of saints, consisting of both Jews and Gentiles, will be present on earth during the tribulation. Therefore, whatever problems pretribulationists may turn up regarding the presence of the Church in a period of divine wrath are their own problems, too; for whether or not the tribulational saints belong to the Church or to another group of redeemed people, they also have escaped God's anger by virtue of the blood of Christ, who underwent their judgment for them (Rev. 7:14). Will Jewish and Gentile saints suffer God's wrath during the tribulation, according to pretribulationism? If not, neither would the Church have to suffer God's wrath in the tribulation. If so, arguments against the suffering of wrath by the Church apply equally to tribulational saints of other sorts.[12]

What then is the ground of this promise? Like salvation, this is a sovereign decision of God. God simply has given this special promise to the church. (At this point in the discussion it does not matter whether the church includes all saints or part of them.) The texts that express this promise are: 1 Thessalonians 1:10; 5:9; Revelation 3:10; and possibly Romans 5:9; Ephesians 5:6; Colossians 3:6. In contrast to trial and tribulation, which the Christian is to expect, there is a promised exemption from divine ὀργή or θυμός. These two terms are roughly synonymous. Where there is a distinction, θυμός is preferred for sudden bursts of anger (Luke 4:28; Acts 19:28), while ὀργή has an element of deliberation.[13]

The wrath of God is an important and much discussed topic in Scripture. God's wrath has been poured out on the wicked in the past (e.g., the wrath of God fell on the Canaanites, Exod. 23:20–33; Deut. 7:1–6). The wrath of God abides presently upon unbelievers (Eph. 2:3; cf. John 3:36; Rom. 1:18–3:20). However, the Bible speaks of a future or eschatological wrath of God. This is unfolded on a grand scale in the New Testament, particularly in Revelation.

Obviously, we are most concerned in our discussion with this future outpouring of divine wrath. Of this Stählin writes: "There are two points in the future where eschatological ὀργή has a place, first, in the tribulation before the end, then in the final judgment itself."[14] While it is certainly true that Christians will not experience the final judgment of God (Rom. 2:5, 8; 3:5; 5:9), 1 Thessalonians 1:10 and 5:10 seem to be speaking of the Tribulation before the end. The Tribulation is a time of great distress for Israel (Luke 21:23) and for those who destroy the earth (Rev. 11:18). However, these two texts teach that the church has not been appointed by God to this wrath.

First Thessalonians 1:10 promises rescue from the wrath of God. There are, I think, three reasons for thinking that the wrath spoken of is that of the Tribulation. First, the general context of the Thessalonian epistles is the day of the Lord. While this includes the final judgment, the focus of these epistles is the judgment of God that precedes and is associated with Christ's coming. Second, the text itself states that it is a "coming wrath" and implies that rescue is related to Christ's return. Third, the wrath of 1 Thessalonians 1:10 seems related to that of 5:9 where the advent of eschatological woes are in view.[15]

The evidence of 1 Thessalonians 5:9 is even more striking. Paul begins by reassuring the Thessalonians that whatever had provoked their concern, they did know the "times and the epochs" accurately (ἀκριβῶς, 1 Thess. 5:1–2). The first three verses are filled with well-known eschatological terminology. "Times and epochs" is one such phrase, as well as the day of the Lord (e.g., Isa. 2:12; Amos 5:18, 20; etc.). Moreover, the expression "labor pains on a pregnant woman" (v. 3) uses the same word, ὠδίν, that is found in Matthew 24:8. The wrath is the same as that of 1:10, the birth pangs of the day of the Lord.[16]

In verses 4–5 the position of the Thessalonians is contrasted with that of the unbeliever. The day of the Lord will overtake the unbelievers as a thief in the night because of their general moral state, which is spoken of as night, or darkness. Believers, on the other hand, will not be surprised as they are of light and the day. Unbelievers will not escape (an emphatic statement). The markedly different relationship the Thessalonian believers had to the day is again expressed emphatically by the insertions in 5:4, 5 of the personal pronoun "you."[17]

There follow, in verses 6–8, exhortations in light of the believers' position. In verse 9 there is the reaffirmation that the Christians hope is a valid one. "For God did not appoint us to suffer wrath but to receive salvation through our Lord Jesus Christ" (5:9). God has not destined the Thessalonians to these eschatological woes, but to salvation. This salvation is not only deliverance from eternal damnation, but also to "live (*ingressive aorist*) together with him" (5:10). Thus, this deliverance (σωτηρίας) is parallel to the rescue (ῥυόμενον) of 1:10.[18]

When taken most generally, as shown above, there seems to be widespread agreement on this principle. Where then does the disagreement arise? It arises with the application of this principle. The debate, or disagreement, concerns two matters: the time of divine wrath in the Tribulation and the nature of the promised protection.

J. Barton Payne, for example, confines the period of divine wrath to the events that immediately precede the Second Coming. However, Payne's view is different from the others cited. He is a preterist, holding historical fulfillments of a good deal of Old Testament prophecy and the Book of Revelation. Scripture passages like Daniel 9:27 and much of Revelation 6–19 do *not* await fulfillment in the events surrounding the Second Advent. There is some judgment connected with the coming of Christ. However, Payne says that as long as it does not cover a large period of time and as long as God protects His children, the promise is not violated. Once Christ has come, the church will realize that it has been in the Tribulation (in a general sense) and will then see who the Antichrist was. There are always those who are persecutors of the church, and who could thus qualify as the Man of Sin.[19]

Payne's general approach to the problem has never attracted many followers. The chief difficulty has been that recent premillennialists have been overwhelmingly in favor of the belief that Daniel 9:24–27 and Revelation 6–19 have not been fulfilled, and are a part of the complex of events connected with the return of Christ to the earth.

George Ladd is not so much concerned with the question of the commencement of divine wrath, but rather with the nature of the promised protection. After suggesting that 1 Thessalonians 5:9 could refer only to the final judgment, he asserts that, if it also includes the Tribulation, it does not necessitate a Rapture. All that is promised is deliverance. He points to the distinction that God made between the Israelites and the Egyptians when the worst of the plagues fell as a prefiguring of what will occur in the future.

> In a similar way it is possible that the Church may find herself on earth during the period of the Tribulation but will by divine protection be sheltered from the sufferings entailed by the outpouring of the bowls of wrath and thus be delivered from the wrath to come. *1 Thessalonians 5:9 says nothing about the Rapture.* That it does is an unjustified inference. It says only that the Church will be delivered from wrath. How the deliverance is to be effected is not suggested. If the Church is on earth during the Great Tribulation but is divinely sheltered from wrath, this verse is fulfilled. This is all it asserts.[20]

At least certain of Ladd's views are included in the thought of Robert Gundry's posttribulationism. Because of the complexity and sophistication of his view, we will do well to try to explain it in detail. We need to understand his view as to the nature of the period and the sequence of judgments. While Gundry accepts the seventieth week of Daniel as future, he begins by distinguishing varieties of distress within that period: the direct retributive judgment of God on sinners for unforgiven sin; the hatred of Satan and his demons; evil and wickedness that is the result of human sin; the persecution of the saints by the Antichrist; and the chastisement of the nation of Israel.[21] Roughly speaking, we may divide the distress into four groups: tribulation or chastisement, man's wrath, satanic wrath, and divine wrath. Gundry does not, as some have supposed, either spiritualize the distress or seek to water down the judgments, rather he claims that God has only promised exemption from *divine* wrath. Saints will die as the result of satanic persecution and man's inhumanity to man, but this makes this period *no* different from any other period of human history. The church has never been exempt from this and neither will it be in the future. All that is required is that there is protection from God's wrath.[22]

To understand the commencement of divine wrath, one must have a grasp of Gundry's structure for the judgments of Revelation. He sees each seventh judgment as reaching Christ's return. Thus, the three sets of judgments are "somewhat concurrent." The seal judgments cover the whole seventieth week. The trumpets begin with the fourth seal, and the bowls commence with the fourth trumpet. The judgments then not only increase in severity but also in number as the period progresses. Gundry feels that such a structure best fits the universally recognized Semitic style of the book; he also mentions several exegetical considerations.[23]

Since, as was said earlier, the saints are exempt only from the direct retributive wrath of God, it is important to determine when divine wrath begins. Gundry thinks it begins with the sixth seal, the fourth trumpet, and the first bowl. In support of this interpretation Gundry offers these considerations: (1) The three woes, the last three trumpets, come on "earth-dwellers" in contradistinction to the saints. (2) The first bowl falls on those who have the mark of the beast (Rev. 16:2). (3) The turning of the sea into blood, and the retribution for the blood of martyred saints in the second and third bowls do not need to involve the saints. (4) The fourth bowl comes on those who do not repent and blaspheme God's name (Rev. 16:9), and so does the fifth bowl (Rev. 16:11). (5) The sixth bowl is related to the kings of the East and the forces that participate in Armageddon. (6) The seventh bowl describes the end of Babylon (from which God's people have been called, Rev. 18:4). (7) There is a remarkable parallel between some of the bowls and certain of the plagues experienced by ancient Egypt (e.g., sores, the turning of water to blood), and there is also the possibility that God's people were protected as ancient Israel was.[24] Their victory song even likens the Second Coming to the Exodus (Rev. 15:3). (8) Protection from the trumpet judgments could be afforded the saints in the Tribulation just as it had been given to Israel in Egypt.

These considerations are supplemented by two arguments that Gundry has given elsewhere. First, he argues that the Day of the Lord does not begin until the close of the Tribulation period, near the time of the sixth seal (Rev. 6:14–17, cf. 2:32–3:1; Zeph. 2:3–3:11, 16). The period of divine wrath is connected with the Day of the Lord.[25] Therefore, the church will be on the earth until the day dawns. Second, Revelation 6:16–17 is the announcement (in connection with the sixth seal) that the wrath of God has broken forth (ingressive aorist) or is on the verge of breaking forth (dramatic aorist).

Gundry concludes, "Divine wrath does not blanket the entire seventieth week, probably not even the latter half of it, but concentrates at the close."[26] It is only from divine wrath that the church is exempt, and Gundry has the church raptured right before the end, before Armageddon. This does *not*, however, mean that the church will be exempt from persecution and death from Satan or from mankind.

Moreover, even if divine wrath began before the bowls, this would not be decisive against posttribulationism, "for the Church would receive protection throughout the whole time just as any other tribulation saint and the 144,000 will receive protection."[27]

The midtribulationism of J. Oliver Buswell bears some similarity at important points to Gundry's posttribulationism. The church will be present during the Tribulation, but this presence does not imply divine wrath against the church. In Matthew 24:29–31, our Lord enumerated signs that will follow the Tribulation. There will be great cosmic upheavals "immediately after the tribulation of those days" (Matt. 24:29; cf. Matt. 13:24–25; Luke 21:25–26). These cosmic upheavals are related to the bowls; they do not come during the Tribulation but *after* it. While the Tribulation will be quantitatively unique, it will not be qualitatively unparalleled. Tribulation is usually man's wrath against God's people. Therefore, it is the lot of His people in all ages.[28]

Divine wrath, for Buswell, is another matter. Salvation

is deliverance from this wrath (Rom. 5:9; 1 Thess. 1:10). Therefore, he believes, "although these references to salvation from wrath do not definitely state, in themselves, that the rapture of the Church will take place before the outpouring of the vials of wrath, yet these references harmonize with that view."[29]

Pretribulationists agree among themselves on two points relating to the question of wrath. First, it is their contention that the *whole,* not just a part, of the seventieth week is a time of divine wrath. Second, the means of protection for the church is *removal* from this period by the Rapture.[30]

Let me summarize the argument to this point. There is general agreement with regard to the principle that God has promised the church exemption from divine wrath. The disagreement arises as to the time that divine wrath commences and as to the method of divine protection. I would like now to turn to examine the first area of disagreement. When does divine wrath begin?

One way in which one might try to resolve the dispute is to observe the usage of the word *wrath* in Revelation. The words ὀργή and θυμός occur six times and ten times respectively in the book. Two occurrences are related to the return of Christ to the earth (in Rev. 19:15, both words appear). In Revelation 12:12 the wrath of the dragon against the woman is in view. Nine uses clearly deal with judgments at the end of the Tribulation (e.g., Rev. 14:8, 10, 19; 15:7; 16:1, 19; 18:3). This would be at a time when midtribulationists and Gundry would have the church raptured.

There are, however, four places where one of the two words appears that deserve comment. The first is Revelation 15:1. The context relates the plagues spoken of to the bowl judgments. In these judgments the wrath of God is "finished" (ἐτελέσθη). The verb "finished" is an aorist; it may be understood as constative, complexive, or effective. This aorist may be conceived as a whole without reference to beginning, progress, or end, and represented as completed.[31] It could refer just to the bowl judgments in which case it would be indecisive with regard to our question as it would assert that they *finish* the wrath. However, it is possible that the plagues have a reference beyond simply the bowls since judgments other than the bowls are called plagues (e.g., Rev. 9:18). As a matter of fact, the judgments of the whole book seem to be spoken of as plagues (Rev. 22:18). If so, then in *all* the judgments of the book the wrath of God is finished.

A second passage is found in Revelation 11:18. Here, there is the announcement that the wrath of God has come (ἦλθεν). On Gundry's scheme this announcement would occur again at the end of the period, and thus would be interpreted as a constative aorist. However, for a midtribulationist, who would place the seventh trump in the middle of the week, this *could* be a dramatic or ingressive aorist (an announcement that the wrath of God is just beginning) making the wrath begin at the middle of the week.

By far the most important two instances are found in Revelation 6:16, 17. The word *wrath* occurs once in each verse. This is the first reference to wrath in the book. Furthermore, it is associated with the seal judgments. This passage gives us a good example of the difficulty connected with resolving theological issues like the one before us. Gundry argues two points with regard to this passage. He contends that the wrath spoken of in this text, as well as others, falls only on unbelievers. Further, the aorist verb ἦλθεν is either an ingressive or dramatic aorist. The ingressive or inceptive aorist expresses a state or condition *just entered*.[32] On the other hand, the dramatic or proleptic aorist functions like a future, taking place after the realization of some condition.[33] This would mean that with the sixth seal the wrath of God has just begun or is about to appear. Since the sixth seal in Gundry's scheme of judgments is near the end of Daniel's seventieth week, the wrath of God only begins at the end of the week. The phenomena in the heavens are those that Jesus said would occur *after* the Tribulation but just *before* His return (Matt. 24:29, 30). In support of an ingressive or dramatic aorist interpretation, Gundry argues that "if the wrath of God has already fallen, how could the wicked be yet fleeing for refuge? Rather, the wrath is at the inception of its breaking forth . . . or on the verge of doing so. . . ."[34]

Gundry's view is exegetically possible. Note, however,

that it rests on these contestable points: (1) Each series of judgments takes one to the end of the Tribulation period. On some views of the judgments, the sixth seal would occur in the first half of the week; for others it would occur about the middle of the week. (2) When the wrath comes, it only touches the wicked. It seems to me that the wrath is so general that it comes on all.[35] The passage speaks of the wrath falling on great men, rich and strong, slave and free, as well as the kings of the earth and commanders. Their response may indicate, however, that they are unbelievers, but the response may simply be chosen from many that could be recorded to show that God is just in bringing His judgment. Revelation 3:10 says that this period of trial comes on the "whole world," again indicating the general character of the wrath. Moreover, if the early seal judgments are the wrath of God, a point yet to be argued, then it is difficult to see how famine, war, and death would fail to touch believers as well as unbelievers. (3) While ἦλθεν may be an ingressive or a dramatic aorist, it could just as well be constative or complexive. This would mean that the wrath of God has come, not just in the sixth seal, but in the six seals viewed as a whole. Moreover, it should be noted that the statement about the wrath of God is in the mouths of unbelievers, not angelic or divine messengers. It may be that with the increased severity of the judgments, people are just beginning to recognize that this is not simply a stroke of bad luck, but the outpouring of God's wrath. Gundry's question as to why the wicked should be seeking refuge has a simple answer. They have no idea how much more judgment or wrath to expect. Therefore, they have no idea if the wrath of God is about to be finished. Suppose there was a great earthquake in Los Angeles; the people would seek safety because they would not know whether there would be further quakes or whether the disturbance was over. Or, if they were to read their Bibles and find out what was ahead in the final judgments, they would understandably flee.

A second possibility for resolving the dispute is to attempt to identify the commencement of divine wrath with the arrival of the Day of the Lord. A number of pretribulationists hold that the Day of the Lord begins immediately after the Rapture or at least with the start of the Tribulation.[36] Probably the strongest argument in support of this view is the identification of the Man of Sin (1 Thess. 2:3) with the prince who makes the covenant with many and begins Daniel's seventieth week (Dan. 9:27). Since, however, there are two satanic masterpieces on the scene during the Tribulation (cf. the two Beasts of Rev. 13), the prince and the Man of Sin may not be the same person. Moreover, Gundry presents some formidable arguments against beginning the Day of the Lord with either the Rapture or the start of the Tribulation. The most significant points he makes are: (1) The events that accompany the arrival of the Day of the Lord in the Old Testament seem to best parallel the judgments in Revelation that relate to Armageddon and the *end* of the period. (2) The Day cannot begin without the revelation of the Antichrist and the apostasy. If the Day of the Lord begins with the Rapture and/or Tribulation, then these events would appear to come before the Rapture, which is supposed to be a signless and imminent event.[37] (3) Revelation 11:1–13, Gundry thinks, requires the appearance and ministry of Elijah. This ministry covers the last half of the Tribulation so that the Day of the Lord could not precede Elijah's appearance.[38]

I think that Gundry is probably right in arguing that the Day of the Lord does not begin with the Tribulation, although I would start the Day of the Lord about the middle of the week (cf. Jer. 30:7; Joel 2:1–11; Matt. 24:15; 2 Thess 2:3–4). Thus, the *terminus a quo* of the Day of the Lord is indecisive unless one assumes that divine wrath coincides with the Day of the Lord. Put differently, divine wrath may not be confined simply to the Day of the Lord.

Is there any evidence that the whole of the Tribulation is the outpouring of divine wrath? I think there is. While it is true that the judgments of the Tribulation period intensify in number and severity, I think that those who try to distinguish varieties of distress or wrath neglect the relationship of Revelation 4 and 5 to the judgments that follow. While our Lord was on this earth He declared that *all* judgment had been committed into His hands (John 5:22). The assumption of this judicial and judgmental authority is strikingly set forth in the scenes of Revelation 4 and 5. True, this authority is not completely discharged until the events of Revelation 20:11–15 are finished. But it does commence with chapters 4 and 5. Christ alone has the authority to take the scroll and to break *its seals.* *Every* judgment from the first seal to the last judgment comes as the *retributive* wrath of God. The early seals relate to the breaking of the seals of this scroll given to Christ. It is the Lamb, Christ, who breaks the seals before the wrath proceeds (Rev. 6:1, 3, 5, 7, 9, 12). To identify the wrath of God simply with His *direct* intervention is to overlook the fact that primary and secondary agency *both* belong to God. Would anyone *deny* that the Northern Kingdom had been judged by God because Assyria conquered her? Did the Southern Kingdom escape the wrath of God for her sin because the instrument of judgment was Nebuchadnezzar and Babylon? Surely the answer is no. Then why should anyone think that because the early seals and trumpets relate to famine and war as well as natural phenomena that they cannot and are not expressions of the wrath of God? Is it not characteristic of God's judgment that He withholds the severest aspects of it until the sinner has shown that he is wholly unrepentant?

Let me make this point in another context; I cannot emphasize it enough. Suppose someone said that divine activity in history is confined to miracle but not to providence. Would we agree? I think not. Providence is every bit as much an *act* of God as is miracle. Even the oppression of Israel by Satan and the tyranny of the Antichrist and the False Prophet are expressions of divine wrath. The incident in David's life where he numbered Israel shows that God used Satan in bringing judgment (2 Sam 24:1; cf. 1 Chron. 21:1). The activity of the *whole* period proceeds from the activity of the worthy Lamb; it is He who breaks the seals (Rev. 5:11–14; cf. Rev. 6:1, 3, 5, 7, 9, 11). One cannot exegetically classify various kinds of wrath and distinguish their recipients, and thus avoid the conclusion that the whole seventieth week is a time of God's retributive wrath. It seems to me that if the church experiences these judgments, this promise to the *church* is vitiated. If I am right on this point, the argument cuts against *both* midtribulationism and posttribulationism since both positions fail to recognize that divine wrath begins with the first seal and the commencement of the Tribulation period.

One might object that the argument just presented does not show the inevitability of a pretribulation Rapture.[39] All that the argument shows is that the church has been promised protection, not Rapture, from divine wrath, and that wrath begins with the commencement of the Tribulation period. Thus, I now turn to the second of the arguments.

The Church Is Promised Exemption Not Only From Divine Wrath but Also From the Time of Wrath

This promise is contained in Revelation 3:10. Townsend observes that no verse establishes explicitly the relationship of the Rapture to the Tribulation, but this one comes close.[40] And it is for this reason that Gundry says that it is the most debated verse in the Rapture discussion.[41] All parties to the discussion agree that it promises protection to the church. The question that divides us has to do with the nature of that protection. Posttribulationists believe that the promised protection is within the Tribulation (internal preservation). Midtribulationists take a mediating position. They see the protection as both internal and external, but the external protection begins at the middle of Daniel's seventieth week.

The key phrase is κἀγώ σε τηρήσω ἐκ τῆς ὥρας τοῦ πειρασμοῦ ("I will keep you from the hour of testing"). The word τηρήσω is usually translated "keep" but most would agree that "preserve" or "protect" is more accurate. Thus, Townsend can write: "Whatever the promise involves, its great fruit will be the genuine preservation and protection of the Church during the hour of testing."[42]

The *nature* of the protection is indicated by the word ἐκ. All lexicons and grammars are in essential agreement that ἐκ means "out of, out from within."[43] Posttribulationists take this in two ways. The church will be *in* the Tribulation or Jacob's time of trouble but protected either by (1) removal from this time or (2) by being preserved through it.[44] Had John wanted to express protection through the period, either ἐν or διά would have served better. Furthermore, since many saints die under persecution at the hands of the Antichrist, Satan, and the wicked, one might wonder in what sense they are "preserved."

This leaves the first view, removal from within the hour of testing. It is a modified form of this view that Gundry defends. He argues that ἐκ is a preposition of motion (thought or physical direction). It means *out from within*. It does not represent a position already taken outside its object. Thus, it cannot represent a stationary position outside the sphere of Tribulation. If ἐκ is ever used without the *idea of emergence,* that use is exceptional. The meaning here is that the church is *in* the Tribulation but is removed from it. Such a view, Gundry contends, fits a posttribulational scheme of eschatology.[45]

Jeffrey Townsend has argued convincingly that "sufficient evidence exists throughout the history of the meaning and usage of ἐκ to indicate that this preposition may also *denote a position outside its object with no thought of prior existence within the object or of emergence from the object*" [emphasis his].[46] I shall summarize his argument.

Liddell and Scott give several examples in classical literature of the preposition, primarily in early writers, under the heading, "of position, *outside of, beyond.*" They cite Murray's rendering of *The Iliad's* ἐκ βελέων (the translation of importance is in italics): "Thereafter, will we hold ourselves aloof from the fight, *beyond the range of missiles,* lest haply any take wound on wound. . . ."[47] In this and other occurrences, although rare, ἐκ clearly *cannot* mean motion "out from within." Gundry is not unaware of this evidence, but confines it to early authors and certain frozen or idiomatic forms of expression.[48] Whether this is so or not, the evidence presented does show that even in the early stages of the development of the Greek language ἐκ could denote a position outside of as well as motion "out from within."[49]

In the Septuagint instances of the outside position of ἐκ continue. An important example is found in Proverbs 21:23. There the verb διατηρεῖ + ἐκ is used: "The one who guards his mouth and tongue *keeps* (διατηρεῖ) his soul from (ἐκ) trouble." The ideas of prior existence or emission are absent.

Moreover, this is a significant example since the verb διατηρέω is a compound of τηρέω, which is used in Revelation 3:10. The preposition δία is prefixed, and only serves to intensify, not change, the idea of the verb.[50]

Proverbs 21:23 is not a unique case. The outside position can be demonstrated in a number of cases where verbs synonymous to τηρέω are used: Joshua 2:13 (ἐξαιρέω + ἐκ); Psalm 33:19 (LXX 32:19); 56:13 (LXX 55:13); Proverbs 23:14 (all three have ῥύομαι + ᾽εκ); and possibly Psalm 59:1–2 (σῶσον + ἐκ, ἐξελοῦ + ἐκ, and ῥῦσαι + ἐκ where the meaning might be "save me by keeping me out of the hand of my enemies who surround me.")[51] Thus, the Septuagint gives us evidence of ἐκ where it has a position outside its object and where the examples are neither early nor frozen. There are also examples in Josephus.[52]

Not only is it possible to find examples outside the New Testament, but the New Testament offers evidence for such a use as well. Acts 15:29 is a case in point. Like Proverbs 21:23 διατηρέω + ἐκ provides the outside position. The brethren in Jerusalem send a letter to Gentiles in Antioch requesting them "to *keep* themselves *from* certain practices that are offensive to their Jewish brethren." The request is for future abstention, not the accusation of practices from which the Gentiles are to abstain in the future.[53]

There are as well at least four other New Testament verses that merit examination because they contain verbs used with ἐκ, where ἐκ reflects a position outside its object.

John 12:27 is important for our discussion, since it is written by the same author; it uses a synonym of τηρέω (in this case σώζω), and the verb is followed by ἐκ. Jesus says, "Father, save me from this hour." The first question that arises is whether Jesus was asking for protection in an hour that He had already entered (inside preservation) or protection from that hour entirely (outside preservation). The verb σώζω is capable of either interpretation. A. T. Robertson is certain that Jesus had already entered that hour.[54]

Against Robertson's view is the way in which the word *hour* is used in John 7:30; 8:20; and in the immediate context, 12:23–24; to refer to Jesus' betrayal and death followed by His

Resurrection. The hour then is future, and Jesus' request is to
be saved from it. The correctness of this interpretation is supported by the way in which other synoptic writers record this
request. Matthew says, "Let this cup pass from me" (26:39),
and Luke writes, "Remove this cup from me" (22:42). It would
thus appear that Jesus is asking for preservation *from* rather
than deliverance *in* or *through* the hour of His agony. If so,
John 12:27 is an example (like Rev. 3:10) of ἐκ indicating the
outside position.[55]

Hebrews 5:7 is a second text that is relevant to our discussion. The crucial Greek words are σώζειν . . . ἐκ θανάτου
("to the one who was able to *save* him *from* death"). From the
description of the prayer (e.g., "with loud crying"), it is fair
to identify this with the Gethsemane prayer (Matt. 26:39; cf.
Mark 14:36; Luke 22:42). Jesus is not asking for salvation *out
of* death because that would be inconsistent with the request
made in Luke 22:42 to have the cup removed. Therefore, if
Hebrews 5:7 is to be harmonized with the other gospel accounts, then the emphasis must be on preservation *from* death,
not on resurrection out of death (this would be the outside
position, not emergence from within).[56]

James 5:20 is another case of σώζω + ἐκ where the meaning of the ἐκ is a position outside its object. The Greek says
σώσει . . . ἐκ θανάτου: "save [the sinner's] soul *from* death."
From verse 19 we learn that this is a brother who has strayed
from the truth, and is in need of being returned (ἐπιστρέφω)
to his former way of life. If this is a brother who has embraced
false doctrine or practice, then the death spoken of in 5:20 is
physical death. Another way of putting it is that if the Scriptures teach the security of the believer, then physical death
must be in view. From 1 Corinthians 11:30 we know that the
church was taught the continuance in sin resulted in sickness
and premature death (cf. James 5:15–16). If then the death in
this verse is physical death, ἐκ cannot mean "out from within"
but must mean "outside" its object.[57]

The final New Testament text to be considered that bears
on Revelation 3:10 is John 17:15. The importance of this text
to the discussion at hand cannot be overestimated. This is the
only other occurrence of τηρέν + ἐκ in either classical or

biblical Greek. It is, moreover, significant that both instances are in the mouth of our Lord and from the pen of John.[58]

There are two petitions in this verse.[59] The first petition in 17:15a is a negative request using αἴρω and ἐκ. Here Jesus asks that the disciples should not be physically removed from the earth. While their removal would be one way of preserving them, it would not allow them to carry out other commands and purposes that God had for them (e.g., witnesses, John 15:27). The presence of αἴρω + ἐκ is of interest here. The verb (αἴρω) naturally lends itself to the idea of motion, even motion out of (cf. οἱ ἐρχόμενοι ἐκ, Rev. 7:14). Thus, it would appear that the postribulation view, which Gundry is defending with Revelation 3:10 could better have been expressed by αἴρω ἐκ. Townsend's comment is to the point as well: "This points up the necessity of considering the verb and the preposition together and not simply isolating the components of the expression. The context is also an important factor in deciding the exact force of the phrase. The disciples were in the world (17:11), so ἐκ must mean 'out from within' in John 17:15a."[60]

In 17:15b we have the second petition. It is a contrast with the first, being introduced by the Greek preposition ἀλλά. The request is for preservation from (τηρέω + ἐκ) the Evil One.[61] Gundry argues that τηρέω ἐκ cannot be the Rapture or the results of the Rapture in Revelation 3:10 since in its only other occurrence it is opposed to αἴρω ἐκ, a verb and preposition that would describe the Rapture (see my comments above about αἴρω + ἐκ). The point, however, that Gundry and other posttribulationists tend to overlook is that pretribulationists claim justification for their position based on *the combined effect of the verb and the preposition in context*.[62] Here the context has the disciples *in* the physical world. This combined with the meaning of αἴρω and its use with ἐκ, gives 17:15a the idea of removal from within. The situation in 17:15b is entirely different. The disciples spiritually were *not* in the Evil One when Jesus prayed. It is this fact in conjunction with the meaning of τηρέω, which has the idea of protection *not* motion, that requires the ἐκ of 17:15b to be understood as preservation in a position outside the preposition's object.[63]

Gundry's interpretation of John 17:15b is at odds with this view. He says that the disciples were *in* the moral sphere of the devil, and that Jesus prays for their protection since they were to be left in the world (John 17:15a).[64] This is an important point of disagreement, but I think that Gundry is wrong. My reasons are as follows. First, Gundry's position best accords with the theme of 17:17–18. There the topic is progression in sanctification and protection from the moral assaults of the Wicked One. On the other hand, the immediate context of 17:15, verses 11–16, is concerned with salvation and the possession of eternal life.[65]

Second, this interpretation seems contrary to the Johannine emphasis of the separation of the believer from the realm of Satan. The believer walks in light as opposed to darkness, and has life as opposed to being dead. First John 5:18–19 expresses this idea. The Evil One does not *touch* (ἅπτω) the Christian because he is born of God. This is contrasted with the unbeliever who *lies* in the power of the Evil One.[66]

Finally, Gundry's view is not in keeping with the general New Testament teaching that the believer has been translated from the kingdom of Satan into the kingdom of God's Son (Col. 1:13). The disciples then were not, as Gundry and some posttribulationists suppose, in the moral sphere, the kingdom, of the Evil One. Jesus prays that God would keep them. This is exactly in keeping with John 10:27–29, where Jesus says that no one is able to snatch believers out of the Father's hand. Thus, if I am right on the point before us, τηρέω ἐκ in John 17:15b is an expression of protection from an *outside* position.[67]

The application of this to Revelation 3:10 is as follows. Just as the disciples were not in the Evil One, so the Philadelphians would not be in the hour of testing. The promise of our Lord is to keep them outside the hour of trial. If this be so, it does not describe the Rapture per se. Instead it looks at the results or consequence of the Rapture. Revelation 3:10 does not describe the manner in which this protection is achieved, it only tells of the condition of the church during that hour.[68]

Having now completed our discussion of the verb and preposition, τηρήσω ἐκ, we are now ready to examine the rest of the promise, the object of ἐκ (τῆς ὥρας τοῦ πειρασμοῦ, "the hour of testing"). It is clear that the promise relates to a specific time; τῆς is the article of previous reference. Jesus is talking about a well-known time of distress and trouble. This was the Tribulation period (Deut. 4:26–31; Isa. 13:6–13; 17:4–11; Jer. 30:4–11; Ezek. 20:33–38; Dan. 9:27; 12:1; Zech. 14:1–4; Matt. 24:9–31). It is further specified by the qualifying phrases of 3:10 as the time portrayed in Revelation 6–18. The combination ἐκ τῆς ὥρας is significant. The promise is a pres-ervation *outside of a time period*. It is this combination of terms that has led pretribulationists to affirm that the church *cannot* be in this period. Thiessen correctly noted that the promise was an *exemption from a period of trial*.[69] Ryrie makes this point, "It is impossible to conceive of being in the location where something is happening and being exempt from the time of the happening."[70]

Gundry tries to undercut the force of "the hour" in three ways. First, he suggests that the hour will elapse in heaven as well as on earth.[71] Some think that heaven is outside time and disagree with Gundry. But what is even more to the point is the fact that this is an hour that is to come on the "inhabited earth" (οἰκουμένης). This is an hour that is clearly related to the earth.[72]

Second, he argues that "hour of testing" emphasizes the trials not the idea of time.[73] While Delling allows for this possibility, he nevertheless gives Revelation 3:10 as an ex-ample of ὥρα in the sense of "the divinely appointed time for the actualisation of apocalyptic happenings."[74] There is the further point that the presence of the article indicates it is identical with a well-known hour (cf. Dan. 9:27). Time and events are intermingled here.

Third, Gundry cites Jeremiah 30:7 (LXX 37:7) as a par-allel promise given to Israel about the same time period. In this case σώζω is used with ἀπό. Israel is promised that she would be saved from the time of Jacob's trouble. His point is that the idea of separation is *stronger* in ἀπό than ἐκ, yet Israel is *in* and not outside the period. Thus, Gundry can conclude, "If a pretribulational rapture was not or will not be required for deliverance from the time of Jacob's distress, neither will a pretribulational rapture be required for preservation from the hour of testing."[75] Is, however, Gundry's suggested parallel a good one? I do not think so. There happens to be an important difference between Jeremiah 30:7 and Revelation 3:10. The context of Jeremiah 30, particularly verses 6 and 7, shows that Israel is *already within* the time of trouble. Therefore, the only kind of deliverance that is possible is deliverance from within the period. Revelation 3:10 does not set the church within the hour. Thus, its deliverance could be an *exemption from the period of time.*

Townsend can conclude:

> This is confirmed in Matthew 24 where the Jews are told to flee the persecution of the one who desecrates the Temple and in Rev. 12 where the dragon persecutes the woman and her offspring. From this trouble, the nation is promised rescue in Jer. 30:7. Thus the promises are different and not comparable. Israel is promised rescue within the time of trouble, the Church is promised preservation from the hour of testing. Only the latter case demands rapture from earth to heaven.[76]

The fact that the church is removed from this period seems to me to be further supported by the two qualifying phrases, "which is about to come upon the whole inhabited earth" and "to test those who dwell upon the earth." The hour of trial here seems to be universal as opposed to a local persecution (cf. Rev. 2:10). Thus, if the wrath is falling *everywhere,* it is difficult to see how preservation could be by any other means than the Rapture, or removal. Furthermore, the purpose of the trial is to test earth-dwellers. The Greek word πειράζω, "to test," is used in both secular and biblical Greek of a test to reveal the true character of someone.[77] There is generally a negative intent, in the word "to break down" or "to demonstrate failure." One of the purposes of this period then is to demonstrate the complete failure of unregenerate men before God. The Tribulation period is thus the final condemning evidence against the wicked.

It should also be noted that this period has a special relationship to τούς κατοικοῦντας ἐπὶ τῆς γῆς ("earth-dwellers"). This designation occurs seven other times in Revelation:

6:10; 8:13; 11:10; 13:8, 14bis; 17:8. In 6:10 the earth-dwellers
are the persecutors against whom the martyrs plead for vengeance. In 8:13 a threefold woe is pronounced against them
because of the final three trumpets, which are to come. They
are the ones who gloat over the death of the two witnesses in
11:10 and worship the beast from the sea in 13:8. In 13:14 they
are the individuals who are deceived by the beast from the
land into making an image of the first beast.

These earth-dwellers gaze in wonder at the scarlet beast
in 17:8, while 13:8 and 17:8 add that their names are not
written in the Book of Life.[78] Charles[79] and Johnson[80] point
out that the phrase comes from the Hebrew idiom ישבי הארץ.
In Isaiah 24:1, 5, 6 and 26:9 this almost becomes a technical
term for those who are the persecutors of the saints in the
Tribulation. These persecutors are the *objects* of the test and
the judgment. They are the emperor worshipers. This does
not, of course, mean that righteous or saints are not present
on the earth during this period. All sides to the debate agree
on this point. However, the *purpose* of this period has a special
relationship to the wicked people. This time of testing demonstrates that they are incorrigible in their opposition to God.
They are the special objects of the testing and wrath.

Because of its importance, let me summarize what I have
argued: (1) I have tried to show that the outside or external
use of ἐκ is well within the range of exegetical possibilities for
the preposition. In every period of the development of the
Greek language examples can be found of this use. (2) The
single other occurrence of τηρέω ἐκ within either classical or
biblical Greek, John 17:15b, supports the outside position of
the ἐκ. (3) The function of the ἐκ is related to the idea of the
verb, some verbs being better suited to motion and emission
than others. (4) The combination of the verb τηρέω plus ἐκ
plus τῆς ὥρας all support the concept of removal or protection
from outside. (5) The qualifying phrases, "which is about to
come upon the whole inhabited world," and "to test those
who dwell upon the earth," show that the universal character
of trial demands removal and that the primary objects of the
judgments are the earth-dwellers, not necessitating the presence of the church. If the first consideration above establishes

the *possibility* of a pretribulation interpretation, then the final four points confirm its *probability* over other alternatives.

The Necessity of an Interval Between the Rapture of the Church and the Second Coming of Christ

A number of reasons have been given for the necessity of an interval between the Rapture and the Second Coming. The rewarding of the saints, the readying of the bride or the distinction between Christ's coming *for* His saints and His coming *with* the saints. These have generally been passed off by those who hold a posttribulational Rapture in one of two ways. Either the events in question could occur in a moment of time, making a lengthy interval of the type a midtribulationist or a pretribulationalist suggests unnecessary, or the differences are harmonizable into distinct aspects of a single complex event. There is one facet of this argument that is not so easily passed off, and I think that it points up the incompatibility between premillennialism and posttribulationism. I refer to the necessity of an interval so that some saints can be saved to go into the Millennium in nonglorified bodies.

Let me develop this argument in some detail. To begin with it is important to see the *need* for saints in nonglorified, physical bodies. While the Millennium will see the radical reduction of evil and the flourishing of righteousness, sin will still exist (cf. the need for sacrifices in Ezek. 43:13–27; Isa. 19:21; and the rebellion that closes the earthly reign of Christ in Rev. 20:7–10). There will be sickness and death (Isa. 65:20). There will be the building of houses and the planting of vineyards (Isa. 65:21–22). All of these are not usually thought of as a part of the life of those who have been glorified.

Why should this cause a problem for the posttribulationist? The difficulty arises from the fact that the Rapture and second coming of Christ are simply aspects of a single event. The righteous who are alive will be raptured at the Second Coming and are thus glorified (1 Cor. 15:51, 52). They will go into the kingdom with those who have been resurrected at Christ's Parousia in glorified bodies. At the same time the wicked, so the pretribulational argument goes, will be prevented from entering the kingdom and bound over for final judgment (e.g., Matt. 25:31–46). If all righteous are glorified before the Millennium and all wicked excluded from the kingdom, where do the people in nonglorified bodies come from to populate the Millennium?[81]

While a number of posttribulationists have not been aware of the problem, many have tried to offer various solutions to this problem. A common response is that numerous Jews will look on their Messiah as He returns to earth after the Rapture, and they will be saved and enter the kingdom in nonglorified physical bodies (Zech. 12:10–13:1; Rom. 11:26). They will populate the kingdom in natural bodies.[82]

Gundry propounds a most interesting variation of this resolution. He suggests that a "plausible" function for the 144,000 is that they may constitute a Jewish remnant who will be physically preserved through the Tribulation. They will resist the enticements of the Antichrist and turn to their Messiah as He returns. They will be both men and women who will populate and replenish the millennial earth. He holds this view in spite of the fact that Revelation 1 4 seems to say that they are celibate; they have not defiled themselves with women. Gundry understands this to refer to spiritual celibacy, not physical celibacy. These are ones who have resisted the spiritual seduction of Satan and the Antichrist.[83]

There are two responses that may be offered to this solution. First, there are some who argue that the repentance of Israel *precedes* the return of Christ (Hos. 5:15–6:3; Matt. 23:29). Israel finds herself under the chastening hand of God. She is the special object of satanic persecution (Rev. 12:13–17). Two-thirds of the nation is annihilated by the Gentiles (Zech. 13:8, 9), and all the nations have laid seige to the city of Jerusalem (Zech. 12:1–5; 14:1–3). The end appears near. The nation turns to God in repentance. Their Messiah now returns. The sight of the One they have rejected does not lead to salvation, rather it is the signal for immense mourning for the years of rejection (Zech. 12:11–14). The return of Christ is *signaled by* an acceptance of their Messiah rather than a *signal for* the acceptance of Jesus as the Christ.[84]

Second, even if the salvation of the nation is during the return of Christ, this in itself will not resolve the dilemma. It raises the question as to why these Jews are not raptured immediately to receive their glorified bodies.[85] Furthermore, there are many passages that speak of Gentiles populating the Millennium in nonglorified bodies (e.g., Isa. 19:18–25; Zech. 14:16–21; Isa. 60:1–3), and the aforementioned solution only allows Jews into the kingdom in natural bodies.

A second attempt to deal with this problem is to deny that all the wicked are destroyed at the coming of Christ to the earth.[86] If all the righteous are raptured and all the wicked are slain, then there would be the dramatic depopulation of the earth. However, Scripture does not demand that *all* unbelievers be destroyed at the Second Advent. Instead, only the *actively rebellious* unbelievers will be slain at Christ's return, fulfilling such passages as Revelation 19:15–18 and Jeremiah 25:31. Therefore, *many,* even *most,* of those who resist the truth will be destroyed but not *all.*[87]

Bell's point is well taken; the only problem is that it accounts for only part of the problem. Pretribulationists can grant his point, but we respond in this way. The *complete elimination* of the wicked from entrance into the kingdom rests *not just* on the destruction of the wicked at the descent of Christ at the Second Advent, *but also* on the separation of the sheep from the goats in the judgment that follows (Matt. 25:31–46). While many unbelievers will be slain at Christ's return, two judgments follow to root out all who remain. Ezekiel 20:37, 38 indicates that when Israel is established in the land at the return of their Messiah, there will be renewal of the covenant (v. 37) and the purging of the rebels from the nation (v. 38). Thus, all wicked will be separated from Israel. All remaining Gentile unbelievers will be eliminated at the sheep-and-goat judgment (Matt. 25:31–46). Therefore, *no* wicked will enter the kingdom.

A third response might be that the wicked enter the kingdom in keeping with a number of passages that teach that wicked live in the kingdom period (e.g., Isa. 37:32; 66:15–20; Joel 3:7, 8; Zech. 14:16–19; and Rev. 20:7–9).[88] The problem with this proposal is that it is really no solution at all. There are two issues related to the question at hand, the *entrance* of nonglorified saints (righteous or wicked) into the kingdom and the *existence* of wicked in the Millennium. Premillennialists all agree that there are wicked in the kingdom. But notice that depends on the entrance of nonglorified saints into the Millennium. If that is not possible, then there is *no* explanation for the existence of the wicked in this period. The arguments that pretribulationists and midtribulationists present are given to show that posttribulationists cannot account for the *entrance* of any people in nonglorified bodies. The righteous are raptured, and the wicked are excluded through death and judgment. Thus, to simply assert that wicked exist in the kingdom age is *no* answer to the problem. How do they enter?

What about the passages cited above? They fall into one of these three categories. First, some passages do not apply. Isaiah 37:32 deals only with deliverance from the seige during the time of Hezekiah. Joel 3:7–8 seems to be talking of the judgment that is to come *before* the kingdom begins. Unquestionably, wicked exist at the time of the Tribulation before the end.

Second, some of the passages teach that there will be those who survive the judgments before the Millennium begins. This is surely so. No one denies this, but it is simply not enough. For the argument is that those who do survive and are wicked, will be excluded from the kingdom as the goats of Matthew 25:31–46. However, do not some of the survivors go into the kingdom? It does appear that way. But they also seem to be righteous, not wicked. In Isaiah 66:19–20 they go forth to declare God's glory and gather others who are called "brothers" to worship God. Zechariah 14:16–19 teaches that Egyptians will survive, and also prescribes a penalty if they fail to celebrate the Feast of Tabernacles. From the threat it might be assumed that these are unbelievers. This, I think, is wrong. Isaiah 19:18–25 teaches that "Egypt" will be converted in that day. They will be God's people. The reason that punishment is promised is that, although redeemed, those who enter the kingdom will not yet be glorified, making them capable of sin. Third, some passages like Revelation 20:7–9 show that at the end of the kingdom evil people will exist and rebel against God. It says nothing about *entrance* into the kingdom.

Because I think this point is so important let me give the positive arguments for thinking that the wicked do not enter the kingdom. There are three lines of evidence. First, the already-mentioned teaching of Scripture is that there are judgments that precede the Millennium (Matt. 25:31–46, Gentiles; Ezek. 20:37–38, Jews). Second, there are passages that teach that the wicked will not escape the judgment of the Day of the Lord at Christ's coming. Isaiah 24:22 not only relates to the kings of the earth, but also to the hosts of heaven. It says that they will be gathered like prisoners in a dungeon and *confined*. Then, after many days they will be punished. Zephaniah 3:8 teaches that God's wrath will be poured out and that "all the earth will be devoured." First Thessalonians 5:3 says that unbelievers will have the woes of the Tribulation come upon them, and that "they shall not escape." Second Thessalonians 2:12 declares that when Christ comes, He will judge those "who did not believe the truth, but took pleasure in wickedness." Between the destruction at Christ's return and the judgment that follows, the wicked will all be judged. Third, numerous passages teach that there is a requirement of righteousness for entrance into the kingdom. Jesus told the multitudes that their righteousness had to exceed that of the Pharisees if they were to enter the kingdom of heaven (Matt. 5:20). In another place Jesus said that simply calling Him, "Lord" would not guarantee entrance into the kingdom. One had to do the will of God (Matt. 7:21). Jesus, talking to Nicodemus, said that if one was not "born again," he would not see the kingdom of God (John 3:3, 5). This surely meant more than simply heaven to Nicodemus.

But is this not also a problem for the pretribulationist or midtribulationist? Not if one distinguishes the conditions that obtain at the inauguration of the kingdom and those that come into existence as the period progresses. Only righteous, glorified and nonglorified, enter the kingdom, but later in the period those in nonglorified bodies will procreate normally. Some of their offspring will not believe. Therefore, the wicked or rebellious in the kingdom, as that period progresses, are the unbelieving children of believing parents. This alone can harmonize all that Scripture says on the matter.

A fourth solution is suggested by Gundry. As a good premillennialist he holds that there are *two* resurrections, one before the kingdom for the righteous and one after the Millennium for the wicked, but he sees only *one general* judgment. Thus, all the righteous are resurrected before the commencement of the kingdom and enjoy its blessings. However, not all the wicked are eliminated. Many will die in the judgments that immediately precede the Second Advent, but not all will be destroyed. Further, if you move the judgment of Matthew 25:31–46 to the period *after* the Millennium rather than *before* it, there will be unrighteous people, though a greatly reduced number, who enter the kingdom.[89]

Gundry's approach is a genuine solution to the problem if it can square with Scripture. The decisive issue is whether the judgment of Matthew 25 can be harmonized with and is identical to that of Revelation 20. There are some obvious differences. In Matthew there are sheep and goats, good and evil, while Revelation speaks of the wicked. Gundry says that these are harmonizable. Further, passages that teach rewards at Christ's coming do not necessitate a *formal* judgment. The punishment pronounced on the goats (everlasting punishment) and the reward given the righteous (eternal life) better accords with the eternal state rather than the millennial kingdom.[90]

In spite of all Gundry's arguments (some are more convincing than others) there is a decisive reason for rejecting his view. He simply does not deal with the opening lines of the judgment scene: "But when the Son of Man comes in His glory, and all the angels with Him, then He will sit on His glorious throne. And all the nations will be gathered before Him" (vv. 31–32a). Here in the passage is the chronological setting for the judgment. It is when Christ comes in *glory* with his angels.[91] When is this? The context is clear. Matthew 24:30 marks the glorious appearing as "after the tribulation of those days," and verse 31 associates that coming with His angels. While an amillennialist can identify Matthew 25:31–46 with Revelation 20:11–15 because the Second Coming comes at the end of the Millennium, a premillennialist *cannot* do this. A judgment that occurs *at* Christ's glorious coming and one that occurs *after* the Millennium are separated by a thousand years.

There is, however, an objection raised by Gundry to my position that needs to be answered. He thinks that the reward, "eternal life," and the punishment, "eternal punishment" (Matt. 25:46), lend themselves to the eternal phase of the kingdom and the final judgment of the wicked.[92]

While there is the mention of "eternal life" and "eternal punishment," this does not constitute a good reason for placing this judgment after the Millennium rather than before it. First, as already mentioned, Matthew 25:31 clearly relates these events to 24:29–31, the Second Coming. Second, a period of confinement and judgment followed by final consignment in hell for the wicked is in keeping with Isaiah 24:21–22. Moreover, the intermediate state of the wicked is pictured as a time of torment (Luke 16:19–31) and therefore is justifiably called eternal punishment, albeit the first phase. Third, if the millennial kingdom is the first phrase of the eternal kingdom or reign of Christ (1 Cor. 15:21–28), then eternal life is not an inappropriate name for the reward of the righteous. Moreover, there are those who think that the righteous who enter the kingdom age will not die, but receive glorified bodies at the end of the age, since the first resurrection is finished at the beginning of the kingdom period. Finally, even if "eternal life" and "eternal punishment" must refer to the *final* state of the righteous and wicked, that does not necessitate our disregard for the one chronological indicator. Often in prophetic literature there is the foreshortening of two events so that they appear to be temporally successive, but in fact are separated by many years (e.g., Isa. 61:1–2 treats as one the Advent and the Second Coming although they are separated by two thousand years; Dan. 12:1–2 and John 5:29 refer to both the first and second resurrections, which will be separated by one thousand years).

There is a final proposal that we should consider. George Rose in *Tribulation Till Translation* postulates a *forty-five* day period between the Rapture and the beginning of the Millennium for people to be saved, and go into the kingdom in nonglorified bodies.[93]

Before commenting on the viability of the approach, it should be noted that this solution concedes the point that both pretribulationists and midtribulationists have made. *There must be an interval,* whether it is forty-five days, three and a half years, or seven years. Having said this, is the proposal a good one? I think not. (1) Why does Rose choose forty-five days? It would seem to me that thirty or seventy-five would have more scriptural support given the differing number of days in Daniel 12:7, 11–12. (2) The point made against Gundry's view above, that the judgment of sheep and goats occurs when the Son of Man comes in glory, not forty-five days later, applies with equal force here. (3) There is a problem that every view that only allows a very small interval at the *end* of the week must deal with. Everyone agrees that the last half of Daniel's seventieth week will see the rule and tyranny of the Beast or the Antichrist. Revelation 13:16–18 makes it clear that extreme economic pressure will be brought on all alive to coerce worship for the Beast and extend his dominion. It will be impossible to either buy or sell without the mark of the Beast. Many who resist him will be martyred, and, on a posttribulation view, those who resist and are not martyred will be raptured right at the Second Advent. Where then will the converts come from? Anyone who takes the mark of the Beast *cannot* be saved (Rev. 14:9, 11; cf. Rev. 20:4 where those who reign with Christ "had not received the mark upon their forehead and upon their hand").

While this argument does not establish a pretribulation Rapture (it is as appropriate an argument for a midtribulationist as for a pretribulationist), it does show that there must be a separation of the Rapture from the Second Advent so that people with natural, physical bodies can be saved and populate the millennial kingdom. Rather than being a problem of pretribulationists' making, it demonstrates the incompatability of the posttribulational view with premillennialism.

The Differences Between Rapture Passages and Second Coming Passages

Both pretribulationists and midtribulationists have pointed out differences between the Rapture and the Second Coming. The central passages dealing with each event reveal these differences. By central passages I mean John 14:1–14; 1 Corinthians 15:51–58; and 1 Thessalonians 4:13–18 for the Rapture, and Zechariah 14:1–21; Matthew 24:29–31; Mark 13:24–27; Luke 21:25–27; and Revelation 19 for the Second Coming.

I think it is helpful to divide these differences into two groups: omissions and inconsistencies.

The major omissions in my judgment are as follows. First, in passages that deal with the Second Advent there are signs or events that lead up to and signal the return of Jesus Christ (e.g., Matt. 24:4–28; Rev. 19:11–21). In each of these passages of Scripture there is the careful and extensive itemizing of details that should alert believers in that day that the Second Advent is about to occur. Matthew 24 is by far the most exhaustive and in my judgment relates events that will occur throughout the Tribulation. In Matthew 24:32–51 our Lord makes it clear that these signs are to alert the believer that His coming is near: "Even so, when you see all these things, you know that it is near, right at the door" (Matt. 24:33).

On the other hand, there is no mention of any signs or events that precede the Rapture of the church in *any* of the Rapture passages. The point seems to be that the believer prior to this event is to look, not for some sign, but the Lord from heaven. If the Rapture was a part of the complex of events that make up the Second Advent, and not distinct from it, then we would expect that there would be a mention of signs or events in at least one passage.

Second, every passage that deals with the Second Coming is set in the context of Tribulation and judgment. Zechariah 14:1–2 tells of a seige of Jerusalem immediately before Christ's return; it results in the capture of the city, the ransacking of property, and the rape of the women of the city. In the Olivet

Discourse the Second Advent follows a time of "great distress, unequaled from the beginning of the world until now—and never to be equaled again" (Matt. 24:21). As a matter of fact, had not the days of the trial been cut short, no flesh would have survived. Finally, the return of Christ as taught in Revelation 19 follows the outpouring of the judgments of chapters 6–18.[94]

Contrast the trial that constitutes the context for the Second Coming passages with the silence about any such distress in the Rapture texts. In each of the Rapture passages there is no mention of trial before the event. Rather, there is the bare promise of Christ's return for His own.

Third, there is no clear, indisputable reference to the Rapture in any Second Advent passage. Pretribulationism, midtribulationism, and posttribulationism are agreed that Scripture teaches clearly a coming of Christ *after* the Tribulation (e.g., Zech. 14:1–3; Matt. 24:4–31), but in neither of these passages is there any clear statement of a catching away of believers at that time.[95] Some of these passages go into great detail concerning the Second Advent, and yet there is no clear mention of a Rapture. On the other hand, there seem to be differences of some significance. In the Rapture saints meet the Lord in the air (1 Thess. 4:17), whereas saints meet Christ on the Mount of Olives at the Second Advent (Zech. 14:3). As a matter of fact, it seems fair to ask what purpose the Rapture would serve in a scheme where the saints immediately accompany Christ to the earth. Gundry, unlike many posttribulationists, does have a purpose for the Rapture. He has the saints raptured just before Armageddon and what he sees as the commencement of the Day of the Lord. The Rapture is the method that God uses to protect the saints from His wrath. It is worth noting that such a view is not unlike pretribulationism or midtribulationism, in that it postulates an interval between the Rapture and Second Advent, and sees the Rapture as the method of escape from the wrath of God. The interval and the wrath are simply confined to a very small portion of the Tribulation period.

To summarize the point being made, in passages like Matthew 24:29–31 and Revelation 19:11–21, which deal in such detail with the Second Advent, it is surprising that there is no indisputable reference to the Rapture.

Fourth, nowhere in the texts that deal with the Second Advent is there the teaching about the translation of living saints. Gundry claims that Matthew 24 is the most complete text on the Second Coming. There is nothing taught anywhere else in Scripture that is not contained in this single passage.[96] Yet, even if we grant for the sake of argument that the gathering of the elect in Matthew 24:31 is a reference to the Rapture, there still remains a silence about the translation of living saints. It is for this reason, I think, that Paul can call it a "mystery" in the strictest sense (1 Cor. 15:51).

Fifth, there is no clear, indisputable mention of the resurrection of the church at the Second Advent. There are two passages that deal with resurrection in connection with the Second Coming. Daniel 12:1–2 is the first. There it is stated that *after* a time of distress, there will be a resurrection. Those who participate in this resurrection are called "your [Daniel's] people." This is a reference to Israel, although some would like to broaden the reference. At any rate, this is not a clear, indisputable reference to the church.

The other reference is in the New Testament. It is found in Revelation 20:4. There, the resurrection is of those "who were beheaded because of their testimony for Jesus and because of the word of God." They are clearly identified with those who have been martyred during the Tribulation period. Now it might be argued that those martyred are simply a part of a larger group called the church, though that larger body is not specified by name.

One cannot rule out that possibility. However, if the martyrs are a part of the church, one wonders why the term "church" never appears in Revelation after chapter 3, and the only clear reference thereafter to this body comes in the benediction (Rev. 22:17). In the first three chapters the term appears regularly, but never again after 4:1. The point is even more striking when one studies the little phrase, "He who has an ear, let him hear what the Spirit says to the churches." This exhortation is to be found in 2:7, 11, 17, 29; 3:6, 13, 22. All of these are in the first three chapters of Revelation. Something similar occurs one other time in the book. In Revelation 13:9 one reads, "If *any one* has an ear, let him hear." For those who think that the church is raptured before the judgments begin, the omission of the word "churches" is significant.[97]

In fairness to those who disagree with me I should note that they have given answers for the absence of the term "church" after Revelation 3. Generally, their response has taken one of two directions. It has been argued that the references to the church in the first three chapters of Revelation are to local assemblies and not to the universal body. This may be. But it still leaves the question as to why there is *no* mention of local assemblies in the last 19 chapters of Revelation. There are references to saints and elect. They are not said to be the church, however.

A second line of response is found in Gundry's work. He points out that this argument is a two-edged sword. While it is true that there is no mention of the church on the earth during the Tribulation period, it is also the case that the book of Revelation takes us into heaven, and there is also no clear reference to the church in heaven.[98] It may look as though the argument comes to a draw. In my judgment this is not quite the case. If one reads Revelation 4–22, he will find that the vast preponderance of the material deals with the *earth,* not heaven. Thus, while the lack of an indisputable reference to the church in heaven counts against a pretribulation or mid-tribulation position, the damage to a posttribulation position is greater because of the greater amount of material.[99]

Sixth, there seem to be changes with the earth associated with the Second Coming. For instance, Zechariah 14:4 speaks of the Mount of Olives splitting and forming a large valley. Furthermore, Ezekiel 40–48, in the distribution of the land of Palestine in the Millennium, assumes some geological changes that could be the result of the Second Coming. On the other hand, from the passages that treat the Tribulation, it does not appear that the Rapture of the church will bring about such changes, at least passages that deal with the Rapture do not explicitly connect changes in geology with that event.

I would now like to turn to the second group of differences. They are much fewer in number, but more troublesome as it seems to me that they are inconsistencies. That is, these differences are not capable of harmonization.

First, there seems to be an inconsistency between the *time* of the resurrection at the Rapture and at the Second Coming. In the central Rapture passage dealing with this issue, 1 Thessalonians 4:13–18, the time of the resurrection of dead saints is clearly stated to be *during* the descent of Christ to the earth. Those raptured, living and dead saints, will be caught up to meet the Lord in the air. Contrast that information with what is found in Revelation 19–20. There, the order seems to be: the descent of Christ, the slaying of His enemies, the casting of the Beast and the False Prophet into the lake of fire, the binding of Satan, and *then* the resurrection of the saints. It seems as though the resurrection of the dead will be *during* the descent at the Rapture, but *after* the descent at the Second Coming.[100]

Second, there seems to be an inconsistency between the destination of those who are raptured in the Rapture and the destination of those who participate in the Second Coming. In the posttribulation understanding of the events that surround the Second Coming, the church will be caught up to meet the Lord in the air and will immediately accompany Him on His continued descent to the earth. Compare that with John 14:3. In the Rapture the Lord is going to come and take those raptured to be with Him. The clear implication is that the raptured saints will be taken to heaven, not earth. If this is so, then the destination of those caught up in the Rapture will be heaven. According to the Second Coming passages, however, the saints involved are headed for the earth.

As I stated at the beginning of this argument, these differences have always seemed weighty to pretribulationists and midtribulationists. That raises the question, why do posttribulationists find such an argument unconvincing? One possible response might go something like this. Differences are insignificant unless the differences constitute contradictions. According to logic, a system that contains a contradiction cannot be true. But, on the other hand, if the differences are not contradictions they can be harmonized as *aspects* of a single, complex event. For example, the oft-heard distinction between Christ's coming *for* His saints and His coming *with* them can be harmonized into one complex event where the Rapture is immediately followed by the return of Christ to the earth.

Such a response is very interesting. It is in my judgment false but quite instructive. It is false because it subjects the differences to too high a criterion of significance. Arguments are usually classified in one of two ways. Some are called *conclusive* arguments. They may be characterized as follows. The premises of such arguments are *known* to be true, and the conclusions follow *necessarily* from those premises. Arguments of this sort are decisive, and leave no question as to the truth of a view. The problem with arguments of this type is that they are difficult to achieve. It is hard to find premises that disputants agree are true, and then the conclusion does not always follow necessarily from those premises. For this reason, a second class of arguments are more common. These arguments are called *reliable* arguments. Their conclusions rest on *good, adequate,* or *appropriate* evidence. Such arguments do not rule out the possibility of all alternative positions. Rather they show that the conclusion has good or adequate warrant. That is, the conclusion is justified.

If the differences mentioned above are contradictions, then we have a *conclusive* argument that two events *cannot* be aspects of *one* more complex event. However, if the differences are not contradictory and thus not conclusive, it does not mean that the differences are insignificant. It simply leaves open the possibility that the Rapture *may* or *may not* be a part of the same event. It is at this point that the discussion becomes instructive as to why men and women of equal commitment to Christ and equal mental abilities differ on this issue. One person may think that the differences are numerous enough and significant enough to warrant taking the Rapture and Second Coming as separate events. On the other hand, another person may judge that the similarities are more numerous than the differences and that the differences are relatively insignificant and harmonizable; this person will take the Rapture and the Second Coming as aspects of a single, complex event.

One final word on this matter. It is only after the event that we can see finally whether the differences or the similarities were the more significant. One can understand the point

I am making by studying the expectation of those who awaited our Lord's First Coming. Some thought that there would be two messiahs, a suffering messiah (Messiah ben Joseph) and a reigning messiah (Messiah ben David). I am sure that there were those who thought that one messiah would perform both functions. It was only after the event that we could know for sure whether there would be two messiahs or one messiah with two comings. Thus, while it may seem "natural" for some like Gundry to harmonize these differences into a single event, it seems just as appropriate, at least at this point in redemption history, to see two events.

CONCLUSION

For me at least, the church will not go through the Tribulation because of the character of that entire period as a time of the outpouring of penal, retributive, divine wrath, as well as the promises of God to the church that exempt it from both the time and the experience of wrath. Further, it is necessary to separate the Rapture of the church from the Second Advent of Christ because of the need for an interval for people to be saved, so that they can enter into the kingdom age in natural, nonglorified bodies. Finally, the differences between Rapture passages and Second Coming passages lead me to believe that there are two separate events referred to in the passages.

My writing has of necessity been argumentative because it has been my responsibility to present as strong a case as possible for my position. However, let me close on a conciliatory note. While we might wish unanimity of opinion on all doctrinal matters, that is not necessarily possible or even best for us. When men and women of the Book disagree, such disagreement can and should serve as a greater impetus to study and clarity. Our effort in this volume will be well spent if it serves that purpose. May our differences never becloud the joy and expectation of seeing our Lord at His visible and personal return. With John we all say: "He who testifies to these things says, 'Yes, I am coming soon.' Amen. Come, Lord Jesus. The grace of the Lord Jesus be with God's people. Amen" (Rev. 22:20–21).

RESPONSE: DOUGLAS J. MOO

THE NEED TO BUILD theological structures on the solid foundation of biblical exegesis is nowhere more apparent than in the area of eschatology. All too often proponents of the various positions on the time of the Rapture argue solely, or mainly, on the basis of theological presuppositions. And while the need to fit texts into a comprehensive, intelligible theological system cannot be denied, it is never admissable to do this without allowing the text to speak for itself. Thus I commend my colleague Paul Feinberg for his desire to establish his position by means of solid exegetical argumentation. It is the validity of this argumentation that I will examine in my reply. Specifically, I will focus on three issues: the extent and significance of divine wrath during the Tribulation; the meaning of Revelation 3:10; and the differences between "Rapture" texts and "Coming" texts. A fourth argument adduced by Feinberg, related to the need for an interval between the Rapture and the Parousia, will be dealt with in my reply to Archer.

As Feinberg indicates, it is commonly agreed that the church has been promised exemption from divine wrath and that the Tribulation will be a period during which divine wrath is evident. Will that wrath be of such extent and duration that it can only be through physical removal (rapture) that God's promise to the church can be kept? To this question Feinberg answers yes, arguing that the entire Tribulation period witnesses the pouring out of God's wrath. But his argument is open to criticism. In fact, I would contend that there is good reason to think that divine wrath is confined to the very *end* of the Tribulation. As he himself notes, the words ὀργή and θυμός are found mainly in descriptions of the climactic judgments just before and at the time of the Battle of Armaggedon. And the four verses cited by Feinberg to prove the existence of divine wrath earlier in the period can be understood more naturally otherwise. Revelation 15:1 states clearly that it is only with "the seven last plagues," not all the plagues recorded in Revelation (as Feinberg suggests) that the wrath of God "is finished." The wrath of God, which continually abides on unbelievers (Rom. 1:18) is brought to its climactic conclusion with the bowl judgments. I deal with the structure of Revelation at greater length in my paper, but it can be suggested here that the bowl judgments are best regarded as occurring rapidly at the end of the Tribulation. Similarly, I would argue that Revelation 11:1, with its mention of wrath, describes the Parousia and associated events. Finally, it seems to me better to confine the wrath mentioned with respect to the sixth seal (Rev. 6:16–17) to that judgment and not to link it with the previous seal-plagues. This is because the martyrs described in the fifth seal cry out, "How long, Sovereign Lord, holy and true, until you judge the inhabitants of the earth and avenge our blood?" (Rev. 6:10). Clearly, God's wrath has not been poured out at that point since the judgment of the "inhabitants of the earth" has not yet occurred. Once again, the sixth seal almost certainly depicts judgments immediately associated with the Parousia, as is indicated by the fact that Jesus specifically says that the astronomical disasters involved with this seal will occur only *after* the Tribulation (Matt. 24:29).

I conclude, then, that the occurrences of the word *wrath* in Revelation do not support Feinberg's contention that divine wrath is present throughout the Tribulation. Consistently, in fact, the inflicting of the wrath of God is confined to the last judgments at the end of the Tribulation.

Feinberg also argues from the relationship of Revelation 4 and 5 to the rest of the book to demonstrate that divine wrath is inflicted throughout the Tribulation. Specifically, he claims that the judgments of the book proceed from the worthy Lamb, who breaks the seals and opens the scroll (Rev. 5), and that all the judgments are therefore expressions of God's retributive wrath. But this does not follow. While it is Jesus, the slain Lamb, who inaugurates the events of the end, not all these events are of God's direct initiative nor is it fair to find in all of them the wrath of God. Granted that, ultimately,

God is responsible for everything, it is also true that God cannot be directly accused of evil (James 1:13). And a number of the judgments of Revelation are traceable to Antichrist, who "utters blasphemies" (Rev. 13:5), takes the place of God, and demands worship. The persecution initiated by this figure cannot in any meaningful sense be attributed to God. What makes this particularly significant is the fact that the sufferings of the saints in Revelation are consistently attributed to this figure and also the fact that none of the judgments initiated by God is said to affect believers. In fact, it is frequently stated that believers are divinely protected from these judgments. Two characteristic texts can be cited. In Revelation 14:9–10, an angel proclaims, "If anyone worships the beast and his image and receives his mark on the forehead or on the hand, he, too, will drink of the wine of God's fury [θυμός], which has been poured full strength into the cup of his wrath." The conditional nature of this warning ("if") demonstrates that the wrath here is inflicted *only* on unbelievers. The fact that Tribulation believers *whoever they are,* will be kept from God's wrath, is indicated also in Revelation 18:4, where God's people are warned to "come out" of the harlot Babylon "so that you will not share in her sins, *so that you will not receive any of her plagues."* In other words, I would argue that not only is it *possible,* it is *necessary* to distinguish between tribulation that has its origin in the wrath of Satan and the judgments that embody God's wrath. In this respect, the Tribulation will be much like the present age: severe tribulations afflict God's people without involving them in the wrath of God against unbelievers.

In response to Feinberg's argument on wrath, one final, but significant point must be made. He argues that the promise of exemption from divine wrath is given *only* to the church and does *not* rest on soteriology. He must do this, of course, in order to explain how it is that saints *do* suffer and die during the Tribulation—these are Jewish saints, not part of the church. But is it possible to claim that exemption from divine wrath is promised *only* to the church and not to *any* believer in Christ? Deliverance from God's wrath seems to be a constitutive part of salvation. To be justified is to be "saved from

God's wrath" (Rom. 5:9) and the sacrifice of Christ once for all accomplished involved the propitiating of God's wrath (Rom. 3:25). To assert that only *some* believers (the church) are delivered from divine wrath would appear to demand the existence of two different forms of salvation—one for believers in this age (the church); another for Tribulation saints. While I am sure Feinberg does not want to go this far, it is difficult to avoid that conclusion if his argument is allowed. But if salvation in Christ *by its very nature* removes the believer from the sphere of divine wrath, Feinberg's whole argument relating to wrath in the Tribulation becomes irrelevant. For he admits, as anyone must do, that believers are on earth during the Tribulation (see Rev. 13:7, *passim*). But if every believer saved by the blood of Christ is exempted from divine wrath, then so, of course, those Tribulation saints will be. Therefore, exemption from divine wrath during the Tribulation will clearly not require physical removal—the divine wrath present during the Tribulation does not logically entail a pretribulational Rapture of the church. At the same time, of course, it does not logically speak against such a Rapture. And the positive *need* to postulate a pretribulation Rapture is found by Feinberg in Christ's promise to the church of Philadelphia.

Revelation 3:10 has always figured prominently in the debate over the time of the Rapture. Proponents of the pretribulational Rapture have often seen in this verse a direct reference to such a Rapture; Christ promises "a removal from the sphere of testing."[1] However, the use of the verb τηρέω ("keep") creates a real difficulty for this view, since removal would much better be conveyed with a verb such as αἴρω (cf. John 17:17a). Therefore, Feinberg, relying heavily on the argument of J. Townsend, seeks to establish a different meaning for the verse, according to which *preservation outside* the time of testing, rather than *removal from* the time of testing, is promised. Such an interpretation still demands a pretribulational Rapture as the event that brings the church into this "outside position." The amount of space Feinberg devotes to this point demonstrates its importance in his argument; our evaluation must be correspondingly thorough.

Basic to the Feinberg-Townsend interpretation is the

meaning "outside position" given to the preposition ἐκ. While ἐκ generally connotes movement or separation of some kind, Liddell-Scott do give as a possible definition "outside of, beyond." However, they give very few examples and state explicitly that this meaning is found "chiefly in early writers."[2] Feinberg is cognizant of this fact, but cites examples from the LXX, Josephus, and the New Testament in an attempt to prove that the connotation "outside position" remained in use and was thus a live option for the apostle John in the first century A.D.

It is extremely important at the outset to determine exactly what is meant by "outside position." Feinberg and Townsend do not clearly indicate what they mean by this phrase, yet the precise definition given it is crucial to the argument. For to provide valid support for the pretribulational interpretation of Revelation 3:10, the word ἐκ must be taken in the sense of physical, or spatial separation. Any other sort of separation will not provide evidence for the pretribulational view, because other views could accommodate other forms of separation. Thus, for instance, if ἐκ is taken in the sense of "separation from the influence of" or "separation from the impact of," no support is given to either of the basic positions. The church could be separated from the impact of the Tribulation by physical removal (pretribulationism), *or* by special divine protection from within the sphere of tribulation (posttribulationism). To put it another way, the problem is incorrectly stated if the decisive issue is made the question as to whether ἐκ can mean separation with no thought of prior involvement. For posttribulationists as well as pretribulationists could claim that the church is never *in* the realm of God's Tribulation wrath. Therefore, as far as the word ἐκ is concerned, support for the pretribulational position will exist only if it can be shown that the word can and *does* in Revelation 3:10 connote physical separation—"outside position" in the spatial sense.

I will not dispute the fact that ἐκ, in classical Greek, can occasionally (though seldom) mean "*physically* outside" with no connotation of prior involvement. But I *do* question whether

Townsend and Feinberg have shown that this meaning is found in biblical Greek.

They cite nine examples from the LXX. Four (Josh. 2:13; Ps. 33:19 [LXX 32:19]; Ps. 56:13 [LXX 55:14]; Prov. 23:14) involve various words for "deliver" with ἐχ, followed by θάνατος ("death"). Apparently the argument is that since the individuals involved had not experienced death, their statements must refer not to removal *out of,* but to preservation *outside of.* But such an argument overlooks the metaphorical sense given to the word "death" in these instances. Von Rad succinctly states this sense of the word as it often appears in the Old Testament. "For Israel death's dominion reached far further into the realm of the living. Weakness, illness, imprisonment, and oppression by enemies are a kind of death." And, with direct relevance to two of the verses cited by Feinberg, Von Rad goes on to say, "This is the point of view from which we have to take what is often said in the Psalms when a suppliant testifies that he was already in death in Sheol, but was 'brought forth' by Jahweh."[3] In other words, "death" in these four verses almost certainly has reference to the difficult straights *in which* the speakers or authors find themselves; removal *out of* the situation is intended.

Feinberg and Townsend also mention the four uses of ἐχ in Psalm 59:1–2 (LXX 58:2–3) as possible examples of the meaning "outside position," but it is difficult to establish that meaning here. Psalm 59 begins with a statement giving the occasion of David's composition: "When Saul sent men, and they watched the house in order to kill him." In such a situation, David's prayer for deliverance from his enemies very likely means, "Bring me *out of* this trap," rather than, "Save me by keeping me out of the hand of my enemies who surround me."

But the most important example from the LXX, because it is closest in language to Revelation 3:10, is Proverbs 21:23: "He who guards his mouth and his tongue, guards (διατηρέω) his soul from (ἐχ) trouble." In this case, I would agree with Feinberg that, "Ideas of prior existence or emission are absent." But I would not agree that ἐχ here means outside position, in the sense of *physical* or *spatial* separation. Solomon is not promising a *spatial* removal of the soul to an "outside position"; he is referring to spiritual protection from the "trouble" of the world—"trouble" from which one in this life is *never physically* separated. Thayer's definition of the phrase τηρεῖν τινα ἔκ fits well here: "to keep one at a distance from."[4]

Thus, eight of the LXX verses cited by Feinberg employ ἔκ with its usual meaning, "out from within." In one, Proverbs 21:23, ἔκ is used with no connotation of previous existence "within," but indicates a metaphorical or "spiritual" separation from impending and ever-present danger. None of these examples provides evidence for the meaning "physical separation" for ἔκ.

Five New Testament verses are cited as providing evidence for the meaning "outside position" for ἔκ. Two, as in the LXX, involve the combination ἔκ θανάτου—Hebrews 5:7 and James 5:20. In the former, Jesus is portrayed as agonizingly praying to "the one who could save him from death." While it is almost certain that the allusion is to Gethsemane and physical death is therefore intended, it would be precipitous to claim that "outside position" must be intended. For, in the first place, it is probable that reference to both preservation *from entering* death and deliverance *out of* death (e.g., resurrection) is intended by the phrase.[5] But, second, even if prevention from entering death is intended, "outside position" in the sense of physical or spatial separation is an inappropriate description of the meaning. As was the case with Proverbs 21:23, a spatial idea is being applied to a situation that is simply not spatial in nature. To be saved from imminent death is not the same as to be placed in a position "outside" it.

The same can be said of James 5:20, in which the turning of a sinner from his error is likened to saving his soul from death. The normal meaning of ἔκ ("out of") is acceptable here. While it is possible, as Feinberg argues, that physical death is intended, it is more probable that *spiritual* death is meant (see the connection James makes between sin and death in this broader sense in 1:15). And the New Testament provides ample warrant for viewing the sinner as *already* "dead" (see John 5:24; Eph. 2:1).

Equally inconclusive are the arguments for viewing John

12:27 as an example of ἐκ meaning "outside position." When Jesus prays to the Father to save Him from (ἐκ) the hour, His words must be seen in light of the immediately preceding context. And in 12:23, Jesus is reported to have stated, "The hour has come (ἐλήλυθεν; perfect) for the Son of Man to be glorified." While the term "hour" in John's Gospel refers to Jesus' death, the reference extends beyond the Crucifixion. As Schnackenburg says, "The moment on the Mount of Olives (v. 27), the betrayal (13:31 νῦν), the lifting up on the cross (12:31) and the glorification (v. 23) are a single event."[6]

Two New Testament texts remain to be examined; they are the most important parallels to Revelation 3:10. The first is Acts 15:29, which employs the verb διατηρέω (which means essentially the same thing as τηρέω, used in Rev. 3:10) with ἐκ. Feinberg is certainly correct in asserting that future abstention is intended when the Gentiles are exhorted to "keep" themselves from the specified immoral and ritually unclean practices. It seems clear, then, that ἐκ in Acts 15:29 implies no idea of prior involvement. But, once again, it is an invalid logical leap to claim that because ἐκ does not denote "emergence from" it must refer to "outside position." The Gentiles, in this life, will never be in an "outside position" with respect to such things as sexual immorality—such vices constitute a perpetual threat and temptation against which careful "guarding" (διατηρέω) is required. "Outside position," on the other hand, suggests removal to a position from which any contact with such temptations is severed.

Finally, John 17:15b, Jesus' prayer that the Father would keep the disciples from the Evil One (or possibly, evil), must be considered. This is the touchstone of the argument over the meaning of τηρέω ἐκ in Revelation 3:10 since John 17:15b furnishes the only other example in biblical Greek of this combination of words. Feinberg claims that here, too, τηρέω ἐκ must denote "preservation in an outside position." But what does "outside position" in this case mean? The object of the preposition ἐκ is "the Evil One." In what sense is it meaningful to speak of being in an outside position with respect to a personal being? Once again, it seems to me that Feinberg is applying a spatial phrase to a context that cannot be understood spatially. One can be separated from the influence of, or protected from the machinations of, or even put physically outside the realm of the Evil One, but one cannot speak meaningfully of being physically outside the *person* of Satan. Jesus' intention is to pray that the disciples be protected from the powerful, raging influence of the "ruler of this age"—an age in which the disciples will continue to live. This is not "outside position" but divine spiritual protection *from within* the sphere of Satan's influence. Galatians 1:4 provides a close parallel in language and thought: Christ "gave himself for our sins, that he might deliver [ἐξέληται] us out of [ἐκ] this present evil age." Believers are indisputably *in* this "present evil age"— Paul asserts that they will be rescued from its influence.

When carefully examined, then, the purported New Testament examples of the meaning of "outside position" for ἐκ vanish. In fact, in checking the over nine hundred occurrences of ἐκ in the New Testament, I could find none that probably has this meaning. In agreement with this conclusion is the fact that none of the major New Testament lexica gives "outside position" as a definition of ἐκ. What *some* of the examples cited by Townsend and Feinberg show is that ἐκ can mean a separation from something with which one has had no prior involvement.

This is the case in each of the three verses which employ διατηρέω or τηρέω with ἐκ. But in each case the separation is not a physical one, in which possibility of contact with that from which one is separated ceases; protection from or guarding against real and continuing danger is denoted. These parallels therefore provide no basis for the assertion that the Philadelphian church is promised protection from the hour of trial in a position outside it. In fact, this interpretation runs counter to the parallels since in each of these the object of ἐκ denotes the thing or person *from* which one is protected, not the sphere *outside of* which one is protected.

But if ἐκ never clearly denotes physical "outside position" in the New Testament, the issue is not conclusively settled. For it could be maintained that the general idea "separation from, with no idea of prior involvement" could demand a physical separation in a given context. And this is precisely what Feinberg finds in Revelation 3:10. He argues that the promise of exemption from a *time period* ("the hour of trial") can be accomplished *only* by means of physical removal. It is impossible to be separate from a time period and still be living during it. It is this temporal aspect in Revelation 3:10 that could place this verse in a different category from the parallel texts, justifying the application of a spatial concept such as "outside position." Two things may be said about this argument.

First, the claim that "hour of trial" designates essentially a period of time must be questioned. G. Delling interprets this particular phrase as connoting "the situation which is characterized by apocalyptic temptation."[7] In other words, the stress lies not on the time period as such, but on the aspect or essential characteristic of the situation. That this is the case is strongly supported by the closest biblical parallel, John 12:27. In this verse, as we have seen, Jesus prays that He might be saved from "this hour." Clearly it is Jesus' desire not to be kept *outside* a time period, but to be delivered from an experience *within* a period of time. In exactly parallel fashion, it would seem best to regard Revelation 3:10 as promising protection from the *experience* of "testing," not removal from a period of time.

Second, the interpretation that stresses removal from a period of time in Revelation 3:10 must reckon with the fact that τηρέω is given a different meaning than it has in the three parallel texts. For while Feinberg wants to define τηρέω in Revelation 3:10 as "protect" or "preserve," such language is incorrectly applied to a temporal period. One can be *kept out* of a period of time, but not *protected* or *preserved out of* a period of time. Either Feinberg must give τηρέω the meaning "keep" or he must insert an idea not present in the text, viz., "I will protect you from the time of trial *by keeping you outside it.*" The first alternative demands that τηρέω be given a meaning it does not have in the parallel texts; the second involves an unwarranted addition to the passage. If τηρέω in Revelation 3:10 means "protect" or "preserve" as the lexica suggest and Feinberg claims, it is very difficult to give "hour of trial" a primarily temporal meaning.

Feinberg finds further support for the notion that physical removal from the *period* of testing is promised in Revelation 3:10 in the qualifiers added to the phrase "hour of trial." It is argued that, since the "time of testing" comes upon the "whole inhabited earth," *only* physical removal can effectively protect the church. This is so, however, only if the Tribulation is of such a nature that its ravages fall indiscriminately upon all men. But we have already argued that this is not the case; many biblical parallels, as well as texts within Revelation itself, demonstrate the selective nature of God's wrath and His ability to keep His people from its effects. The purpose of the "hour of trial" is to "test those who dwell on the earth" a characterization that, as Feinberg notes, shows the selective nature of the trial.[8] But, as Feinberg admits, this can hardly be used to deny the presence of believers during this time; and if the 144,000 can be present during the Tribulation, yet protected ("sealed") by God, there is nothing to prevent the church from being there also. It is precisely because the period of the Tribulation has special reference to unbelievers that Christ promises to protect His church from its onslaught.

We conclude our response to Feinberg's treatment of Revelation 3:10 with a summary: (1) The evidence that ἐκ can mean "outside position" in a spatial sense is nonexistent in biblical Greek; (2) The combination τηρέω or διατηρέω ἐκ denotes protection from, or guarding against a real and threatening danger; (3) "The hour of trial" connotes primarily the eschatological experience of tribulation rather than a period of time; and (4) The phrases qualifying "the hour of trial" imply nothing at all about the presence or the removal of the church. The lexical and contextual evidence strongly favors the interpretation according to which Christ in Revelation 3:10 promises His church protection from the real and present danger of affliction when the "hour of trial" comes. Thus, we reject four different meanings commonly attached to the phrase τηρέω ἐκ: "removal from" (Pentecost); "keeping outside of" (Townsend, Feinberg); "removal from the midst of"; and "Protection issuing in emergence" (Gundry). The first and third rest on an incorrect rendering of τηρέω; the second on an unestablished definition of ἐκ; the fourth, while possible, does not do justice to the parallel texts. The rendering of the phrase suggested by our interpretation, "protection from" (with the implication that the danger from which one is protected is present) best accounts for the lexical data and the sense the phrase has elsewhere in biblical Greek.

Finally, we consider Feinberg's argument to the effect that the differences between New Testament depictions of the Rapture and of the Second Coming strongly suggest that the events are separated *in time.* I emphasize these last two words because it is only a *temporal* difference that would constitute evidence against a posttribulational view. That is, a posttribulationist readily concedes that the Rapture and the Second Coming in *judgment* are not identical, in the sense that they have different purposes and effect different groups of people. All that the posttribulationist affirms is that these two events are part of one complex event, the Parousia, and that it will occur after the Tribulation. With this important distinction in mind, let us turn to Feinberg's argument.

With respect to *omissions,* aspects of the Rapture not mentioned in passages dealing with the Second Coming, and *vice versa,* the following points can be made. First, much depends upon certain debated texts. Feinberg claims, for instance, that "There is no clear indisputable reference to a Rapture in any Second Advent passage." But I argue in my chapter that precisely such a reference is found in Matthew 24:31. To be sure the reference is not "indisputable," but can *any* argument in this tangled debate be put in such a category? Similarly, I have maintained that normal methods of exegesis demand that the church be included in the second person plural address of the Olivet Discourse. If that be so, the church is "indubitably" told to watch for signs to precede its deliverance. Equally clear, it seems to me, is 2 Thessalonians 2:1–10, where the *church* is told of events to be expected *before* the Rapture.

Second, with respect to omissions, it is not true that the Second Advent is always portrayed as coming immediately in association with the Tribulation. First Thessalonians 5:1–10 not only fails to mention tribulation, but characterizes the time when judgment falls on unbelievers as a time when people are saying, "Peace and safety" (v. 3). Again, the claim that tribulation is not found in texts dealing with the Rapture depends greatly on which texts one places in this category. Thus, I would argue that the "rest" to be given the Thessalonian church (2 Thess. 1:7) involves the expectance of the Rapture. Yet this rest comes immediately in conjunction with severe tribulation (vv. 4–6). Likewise, 1 Thessalonians 4:13–18, which clearly describes the Rapture, is directed to a church already undergoing severe tribulation (cf. 2:14, 3:3–4). In other words, Paul does not need to specify in the immediate context of 1 Thessalonians 4:13–18 that tribulation is to precede the Rapture because he and the Thessalonians are *already* suffering tribulation. The persistent tendency on the part of pretribulationists to confine tribulation only to a climactic seven-year period at the end of history seriously distorts the New Testament perspective.

Another omission noted by Feinberg is the lack of mention of the resurrection of the church in conjunction with the Second Advent. But for this point to stand, a reference to the resurrection of the church in Revelation 20:4 must be denied. This means, however, that in the book that describes in most detail the events of the end, and whose purpose is to comfort churches undergoing suffering, no mention whatever is made of the Rapture *or* the resurrection of saints. I find this possibility unlikely. The grammar of 20:4, the specific mention of two (and *only* two) resurrections, and the purpose of Revelation make it overwhelmingly probable that the resurrection of *all* saints is depicted in 20:4. If so, the resurrection of the church is explicitly linked to the Second Advent.

Before turning to the next general point, it is important to keep in mind an important point with respect to suggested omissions. New Testament texts are almost universally directed to rather specific situations in the life of the church. This means, however, that the author will generally include only what he wants in order to make his point and he will omit much that is unnecessary for his immediate purposes. The omissions to which Feinberg has pointed in eschatological passages are best understood in this same way. When Paul, let us say, in 1 Thessalonians 4:13–18 seeks to comfort the believers with respect to departed brothers and sisters, he naturally focuses upon that aspect of the Parousia that meets his purpose here—he speaks of rapture and resurrection. And when he attempts to encourage the same church in the midst of tribulation, he emphasizes the judgment upon unbelievers that will also accompany the Parousia (2 Thess. 1:3–10). Scripture abounds with clear parallels to this procedure. Thus, for example, consider the very different ways in which Christ's death is described in the four Gospels. The "cry of dereliction" is omitted in Luke and John, Jesus' prayer of committal to the Father is omitted in Matthew, Mark, and John, the spear thrust into Jesus' side is found only in John, and so on. Do we conclude that Christ was crucified two times? What the Evangelists do in including and omitting certain events in order to make a point to their respective audiences is exactly what occurs in texts related to the Parousia.

A greater problem, as Feinberg points out, are inconsistencies. Omissions *can* suggest that different events are involved; irreconcilable differences virtually demand it. But are the inconsistencies brought up by Feinberg "irreconcilable?" I think not.

To say that there is a difference between 1 Thessalonians 4:13–18 and Revelation 19–20 as to the precise *time* of the resurrection is to assume that Revelation 19–20 intends a clear temporal progression. But there seems to be no intention of such a clear progression. The binding of Satan (20:1) and the resurrection (v. 4) are introduced with a very general "and" (καί)—contrast the clear temporal indicator in verse 7. It seems most reasonable to think that the events depicted in 20:1–6 occur in conjunction with the Second Advent (19:11–21).

The second suggested inconsistency involves the destination of raptured believers. According to the posttribulational interpretation, raptured saints descend with Christ to earth, but John 14:3 implies that saints are raptured to *heaven*. But, in fact, the word *heaven* is not used in John 14:1–3 and, although John's language *may* imply it, the stress of the text is on the promise that "Where I am, you may be also" (v. 3b). Furthermore, the pretribulational scheme demands that raptured believers spend only seven years in heaven before descending with Christ to earth—this is not much of an improvement on the posttribulational conception!

What strikes me as interesting is that Feinberg can point to only two (to me) insignificant inconsistencies between Rapture and Second Advent texts. If, indeed, these two are distinguishable in time, one would have expected many more differences than this. I could name several apparent inconsistencies in the Resurrection narratives of the Gospels—yet we *know* these all depict the same event. The failure to indicate *more* inconsistencies than those two suggests that it is not difficult at all to view the Rapture and Second Advent as part of a single event.

RESPONSE: GLEASON L. ARCHER

Dr. FEINBERG HAS presented the most scholarly and persuasive case for the pretribulation position that I have yet seen. The combination of firm conviction in the light of the scriptural evidence and a constant appreciation of the insights and sincere motivation of those with whom he cannot agree is admirable. The thoroughness of his research into the range of possibilities for the use of the preposition ἐκ, so crucial to the interpretation of Revelation 3:10, leads to a far better understanding of its versatility than can be obtained from any lexicon with which I am acquainted. It seems to me that he has firmly established the possibility of an outside locus for ἐκ that is independent of the "out from within" connotation generally attributed to it. My own discussion lays emphasis on the essential meaning of τηρέω (without implications as to motion) rather than furnishing detailed proof of the outside locus of ἐκ. I feel that the wealth of examples he has assembled clinches the matter in a satisfying way.

There are a few paragraphs of the presentation that I would like to comment on by way of confirmation or of corrective criticism. I will not attempt to follow any careful topical arrangement but will simply make observations in the sequential order followed by Feinberg himself.

On page 57 he brings up the interesting question of the point during the final seven years before Armageddon at which the "wrath of God" (from which believers are to be kept according to Rev. 3:10) begins. The pretribulation position assumes that the wrath of God begins at the commencement of Daniel's seventieth week (Dan. 9:25–27). The deferral of this stage of the Tribulation until near the end of the seven years, as Robert Gundry maintains, necessitates placing the seven bowls and the seven trumpets very late in the scheme, as a sort of preliminary to the final conflict at Armageddon. But the mid-seventieth-week interpretation places the outpouring of God's wrath in a climactic series of destructive judgments right after the commencement of the second half of the "week," not long after the church has been removed from the earth scene by the Rapture. This raises the interesting point as to where in the Apocalypse this point of division appears. Various adherents of this midway approach have offered differing suggestions in regard to this bifurcation. One of the most interesting of these is the proposal by J. Oliver Buswell, Jr., that the resurrection of the two witnesses predicted in Revelation 11 is identifiable with the Rapture. But this suggestion carries with it a possible assumption that the two witnesses are not really individuals, but rather symbolic figures or personifications of the church. To me this theory suffers from the lack of contextual evidence.

To my mind a more plausible bifurcation point for Revelation is to be found between the end of chapter 7 and the beginning of chapter 8. Chapter 13 presents the ten-horned, seven-headed beast in his progressive rise to supreme power. Upon attaining his position, he proceeds to "make war on the saints and overcome them" (13:7). The strongest kind of economic pressure is directed at believers. They must receive the "number of the beast" on hand or brow in order to buy or sell, and all his subjects must worship his image. But all of this will result from the wrath of man, not from the wrath of God.

In Revelation 14 we find that decisive intervention from God has begun to manifest itself on the earth. The 144,000 faithful witnesses, who may be recent converts that came to personal repentance and faith soon after the disappearance of their Christian friends and neighbors at the Rapture, are depicted as continuing objects of the tyranny of the Beast. At verse 6 a mighty angel proclaims the imminent downfall of the world-capital, "Babylon," saying, "Fear God and give Him glory, for the hour of His wrath has come" (v. 7). This is immediately followed by the declaration: "Babylon the great has fallen!" Here we meet with a decisive counterthrust against the Beast and his world government: the wrath of God has made its appearance upon the scene. Then in verses 14–19 we see the Son of Man enthroned on a white cloud above the earth and sending forth His terrible sickle to mow down the harvest of rebellious mankind, with a resultant spilling of blood that pours out past the limits of the doomed city.

In chapter 15 the mighty angels who administer the seven plagues join with the shining saints in the glorious realm of heaven, looking down with satisfaction upon the long-delayed justice of God at last breaking forth upon the world. The intense suffering, devastation, and loss of life occasioned by the seven bowls of wrath furnish the theme for chapter 16. That next chapter dramatically portrays the downfall of Babylon, drunk with the blood of the postrapture (and possibly also the prerapture) saints she has martyred for their faith in Christ. It devotes special attention to the characteristics of the Antichrist as the supreme lord whom Babylon worships and exalts. Five of his seven heads represent the five kings (or kingdoms?) who have already fallen (Egypt, Assyria, Babylon, Persia, Greece) and the Roman Empire "which now is," is followed by the ten-kingdom confederacy of the New Rome as "the one which is yet to come." The Beast himself constitutes the eighth world-empire as a completely totalitarian dictatorship. Chapter 18 summons the postrapture believers to separate completely from the doomed civilization of Babylon, which is about to be overthrown—much to the distress and grief of all the nations who serve as her trading-partners. Chapter 19 describes the songs of triumph and joy coming from the prerapture saints and the angels in glory just prior to Christ's Second Coming in splendor and power to crush the rebellious forces of men at Armageddon. Thus we see that chapters 8–19 (apart from 13, which sums up the program of the Beast during the first three and a half years) relate to the terrible strokes of judgment by which the wrath of God is poured out upon man. These stand in clear contrast to the preceding block of chapters (6–7), which relate the period of the wrath of man against the loyal, Christ-confessing church.

We have suggested that chapters 6 and 7 pertain to the first half of the final seven-year period preceding Armageddon. But we should be careful to observe that within chapter 6 we find an introduction to *both* periods of wrath (the wrath of man and the wrath of God) that are decreed in the seven-sealed scroll of chapter 5 opened by the Lamb. The series of seven seals contains the whole destiny appointed for the seven last years, and it turns out upon careful examination that the first four seals include the major developments of the first half of the heptad; the fifth seal gives a glimpse of heaven (where the already martyred saints are assured that vengeance upon their persecutors will come very shortly [ἔτι χρόνον μικρόν, 6:11], that is during the last three and a half years). The sixth seal ushers in the final phase of the wrath of God upon the Antichrist and all his realm. The heavenly interlude continues in chapter 7 with its remarkable vision of the 144,000 martyred saints, who seem to belong to the Christ-professing Jewish believers already executed by the Antichrist and his henchmen. The group includes the innumerable hosts of the Gentile converts of the postrapture period who have also been slaughtered in this bloody purge. Chapter 8, with the breaking of the seventh seal, shifts the focus back to earth and the successive plagues inflicted by the wrath of God upon the empire of the Beast. Each plague is heralded by trumpet blasts from death-dealing angels—a theme which is continued in chapter 9, which describes the assaults of the falling stars, the hell-spawned locusts, and the lion-headed cavalry. Chapter 10 records a personal confrontation between John and the angel who gives him a scroll of destiny to ingest. But the account of the final events is resumed in chapter 11 with the episode of the two witnesses, who are finally slain, but are raised again after three and a half days with resultant joy and praise in heaven. The joy is shared by angels and the already raptured saints. Chapter 12 gives a diachronic survey of the entire battle between Christ and Satan set forth in the dramatic figure of a woman who gives Him birth under the baleful gaze of the satanic dragon who attempts to destroy both the Messiah and all His people. Since this mother of the Savior is arrayed with the splendor of the sun and crowned with twelve stars, she is probably representative of believing Israel, united with the New Testament Israel of God. Daniel 12:3 refers to true believers as stars, and the flight from persecution for three and a half years (Rev. 12:6) points to the Tribulation period rather than to the sojourn of the holy family in Egypt. There is, after all, no record of Mary's ever fleeing into a desert after Christ's resurrection (vv. 5–6) and remaining hidden there for that period of time. At the end of this contest Christ is locked in combat with Satan, who is cast down to earth, to the plaudits of the heavenly choir as they laud the faithfulness of all who were slain for Christ's sake. Meanwhile down on earth the postrapture saints are subjected to even fiercer persecution than before by the malignity of the satanic dragon, who vainly tries to destroy the people of God ("the woman") altogether.

On page 61 Dr. Feinberg concedes that the "Day of the Lord" referred to in 2 Thessalonians 2:3–4 does not start until the middle of the week. I find this a very significant observation, because it serves to coincide with the very same bifurcation for which we have been arguing. There is really not too much difference between holding that the Tribulation continues throughout the whole seven-year span, with the Day of the Lord commencing at the middle of the week—and holding that the first half relates to the wrath of man (which of course does entail mounting persecution and distress for God's people under the rising power of the Beast), and that the second half is to be regarded as the Great Tribulation, during which the fury of the Lord Himself is vented upon the Satan-dominated civilization of Antichrist. I personally see no difficulty in describing this final half as the Day of the Lord. The pretribulationist and the mid–seventieth-week approaches both agree that the New Testament church has been safely raptured and out of the way before this grim finale is ushered in.

As for the objection raised by Dr. Feinberg (p. 63), I get the impression that he misses the point of the distinction between the wrath of man and the wrath of God. It would be a grave misunderstanding to conclude from this antithetic terminology that we regard God as totally inactive during the first three and a half years, or that His sovereignty is in any way held in abeyance. On the contrary, it is perfectly clear that God never ceases His activity as supreme ruler over the entire universe. He knows how to use even the wicked and disobedient (like Pharaoh back in the days of Moses) to further His ultimate, all-wise purpose. But when we speak of the "wrath of man" as the distinctive feature of the first half of the "week," we mean that the wrath of the Antichrist and his associates in government is the dominating feature on the stage of this drama. The cruel and coercive measures taken to compel the submission of all mankind to this idolatrous dictatorship are solely the responsibility of the Beast and the False Prophet and all of his collaborators. In no way can the guilt of this brutality be attributed to God. But as the second half of the week comes into play, with the church safely removed from the scene, the indignation of the Lord breaks forth with overwhelming, supernatural power. It is now God who dominates the stage, not the Antichrist. Hence we rightly speak of this period as the "wrath of God." While it is true that the first four seals of Revelation 6 are components of the book of destiny unrolled by the Lamb, it would be unjustified to label these first four developments of the earlier half of the "week" as manifestations of the *wrath* of God, as Feinberg seems to imply (p. 63) even though they may be included in the *plan* of God. The white horse of Revelation 6:2 is generally understood to be descriptive of the rise of Antichrist to power, with the white horse itself symbolic of victory. The rider on the red horse referred to in 6:4 suggests the carnage of warfare that will mark his progress toward world domination. The third seal portends the near-famine conditions resulting from this widespread conflict and the damage it inflicts on the food supply. The fourth seal (v. 8) relates to a widespread and terrible pestilence that will bring about a huge mortality throughout the world. As we have suggested above, it is these four seals that pertain to the first half of the "week," and they do not give expression to the wrath of God on a miraculous or apocalyptic scale. They merely present on a somewhat intensified scale the same sad story that earlier centuries have often witnessed during the history of mankind. Not until we move into the sixth and seventh seals, as indicated in our previous discussion, do we encounter features which relate specifically to the wrath of God which descends upon the earth during the final three and a half years.

On page 63 Dr. Feinberg raises the question of how the protection promised to the saints in Revelation 3:10 can be reconciled with an initial three and a half years during which many of them are martyred by the government of the Beast. "One might wonder," he says, "in what sense they are preserved." Well, the answer is that they are to be preserved from, according to Revelation 3:10, "the hour of trial that is going to come upon the whole world." And this "trial" must refer to something more intense than, or qualitatively different from, the kind of persecutions that have characterized the entire history of the Christian church during times of great persecution. Thus, the afflictions and martyrdoms predicted for the first three and a half years are not essentially different from the severest periods of Roman persecution prior to the reign of Constantine the Great. But Revelation 3:10 must be referring to a level of horrible and overwhelming destruction surpassing anything ever known before. As Jesus described it in the Olivet Discourse: "For then there will be a great tribulation, such as has not occurred since the beginning of the world until now, nor ever shall" (Matt. 24:21, NASB). Just previous to this statement, Christ had indicated that many of the same persecutions afflicted the saints prior to the Tribulation (vv. 7–11, 15–19). Unquestionably the church *did* go through such testing experiences long before the beginning of the seventieth week—the same type of trials are detailed in *Revelation* for the first half of that week. Therefore we conclude that this objection regarding Revelation 3:10 is without force.

On page 63 Dr. Feinberg speaks of the revival of sacrifices during the millennial period as reflecting a need of finding atonement for sin (Ezek. 43:13–27). While this is not exactly germane to the matter of the timing of the Rapture, I should like to register emphatic dissent. In view of the explicit assurance in Hebrews 10:12 that the atonement of our Lord Jesus Christ was, is, and ever shall be sufficient to cover the sins of all believers, it would take nothing less than the canceling out of the effectiveness of the Cross during the Millennium for *atonement* sacrifices to be either necessary or appropriate. Yet the emphasis laid on His atoning deed by the choirs of saints and angels up in heaven (Rev. 5:6–10) right on the threshold of the Millennium renders this interpretation untenable. While it is true that the Old Testament term for sacrifice used in Ezekiel 43 is characteristically עוֹלוֹת ("burnt offerings"), nevertheless we should see in this expression simply the employment of a term intelligible to an Old Testament audience at the level of their understanding of atonement prior to the Cross, but interpreted in harmony with the changed conditions that will obtain during the time of the prophetic fulfillment. There are many examples of this principle in prophecy; for example, those references to the role of "Assyria" in Zechariah 10:10–11 long after the historic empire of Assyria had been permanently destroyed. Or the prominence of "Babylon" in the Book of Revelation, even though the historic Babylon was nearly uninhabited by the end of the first century A.D. and was destined to become so totally deserted and abandoned a few centuries later that its very location was nearly forgotten. (Cf. Isa. 13:20, which states that Babylon shall never be inhabited again after its destruction.) So it is with these burnt offerings. They will have no atoning efficacy—atonement has been accomplished by Calvary—but they will serve as elements in that form of *holy communion* that will be instituted during the Millennium. That the present form of bread and wine is to be maintained only until the Second Advent is clear from what Jesus Himself said (according to 1 Cor. 11:26). It is therefore only to be expected that after the Second Coming some different elements should be appointed for the Kingdom Age, and very naturally also, elements reminiscent of those God appointed for His ancient people in Moses' time.

On page 75 Dr. Feinberg raises a most interesting point in regard to the timing of the conversion of latter-day Israel to faith in Christ. The repentance for the guilt of the Crucifixion that overwhelms the consciences of the Jews in that day is not mentioned in Zechariah 12 until after their heroic, God-empowered defense of Jerusalem against heathen attack had been described in the first nine verses. Feinberg seems to assume that their conversion will not actually take place until Christ returns bodily to earth and they behold Him with their physical eyes. If the arrangement of Zechariah 12 is chronologically sequential, this would be a valid deduction to draw, but it is impossible to suppose that God would have so remarkably delivered the Jewish people if they persisted in rejecting Christ as Savior until the very end of the seventieth week. It was, after all, precisely because they rejected Jesus before Pilate's judgment throne that the Lord condemned them to total defeat as a state and the destruction of Jerusalem as a city at the close of the First Revolt in 70 A.D. It is therefore inconceivable that the Lord would have put them back under His special protection and favor while they still persisted in rejecting Christ. The apostle Paul himself affirms in Romans 11:23 concerning his own countrymen: "And they also, if they continue not in their unbelief, shall be grafted in; for God is able to graft them in again" (KJV). In other words, unbelief in Jesus keeps the Jewish people from restoration to God's protection and favor.

It appears to me that we may choose one of two alternatives in dealing with this apparent difficulty. Either we must understand Zechariah 12:10–14 as referring to a conversion experience earlier than the successful withstanding of attack against Jerusalem as described in verses 1–9 (and this is entirely possible, since Zechariah does not always observe a strictly chronological pattern; cf. Zech. 13:7 and Matt. 26:31) or we may take these verses to refer to a revival experience among them when they actually behold the Lord in His glorified body, at the time of His return to earth in order to crush all rebellion against God. A close examination of these verses does not necessarily demonstrate a first-time conversion experience. The verses may indicate rather a soul-shaking experience of deepened horror at the crime of the Cross such as occasionally befalls even those who have been true believers for many years.

On page 74 Dr. Feinberg takes up the interesting question of the appearance of unregenerate citizens in the Kingdom Age. Theoretically there should be no unregenerate people in the Millennium. As God promises in Isaiah 60:21, "Thy people also shall be all righteous." Nevertheless we find in Zechariah 14:17–19 that certain severe sanctions will be leveled by God against any of the "families of the earth" who fail to go up regularly to Jerusalem to celebrate the Feast of Tabernacles; they will experience complete drought and deadly disease. Such disciplinary measures strongly suggest that some of Christ's earthly subjects during the Millennium will not be true believers. This is definitely confirmed by the success of Satan after his release from a thousand years of imprisonment at the end of the Millennium; he will achieve the organization of one final rebellion against the rule of Christ (Rev. 20:7–9). This suggests that some who grow up during the Millennium will rebel against the Lord, even though their parents may be truly regenerate believers. Probably Paul Feinberg's suggestion is the best explanation available: even though no unbelievers will be allowed into the kingdom after Christ establishes Himself upon the throne of David, it is quite possible that their children may covertly, at least, turn against the Lord in their hearts, and thus will be ripe for enlistment in Satan's earthly army against the Lord and His kingdom. This will result in a second conflict like that of Armageddon a thousand years before (Rev. 20:8–9).

3

THE CASE FOR THE MID–SEVENTIETH-WEEK RAPTURE POSITION

Gleason L. Archer

Gleason L. Archer is Professor of Old Testament, Trinity Evangelical Divinity School. He holds degrees from Princeton Theological Seminary (B.D.), Suffolk University Law School (LL.B.), and Harvard Graduate School (Ph.D.). Among other books, Dr. Archer has written *In the Shadow of the Cross, Survey of Old Testament Introduction,* and *Encyclopedia of Bible Difficulties.* He has served as president of the New England Association of Christian Schools and is a member of the Council of the International Council on Biblical Inerrancy.

INTRODUCTION

In the light of current world events it is only natural for earnest attention to be directed to the teaching of Scripture concerning the return of the Lord Jesus for the Rapture of His church. This doctrine is set forth in 1 Thessalonians 4 and related passages. Does the Bible teach that this momentous event will take place on the threshold of the seventieth week of Daniel's vision (Dan. 9), which is the pretribulation view, or will it take place at the conclusion of that seven-year period, just prior to the Battle of Armageddon, which is the posttribulational theory? Within the ranks of sincere Evangelicals, who believe in the inerrancy of Holy Scripture and the fulfillment of all biblical prophecy, there is a difference of opinion. There are energetic advocates of each interpretation. Between these two views there stands a third, the view that the Rapture will occur at the midway point between the beginning of the final seven-year period and its end. This mediating approach succeeds in avoiding the difficulties of each of the other two theories and also does justice to the two periods of three and a half years each that are mentioned in Daniel 7:25; 9:27; 12:7, 11; and also in Revelation 11:2. Neither the pretribulationists nor the posttribulationists have been able to furnish a convincing explanation for this emphasis on the midpoint of Daniel's seventieth week.

THE RAPTURE WILL PRECEDE THE SECOND ADVENT OF CHRIST

The posttribulation theory holds that the church will have to endure all of the persecutions and plagues to afflict the world prior to Christ's return. The Rapture (1 Thess. 4:14–18) will be a preliminary stage to the appearance of the Lord Jesus who comes to impose His righteous judgment upon all of rebellious mankind. There will be no significant interval between the coming of Christ in the clouds to receive up His church and His return to earth for the punishment of the Beast and all his armies at Armageddon. The church will have been purged and purified in the fires of persecution. The saints must be prepared to face their trials as bravely and nobly as did their forebears prior to the reign of Constantine the Great.

There seem to be at least five objections to the posttribulation view: (1) It fails to account for that attitude of eager personal expectation that was characteristic of the first-century apostles and saints as they looked forward to the Lord's return. (2) It hardly does justice to the sequence of events in the Rapture passage (1 Thess. 4) and the Day of the Lord passage (1 Thess. 5). (3) It fails to give sufficient weight to those New Testament passages that speak of the church as being delivered from the wrath of God to be experienced by the unbelieving world. (4) It can furnish no satisfactory explanation for the white-clad saints who accompany the Rider on the white horse described in Revelation 19, who returns to earth in order to crush rebellion and punish sin. (5) Several passages in Isaiah refer to the population of the millennial kingdom as consisting of flesh-and-blood believers who will enjoy prosperity, peace, and a long, happy life. But if *all* believers will be included in the Rapture just prior to the Battle of Armageddon, and if *all* the saints who are raptured will be clothed upon with their resurrection bodies (1 Thess. 4; 1 Cor. 15), where are these untransformed earth-dwellers going to come from that will make up the citizenry of Christ's earthly kingdom? We shall discuss these difficulties in the order named above.

The First-Century Attitude of Expectation

The posttribulation view posits an interval of seven years between the commencement of the seventieth week of Daniel's prophecy and the Rapture of the church. Even though there may be signs of the Lord's coming that are to be fulfilled before the church is taken up to glory, it is difficult to reconcile a period of seven years with the sense of excitement and expectancy conveyed by passages like 1 Thessalonians 4 and 1 Corinthians 15. Paul seems to include himself among the potential participants in this great event. First Thessalonians 4:17 states: "We who are still alive and are left will be caught up with them in the clouds to meet the Lord in the air. And so we will be with the Lord forever." Again, in 1 Corinthians 15:51, we find this expressed even more vividly: "Listen, I tell you a mystery: We will not all sleep, but we will all be changed—in a flash, in the twinkling of an eye, at the last trumpet." It is conceivable that Paul was using the pronoun "we" simply to convey his solidarity with the rest of the Christian church, including even those who are to be converted in the distant future. But the distinct impression is given that Paul thought of himself as a possible candidate for this thrilling experience. A similar inference may be drawn from Romans 13:11–12: "The hour has come for you to wake up from your slumber, because our salvation is nearer now than when we first believed. The night is nearly over; the day is almost here." To be sure, there is no specific reference to the Rapture, but the potential immediacy of the Lord's return seems to be implied by the term *salvation* in this particular context. These passages point in the direction of an "any-time-now" expectation on the part of the apostle. But even if the fulfilment of signs must precede the Rapture, the interval of three and a half years fits better with the idea of imminence than does the full span of seven years posited by the postribulationist.

The Sequence of Events in 1 Thessalonians 4–5

First Thessalonians 4:14–18 sets forth a prediction of the Rapture of the church, and 5:1–9 describes the "Day of the Lord" as a separate and subsequent event. "Now, brothers, about times and dates we do not need to write to you, for you know very well that the day of the Lord will come like a thief in the night. While people are saying, 'Peace and safety,' destruction will come on them suddenly, as labor pains on a pregnant woman, and they will not escape." While it is true that no clear lapse of time is here specified between the Rapture and the wrath of God upon unbelieving mankind, nevertheless the mention of "times and dates" in verse 1 strongly suggests that a significant interval is involved. The Rapture and the Day of the Lord can hardly be parts of the same event in the manner assumed by the posttribulation interpretation.

The Church Delivered From the Wrath of God

Although there is no passage that explicitly affirms this, there are several statements in the New Testament that suggest that born-again believers will be delivered from the outpouring of the wrath of God in the final years before Armageddon. First Thessalonians 5:9 declares: "For God has not destined us for wrath, but for obtaining salvation through our Lord Jesus Christ" (NASB). This may be taken as referring to the wrath of God in general against sin and culminating in the condemnation of the unrepentant to eternal hell. The same can be said of Romans 5:9: "Since we have now been justified by his blood, how much more shall we be saved from God's wrath through him!" Perhaps 1 Thessalonians 1:10 is also general, ". . . and to wait for his Son from heaven, whom he raised from the dead—Jesus, who rescues us from the coming wrath." But the promise given in Revelation 3:10 to the church of Philadelphia can hardly be interpreted in such a general fashion. "Since you have kept my command to endure patiently, I will also keep you from the hour of trial that is going to come upon the whole world to test those who live on the earth." If this verse means anything at all, it guarantees that true and faithful believers will be rescued from a period of great testing and trial that is going to come upon the world as a whole. But upon posttribulational presuppositions there could be no such differentiation at all; what comes upon the world in general will have to come upon the church, which is still living in the world. There seems to be no way of reconciling this verse with the posttribulational approach.

This passage calls for special comment in regard to the diachronic interpretation commonly given to the seven churches of Asia. In this interpretation each successive church from Ephesus to Laodicea represents a successive phase in the history of Christianity from late apostolic times to the last days. According to that schema the Philadelphian church would represent the modern missionary movement of the nineteenth and early twentieth century, and the Laodicean church would stand for the final stage of lukewarmness and apostasy that will precede the return of Christ. But since the promise of deliverance from the hour of temptation (Rev. 3:10) is addressed to the Philadelphian church rather than the Laodicean, the diachronic interpretation cannot stand. We can only infer that in the last days there will still be faithful, Bible-believing churches like that of Philadelphia in Asia, and that Christians of such firm commitment to God's Word will be rescued by His intervention from the terrible "hour of temptation" that is to try the rest of the world. This rescue is most reasonably to be identified with the Rapture, which will precede the outpouring of God's penal wrath upon the sin-cursed earth, as set forth in Revelation 6:9–19.

The Rider on the White Horse

In Revelation 19:11–15 we are presented with the magnificent scenario of the triumphant return of the Lord Jesus Christ, who comes to subdue the rebellious earth and establish His rule over all the kingdoms of mankind. In verse 14 we are told, "The armies of heaven were following Him, riding on white horses and dressed in fine linen, white and clean." Who will these white-clad cavalrymen be? Undoubtedly they will include the angels of heaven, since Jesus Himself refers to His return in Mark 8:38 as coming "in his Father's glory with the holy angels" (cf. also Jude 14). But in this context emphasis is laid upon the fact that redeemed saints are clothed in fine white linen as a symbol of their sincere faith and holy life. Revelation 19:7–8 makes this unmistakably clear, for it is the bride of the Lamb who has been given these shining white garments to wear, and this "fine linen stands for the righteous acts of the saints." Therefore we must conclude that the primary reference in verse 14 is to the hosts of redeemed believers who follow in Christ's train as He comes down from heaven to subdue the earth.

At this point we must deal with the question of where these white-clad saints are coming from. From heaven, obviously, but how did they get there? According to the posttribulational view the only saints up in glory are those who have died in the faith and who are awaiting the day of resurrection when they shall be clothed upon with their resurrection bodies (2 Cor. 5:2). Yet this mighty army of saints are vested in white garments like Christ Himself. It is hard to avoid the inference that they have already seen the Lord, as we read in 1 John 3:2, "We know that when he appears, we shall be like him, for we shall see him as he is." They are apparently of the number who have already been "caught up . . . in the clouds to meet the Lord in the air" and who are "with the Lord forever," according to the promise of 1 Thessalonians 4:17. But this could only be true if these white-clad saints had already been raptured and had joined the hosts of heaven at some time prior to Christ's triumphant return to earth. These considerations seem to eliminate effectively the possibility of a posttribulation Rapture.

Flesh-and-Blood-Believers in the Millennium

Isaiah 65:17–25 describes the new order of the millennial kingdom. "Behold I will create new heavens and a new earth. . . . I will create Jerusalem to be a delight and its people a joy. I will rejoice over Jerusalem and take delight in my people; the sound of weeping and of crying will be heard in it no more." There are parallels here to the new earth described in Revelation 21:1–4, which culminates in verse 4: "He will wipe away every tear from their eyes. There will be no more death or mourning or crying or pain, for the old order of things has passed away." Clearly Revelation 21 describes a new order, which will ensue after the suppression of the final rebellion of Christ-rejecting mankind at the *close* of the Millennium rather than at its inception. Revelation 20:7–10 specifies: "When the thousand years are over, Satan will be released from his prison and will go out to deceive the nations in the four corners of the earth—Gog and Magog—to gather them for battle. But fire came down from heaven and devoured them." Then the final verses of this chapter foretell the final judgment of the "great white throne," which will seal the doom of the millennial population who have joined with Satan in his rebellion against God. But I conclude that Isaiah 65 does not refer to the postmillennial phase as such, because Revelation 21:4 clearly affirms that "there will be no more death," whereas Isaiah 65:20 refers to old men who will fully live out their days to the age of one hundred or more, and speaks of youths as being at least a century old. We must therefore conclude that in this latter-day city of God on earth there will still be physical death whereas in heaven death will be no more.

Now then, if the millennial kingdom is to be populated by believers only ("Then will all your people be righteous and they will possess the land forever," Isa. 60:21), where will these saints come from? To be sure there will be many resurrected saints who will live and reign with Christ during the Millennium (Rev. 20:4), but who will be the citizens of the kingdom who will not die until they are at least a hundred years old? According to posttribulation presuppositions *all* true believers will be caught up to meet the Lord in the clouds at the *end* of the Tribulation. As such they will be given their imperishable resurrection bodies ("The trumpet will sound, the dead will be raised imperishable, and we will be changed. For the perishable must clothe itself with the imperishable . . ." [1 Cor. 15:52–53]). There will be no interval of time in which new believers could be won to the Lord after the Rapture, and thus live on to people the earth during the Millennium. This factor speaks decisively in favor of a significant lapse of time between the Rapture and the return of the Lord Jesus to impose judgment on the earth. If the Rapture takes place either seven years before or even three and a half years before the Battle of Armageddon, there will be adequate opportunity for the impact of the sudden disappearance of all regenerate believers to make itself felt. Almost inevitably the large numbers of friends and relatives and business associates to whom these believers have previously witnessed will become convinced of the truth of the gospel and turn to the Lord in large numbers, despite the fierce opposition of the Beast and all of his minions. These converts will furnish a substantial base upon which to build up the population of the millennial kingdom. But on posttribulational presuppositions such a development becomes impossible.

CERTAIN SIGNS WILL PRECEDE THE RAPTURE

Under this general heading we will discuss seven problem areas in connection with the pre–seventieth-week Rapture theory. (This term is used in order to distinguish the pretribulation view from the mid–seventieth-week form of pre-tribulationism.)

The Olivet Discourse Foretells the Rapture

It is generally held by advocates of this view that the Olivet Discourse of Matthew 24 and Mark 13 refers only to the second coming of Christ and has nothing to say about the Rapture. By this interpretation the various references to signs that portend the Second Advent have no bearing upon the time or circumstances of the Lord's earlier return for His church. The Rapture, then, is to be heralded by no warning indications whatever. It may come at any moment, totally unexpected, like a thief in the night (1 Thess. 5:2; 2 Peter 3:10). But once the Rapture has taken place, then all of the signs predicted in the Olivet Discourse and similar passages (such as 2 Thess. 2) will start to appear, and after the seven years are up, all will explode like a time bomb and the world-powers will be completely crushed at Armageddon. The Rapture itself will be totally unobserved by the unsaved; only true believers will observe its occurrence and participate in its blessed results. The only thing that the world will see will be the sudden and unaccountable disappearance of all the Christians.

In order to sustain this thesis that the Olivet Discourse contains no reference whatever to the Rapture it is absolutely essential to demonstrate that the disciples to whom He revealed this prophecy were not addressed as members of the

New Testament church, but only as representatives of the converted Israel of the last days. As such they could be encouraged to look for the fulfillment of the signs predicted by our Lord summarized by the budding of the fig tree (Matt. 24:32). But to maintain such a position as this seems to run counter to the most basic postulate of evangelical hermeneutics, namely, the perspicuity of Scripture.

If the apostles and disciples who constituted the Christian church at the descent of the Holy Spirit on the Day of Pentecost were not true members or representatives of the Christian church, then who ever could be? Apart from the two books composed by Luke, the entire New Testament was composed by Jewish believers. For the first five years of the existence of the Christian church, during which several thousands of believers were added to its ranks, there was scarcely a non-Jew to be found in the entire company. All of the other admonitions and warnings addressed to the Twelve were unquestionably intended for them personally and found fulfilment or application in their later careers. How could it be that the Olivet Discourse, and that alone, was an exception to this principle? How can we possibly imagine that when Christ said to His disciples, "These are the signs you are to look for," He really meant, "You will never see these signs at all, but 1900 years from now some distant descendants of yours are to look for these signs"? Such an interpretation as this appears to violate completely the principle of literal or normal interpretation that underlies the grammatical-historical exegesis of Scripture. We must of course compare other passages which bear upon this same theme as an aid to understanding this chapter aright, but we can scarcely go to the extreme of saying that Christ really meant the opposite of what He said. Yet if He addressed His remarks to nonexistent people who would not even be born until nineteen centuries later, then His Olivet Discourse boils down to: "Here are the signs you are to look for; but when I say 'you' I don't mean *you* but a future generation almost 2000 years in the future. And when I say, 'Look for these signs,' you are not to look for them, because you will not survive long enough to see them.' " This kind of interpretation adds up to a serious violation of the perspicuity of Scripture. We are bound to believe that when Jesus gave a prediction or a command, it was to be believed in and obeyed just as He expressed it, rather than in some arcane fashion discoverable only to those who were initiated into some specialized mode of interpretation not derivable from the text itself.

If, then, we are to follow the normal usage of language and take the wording of the Olivet Discourse in its ordinary and obvious meaning, we have no choice but to understand it as addressed to representatives of the Christian church, namely the apostles themselves. And if the Christian church is to look for the signs of Christ's coming, then we can scarcely speak of an any-moment Rapture as a teaching of Christ or His apostles. It is confessedly difficult to pick out any certain point in the Olivet Discourse as indicating the disappearance of the church during the middle of the final seven years. Perhaps it is to be found after verse 14, which declares that, "The Gospel of the kingdom will be preached in all the world for a witness to all the nations, and then shall the end come." In view of the worldwide outreach of Christian missions within the last century and a half, and that too prior to the Rapture of the church, this would be an attractive thesis to maintain. If so, then there are at least eight signs which will precede the Rapture, and which the Christian church is to look for. They are, according to Matthew 24:4–14, as follows: (1) false Christs (such as did appear in the apostolic and postapostolic ages); (2) wars and rumors of war (to which the subsequent history of Europe and the Near East give abundant confirmation); (3) famines; (4) earthquakes; (5) hatred, persecution, and martyrdom directed against the true followers of Christ; (6) apostasy and treachery within the ranks of the professing church; (7) the triumphant survival of a remnant of true believers to the very end; (8) the worldwide spread of the gospel. After all of this the *end* (τέλος) will come—by which our Lord may have meant the final horror of the three and a half years during which the wrath of God will be poured out upon the earth.

Yet it must be admitted that the cut-off point after verse 14 is only one of several possible interpretations. It is intriguing that the Great Tribulation is not mentioned as such until verse 21, which would make it pertain specifically to the last half of the "week" rather than to the entire seven years prior to Armageddon. In verse 27 the Parousia of the Son of Man is specifically mentioned, and this is the same term as is used in 1 Thessalonians 4:15 in connection with the Rapture ("those who are left until the *coming* of the Lord"). But this Parousia seems to be connected more definitely with a startling public display, like the flash of lightning, followed by a scene of carnage (such as the Battle of Armageddon) to which the birds of prey are invited (v. 28). At the end of the Tribulation (v. 29) will come the terrifying signs in the heavens, such as the darkening of the sun and the moon and the falling of the stars. After mankind has been thrown into despair and panic, then the triumphant Christ will send out His angels to gather together His elect from the four compass directions (which could either refer to the saints at the Rapture, or to the saints converted during the Tribulation) in response to the signal of a celestial trumpet (which also figures in the 1 Thess. 4 passage and in 1 Cor. 15:52). Perhaps such a trumpet blast might be appropriate for both occasions, both the Rapture and the Second Coming for judgment.

But if the precise timing of the Rapture cannot be clearly ascertained from the text of the Olivet Discourse—beyond the conjectural suggestion of verse 14 offered above—there can be little debate as to 2 Thessalonians 2:1–4, which specifies signs preceding the Rapture.

> Concerning the coming [*Parousia*] of our Lord Jesus Christ and our being gathered to him (surely a reference to the Rapture), we ask you, brothers, not to become easily unsettled or alarmed by some prophecy, report or letter supposed to have come from us, saying that the day of the Lord has already come. Don't let anyone deceive you in any way, for [that day will not come] until the rebellion [*apostasia* should really be rendered *the apostasy* here] occurs and the man of lawlessness [*anomias*] is revealed, the man doomed for destruction.

Actually the word translated "has already come" is the Greek ἐνέστηκεν, which in 2 Timothy 3:1 and 1 Corinthians 7:26 clearly means "impend, be imminent"—and it may have that meaning here. The KJV renders it here as "the day of

Christ is at hand," and the ASV has "the day of the Lord is just at hand." If this is so, it seems clear that the teaching Paul was rebuking as erroneous was an any-moment Rapture! Some were arguing that the Day of Christ, involving the gathering together of all Christian believers to Himself, was impending already. But the apostle here responds with a firm negative. He says, No it is not now at hand, nor can it be until certain signs are first fulfilled, namely the outbreak of apostasy in the church and the rise of the Beast ("the man of lawlessness"). He then goes on to specify how this agent of Satan will manifest himself. "He opposes and exalts himself over everything that is called God or is worshiped, and even sets himself up in God's temple, proclaiming himself to be God" (v. 4).

From this passage in 2 Thessalonians 2:3–4 we deduce that there are two more signs that must be fulfilled before the Rapture: the erection of a temple of God—presumably on the site of Solomon's temple in Jerusalem—and the enthronement of the Antichrist in that temple as the embodiment of the divine. Paul clearly notifies his contemporaries in the Christian church of his day (a predominantly Gentile church in the Greek city of Thessalonica, at that) that they cannot expect the Rapture until the apostasy (already foretold in the Olivet Discourse) takes place, and with it the desecration of the rebuilt temple of the Lord through the arrogance of the Antichrist, who will there display himself as God. Thus we now have a total of possibly ten signs that are to be fulfilled before the Lord comes to receive up His church. We also have a clear denial of the doctrine of the any-moment Rapture, for Paul unequivocally denies that the Day of the Lord is at hand (ἐνέστηκεν).

The Removal of the Restraining Power of the Holy Spirit

It is argued by most advocates of the pre–seventieth-week Rapture theory that the reference in 2 Thessalonians 2:6–7 to the restraining power of the Holy Spirit as being removed from the world empire of the Beast points to the total removal of the church as well. That is to say, the Holy Spirit resides within the church as the spiritual temple of the Lord (1 Peter

2:5), a status that pertains to each individual believer as well (1 Cor. 6:19). If therefore the Holy Spirit is removed from the earthly scene, it necessarily follows that the church will be removed likewise. But a more careful examination of the text and of related passages make it clear that this was not the meaning intended by the biblical author.

In the first place, 2 Thessalonians 2:7–8 does not really say that the Holy Spirit will be removed from the world scene during the seventieth week. What it does say is that His restraining influence will be removed. "For the secret power of lawlessness is already at work; but the one who now holds it back will continue to do so till he is taken out of the way. And then the lawless one will be revealed, whom the Lord Jesus will overthrow with the breath of his mouth." The Greek phrase used here is ἕως ἐκ μέσου γένηται, which more literally means "until he gets out of the way." In other words, the Holy Spirit, operating through common grace (to use the technical theological term) so as to restrain unredeemed human society from a total disregard of the moral law, will at the commencement of the final seven years remove His restraining influence, with the result that human society and government will progressively degenerate to the depth of depravity that characterized the generation of Noah (when the Spirit ceased to strive with that fallen and utterly corrupt society, Gen. 6:3). He will suspend His efforts to restrain the outbreak of immorality and depravity that will characterize the reign of Antichrist, and thus will give the Beast a free hand in vaunting himself as God in the temple of the Lord. But this does not mean, and cannot mean, that the Holy Spirit has removed Himself from the world, for apart from the influence of the Holy Spirit there can be no such phenomenon as conversion. The account in Revelation indicates that converted Jews, and doubtless Gentile converts as well, will be amazingly successful in evangelistic outreach during the Tribulation. Paul suggests this in Romans 11:15, where he speaks of a national turning to Christ on the part of the Jewish race during the last days: "For if their rejection [during the present apostolic age] is the reconciliation of the world [i.e., the extension of the gospel invitation to all the nations of earth], what will their acceptance be but life from the dead?" In the context this can only imply an amazing burst of evangelistic energy and power leading to the enrichment of the world as a whole. Compare verse 12: "But if their transgression means riches for the world, . . . how much greater riches will their fulness bring!" So also in Revelation 7:9 there is a reference to "a great multitude that no one could count, from every nation, tribe, people and language, standing before the throne and in front of the Lamb." A little later on, in verse 14, this innumerable host is identified as "they who have come out of the great tribulation; they have washed their robes and made them white in the blood of the Lamb." In other words, during the Tribulation there will be more astonishing success in evangelistic outreach than has ever yet occurred in the history of the church. Since no sinner can ever be brought to repentance, faith, and surrender to the lordship of Christ except by the power of the Holy Spirit, it is utterly inconceivable that during an era of total removal of the Spirit Himself from the world scene there could be so much as a single conversion, to say nothing of such a numerous company as this!

If then we are to conclude, as surely we must, that the Holy Spirit is not personally removed from human society during the reign of the Beast, but only His restraining influence toward evil is removed, then there can be no inference drawn as to the removal of the church. Though He withdraws His restraining hand at the commencement of the seventieth week, He is still very much present to give power to the saints to maintain their steadfast faith in the face of all satanic pressure. He will be present during the Tribulation of the last half of the week as well, and large numbers of people from every race and tribe will be converted. This will remain true even after the church itself has been raptured, whether at the beginning or in the midpoint of the final seven years.

The Apostolic Attitude Concerning the Imminency of the Rapture

We have already seen that Paul rejected the idea of the any-moment Rapture in his specification of prior signs in

2 Thessalonians 2:2–3. Yet he certainly cherished also a hope that he himself might participate in the Rapture as a believer who had not yet died. "According to God's own word we tell you that we who are still alive, who are left till the coming of the Lord, will certainly not precede those who have fallen asleep." He seems to include himself as a possible actor in this dramatic scene. The same is true of 1 Corinthians 15:51: "We will not all sleep, but we will all be changed—in a flash, in the twinkling of an eye, at the last trumpet." While it is possible to argue that Paul used the first person pronoun only in order to illustrate that when the Lord comes, He will raise up to Himself people who are still alive (as Paul and his readers are at the time of the composition of the epistle) and have not yet passed through physical death, yet other passages, like Romans 13:12 ("The night is nearly over; the day is almost here") and the verse preceding ("Our salvation is nearer now than when we first believed") strongly suggest the same eagerness about the possible return of the Lord in his own lifetime.

How are we to understand this attitude on the part of the apostles (for John seems to reflect the same hope in 1 John 2:8)? Was this merely a subjective outlook of joyous anticipation on their part? Or did they have any objective basis for such optimism? Since this is a factor strongly emphasized by pretribulationists, it deserves careful attention. Can such an explanation be reconciled with an awareness of the fulfillment of prior signs? Yes it can, provided the world situation in apostolic times presented a set of factors resembling those described in the Olivet Discourse. Were there false messiahs at hand? Yes, there were some already at hand among the Jewish patriots during the build-up of resistance to Roman tyranny that culminated in the First Revolt (A.D. 66–70). During the Second Revolt, which occurred during the reign of Hadrian, Rabbi Akiba acclaimed Simon Barcochba as the Lord's Messiah. Were there wars and rumors of war? Even in the reign of Claudius and Nero there were frequent invasions and revolts that troubled the Empire. Were there famines? Yes, there was one so severe in Judea that Paul had to appeal to his new converts in Macedonia and Achaia to gather a relief fund for

the starving Christian Jews of Palestine. Were there earthquakes? L. E. Toombs in *Interpreter's Dictionary of the Bible*
3:4, states, "Classical and modern authors record at least seventeen major earthquakes in the Palestine area during the
Christian era." The geologic instability of the Jordan fault and
the Mediterranean basin were illustrated by the earthquake
that accompanied the crucifixion and resurrection of Jesus
(Matt. 27:54; 28:2) and the one that occurred at Philippi when
Paul's jailor became converted (Acts 16:26). As for hatred,
persecution, and martyrdom of the saints, these were already
shaping up during Paul's own career of service, even prior to
his ultimate execution in Rome under Nero. There were serious factions in the church at Corinth and bitter contention
between leaders in various other centers. Hymenaeus and Phi-
letus were teaching heresy (1 Tim. 1:20), and incipient Gnos-
ticism gave rise to the Epistle to the Colossians. The gospel
was spreading throughout the Roman Empire and even into
Parthian domains with gratifying rapidity. All of these developments fell into a pattern resembling the signs set forth in
the Olivet Discourse, and so it was quite reasonable for the
apostles themselves to consider the return of the Lord as a
distinct possibility even in their own lifetime.

Events Predicted to Precede the Rapture

We now come to a consideration of events foretold by
Christ Himself that necessarily had to precede the Rapture of
the church. These predictions definitely precluded the possibility of an any-moment Rapture. There are at least three
examples of such predictions.

1. In John 21:18–19 Jesus said to Peter: " 'I tell you the
truth, when you were younger you dressed yourself and went
where you wanted; but when you are old you will stretch out
your hands, and someone will dress you and lead you where
you do not want to go.' Jesus said this to indicate the kind of
death by which Peter would glorify God." Both Peter and
John and the rest of the disciples involved in that fishing party
knew that Peter would live to be an old man, that Peter would
not be personally involved in the Rapture as a living person,

and that Peter would have to die by crucifixion (ca. A.D. 67). This necessarily precluded Peter from the hope that he would be included in an any-moment Rapture, and it served notice on the rest that they could not look for the Rapture until after Peter had laid down his life after he had become old.

2. In Acts 23:11 Paul is told by the risen Christ in a vision at Jerusalem after his arrest in the temple: "Take courage! As you have testified about me in Jerusalem, so you must also testify in Rome." This prediction left no doubt but that Paul would survive to journey all the way to Rome and witness for Christ in the capital of the Empire. There was therefore no possibility of the Rapture taking place before Paul got to Rome. Hence there could have been no justifiable expectation of an any-moment Rapture until that event, which probably took place in 63 A.D. A shorter time-interval is involved, but the same general principle is involved in Acts 18:10, where the Lord appeared to Paul in a vision and said to him, "I am with you, and no one is going to attack and harm you, because I have many people in this city [i.e., Corinth]." This meant that no Rapture could occur until there had been a sizable ingathering of new believers at Corinth. Again, in connection with the storm at sea that threatened shipwreck to Paul and his fellow passengers, an angel of God appeared to him and said (Acts 27:24): "Do not be afraid, Paul. You must stand before Caesar; and God has graciously given you the lives of all who sail with you." Paul therefore knew that the Rapture could not occur before he had made it to Rome and would be presented before Nero Caesar on appeal from the provincial court at Caesarea. Until after that happened, there could be no possibility of an any-moment Rapture.

3. In Luke's version of the Olivet Discourse Jesus foretells the destruction of Jerusalem by the Romans in A.D. 70. Luke 21:24 ends this paragraph with this prediction: "They will fall by the sword and will be taken as prisoners to all the nations. Jerusalem will be trampled on by the Gentiles until the times of the Gentiles will be fulfilled." The events following the destruction of Jerusalem and the sale of its 97,000 survivors on the slave market are certainly involved in this prophecy. The statement following makes it clear that the subjugation

of Jerusalem to the Gentiles will continue until the end of the age—i.e., the "times of the Gentiles." This prediction has been fulfilled until our own generation, for it was only in 1967 that the State of Israel gained full control of the walled city of Jerusalem. Here, then, is a prophecy that extended to A.D. 70 and the centuries following that disaster even until our present century. It necessarily follows, then, that there was no possibility of the Rapture's occurring before 1960, or seven years before the Six-Day War. In what sense could there be any objective basis for belief in an any-moment Rapture until 1960? Only if the Lord Jesus was a fallible prophet of the future could there be an any-moment Rapture legitimately expected by any believer until our own generation. Since the errancy of Christ is too high a price to pay, we shall simply have to give up the doctrine of an any-moment Rapture altogether. Only in the form of an attitude of eager desire or longing for Jesus to come quickly (as Rev. 22:20 suggests)—despite the adverse indications in Scripture—can the hope of an any-moment Rapture be justified.

On the other hand, in the light of the present situation in the Near East it should be observed that we now have good and sufficient grounds to look for the return of our Lord within our own time. In the late 1940s there was a regathering of dispersed Jews from all over the world in apparent conformity to the divine promise in Isaiah 11:11. All eight of the signs specified in the Olivet Discourse up to and including Matthew 24:14 have been fulfilled. The next significant sign that awaits fulfillment—possibly during the first half of the seventieth week—is the rebuilding of a temple to the Lord on Mt. Moriah in Jerusalem along with a national conversion of Israel to Christ as their Savior and Lord in the manner predicted in Zechariah 12:10. There will of course be no bestowal of kingdom blessings on the basis of a covenant relationship with God until the nation of Israel accepts Jesus as their Redeemer and King. But the important point to be observed is that all of these developments could easily take place within our lifetime. In that sense we may now declare our faith in the possibility of the Lord's soon coming and affirm that the Rapture is indeed imminent.

The Nature of the Comfort Derived From the Rapture

One of the most prominent factors emphasized by the advocates of the theory of the any-moment Rapture consists of the comfort this doctrine bestows upon the believer who embraces it. James M. Boice argues:

> The view of a posttribulational rapture is impossible for the simple reason that it makes meaningless the very argument that Paul was presenting in the Thessalonian letters. Paul was arguing for the imminence of the Lord's return. This is to be the major source of comfort for suffering believers. If Christ will not come until after the great tribulation (that is, a special period of unusual and intense suffering still in the future), then the return of the Lord is not imminent and tribulation rather than deliverance is what we must expect (*The Last and Future World* [Grand Rapids: Zondervan, 1974], pp. 41–42).

This statement raises some basic issues in connection with the comfort afforded by the doctrine of the Rapture, and these are issues that require careful examination.

Proponents of the pre–seventieth-week Rapture argue that the coming of the Lord to receive up His church is devoid of real comfort for the final generation of Christians if it does not entail escape from the Tribulation itself. Walvoord says that 1 Thessalonians 4:18 ("Wherefore comfort one another with these words") is "devoid of real meaning if they had to go through the great tribulation first. While many generations of Christians have died before the rapture, it is evident that the exhortation given to the Thessalonians applies to each successive generation which continues to have the bright hope of an imminent return of the Lord for his own" (*The Blessed Hope and the Tribulation* [Grand Rapids: Zondervan, 1976], p. 165). He adds that the exhortations of 1 Corinthians 15:51–58 concerning the Rapture have similar implications. Not a word of warning is given there concerning a Great Tribulation, "but they are exhorted to be living in the light of the imminent return of Christ." It cannot be denied that this line of reasoning has considerable appeal, for it sounds very reassuring to be guaranteed exemption from the griefs and horrors of the Tribulation described in the Olivet Discourse (Matt. 24:15–22) and in Revelation 6–18. This element of comfort is also built in to the mid-seventieth week theory as well, in that the raptured church will not be present on earth to experience the unparalled disasters and afflictions of the last three and a half years while the wrath of God is poured out in successive strokes of judgment upon the guilty earth.

Nevertheless it is highly questionable whether personal escape from the agonies of the Tribulation is what the Scripture is really talking about when it refers to the comfort and encouragement afforded by the Rapture. Even in our own age, prior to the commencement of the seventieth week, there are many of God's beloved saints who are allowed to pass through the agonies of malignant cancer or heart disease. These things involve excruciating anguish like that described for those who pass through the Tribulation. Those hundreds of Korean Christian ministers who were compelled by their Marxist captors to march on the road for days on end until they finally dropped from exhaustion and one by one were bludgeoned or bayoneted by their tormentors—these noble martyrs of the faith surely went through suffering as cruel as the suffering of those who live through the Tribulation. According to tradition, at least, most of the apostles themselves passed through an agonizing mode of death—Paul by strangling and Peter by crucifixion. The avoidance of suffering and distress on earth is hardly the highest level of comfort that the Scripture has to promise us. On the contrary, it teaches us that "our light and momentary troubles are achieving for us an eternal glory that far outweighs them all" (2 Cor. 4:17). But surely the highest and truest level of comfort and encouragement for the Christian is the prospect of going to be with Christ. Jesus said, "Let not your heart be troubled . . . If I go and prepare a place for you, I will come back and take you to be with me, that you also may be where I am" (John 14:1–3). To this assurance the true lover of Christ responds as Paul did in Philippians 1:23, "I desire to depart and be with Christ, which is better by far." Should we not therefore understand the comfort of the Rapture to consist in our meeting with Christ and bathing ourselves in the glory of His love and

seeing His face? Is this not far more significant than our escaping a few years of earthly agony through which the rest
of our generation must pass? Even if the posttribulationists
were right, could we condemn the Rapture promises of
1 Thessalonians 4, 1 Corinthians 15, and Titus 2 as "devoid of
comfort" when they assure us that our risen Redeemer is
going to return to earth to vindicate His righteousness, to
crush the wicked, and to establish His rightful authority over
all the earth for a thousand years? A temporary period of
struggle and pain does not necessarily cancel out the joy of
ultimate victory after the trial is over. Concerning the Lord
Jesus Himself, we read in Hebrews 12:2, "Let us fix our eyes
on Jesus, the author and perfecter of our faith, who for the
joy set before him endured the cross, scorning its shame, and
sat down at the right hand of the throne of God." From this
standpoint, then, the glorious vindication and triumph of our
Savior would be of immeasurable comfort to us, whether or
not we escape passing through the Tribulation. Therefore we
must discount this argument for pretribulation Rapture as of
little weight. Other considerations of a far more compelling
nature have already been cited in its favor.

"There Is No Mention of the Church in Revelation 4–18"

Pretribulationists rely heavily on an argument from silence concerning the church in those chapters of Revelation
that describe the course of the Tribulation, namely 4–18. It
is perfectly true that ἐκκλησία occurs in Revelation 1–3 at least
seventeen times (always in the sense of the individual congre-
gations of the seven cities of Asia), but never again until 22:16,
where it refers to these same local churches. Yet it should be
noted that John never uses ἐκκλησία in the collective sense of
the temple of the Holy Spirit or the body of Christ anywhere
in the entire book. Therefore his failure to mention it by that
specific term in chapters 4–18 is of no great significance to the
question of its existence on earth during the Tribulation period. But it should also be observed that the term *church*
never occurs in any of the main Rapture passages either (1 Cor.

15:51–57; 1 Thess. 4:14–18; Titus 2:11–14). Since all agree that the church is nevertheless the subject involved in all of these passages, even though the word ἐκκλησία appears in none of them, this argument from silence is robbed of any possible validity. On the contrary, we must determine on contextual grounds whether the church is present on earth during the Tribulation, just as we determine its involvement in the three Rapture passages cited above—on the basis of context. Consider Revelation 6:9, where "the souls of those who had been slain because of the word of God and the testimony they had maintained" are depicted as crying out for God to inflict judgment on their murderers; this sounds very much like a group of martyred Christians who stand on a par with those who were slain in the Roman persecutions prior to Constantine the Great. The same is true of "their fellow servants and brothers who were to be killed as they had been." These victims of the persecution waged by the Beast during the first half of the seventieth week would appear to be members of the New Testament church, in the absence of any positive evidence to the contrary. But after the opening of the sixth seal in Revelation 6:12 the scene changes quite drastically, and the establishment leaders begin to feel the weight of the wrath of God coming down upon them. In terror and anguish they cry out to the mountains and rocks, "Fall on us and hide us from the face of him who sits on the throne and from the wrath of the Lamb!" It would appear that the first phase, the wrath of man (i.e., of the Antichrist), has now given place to the second phase, the wrath of God. If this change occurs in the middle of the final "week," then we may conclude that the church has been raptured at some point between verse 11 and verse 12, that is, between the opening of the fifth seal and the opening of the sixth.

The Radical Distinction Between Israel and the Church

We close our discussion of the pre–seventieth-week Rapture with a few comments concerning the radical distinction drawn between the church and Israel by the advocates of this theory. That a distinction does exist is made perfectly clear by various passages in both Testaments. Thus, in Isaiah 11:10–12, we read of the impact of the crucified and risen Christ upon (1) the Gentiles who become converted to faith in Him, and (2) the remnant of the Jews, who will be regathered to Israel from all the lands to which they have been dispersed. But verse 12 seems to suggest that these two groups will be merged into one covenant people, "He will raise a banner for the nations (גוים) and gather the exiles of Judah from the four quarters of the earth." A similar impression is made by Isaiah 49:6–7, which addresses the Messianic Servant of the Lord as the Restorer of the tribes of Jacob and also a light of salvation to the Gentiles—"that you may bring my salvation to the ends of the earth."

In Romans 11:16–24 the Gentile and Jewish constituents of God's covenant nation are referred to under the analogy of an olive tree. First the branches of the Christ-rejecting Jews are lopped off from the tree, and grafts from wild olive trees (representing the converted Gentiles) are inserted into the trunk of the good olive itself (v. 17). Paul then comments that the original branches were broken off "because of unbelief" (v. 20), and that the newly ingrafted branches can remain part of the tree only on the condition of evangelical faith. Paul closes this paragraph by suggesting that if the lopped-off branches of the Christ-rejecting Jews "do not persist in unbelief" they too may be grafted into the parent tree from which they were earlier removed (v. 23). The final sentence reads: "After all, if you were cut out of an olive tree that is wild by nature, and contrary to nature were grafted into a cultivated olive tree, how much more readily will these, the natural branches, be grafted into their own olive trees?" (v. 24). Thus this passage teaches two principles: (1) that national restoration is in store for Israel in the latter days, and (2) that both the Gentile branches and the Jewish branches belong to the one and same organism, the church of the living God. Both of them belong to this covenant people of God by faith (rather than by human descent) and therefore belong to one another. From this we deduce that this principle still prevails during the final seven years before Armageddon. There is no special arrangement to accommodate a Jewish nation which rejects the atonement and lordship of Christ, even during the Tribulation, and certainly not during the Kingdom Age. Israel can only receive the personal benefit of God's gracious promises of salvation through faith in the Messiah Jesus, whom they once rejected in the presence of Pontius Pilate. Zechariah 12:10 states that they will do so in the end time. This observation has implications for the present political state of Israel. The preservation and military victory that God has granted them up until this point has not been vouchsafed to them because they are now pleasing in God's sight, simply as descendants of Abraham, but only in contemplation of what they will become after they have yielded to the call of the gospel and repented of the crucifixion of their only true Messiah on the Cross. From this standpoint, then, it is highly questionable whether we may speak of the church as being completely and permanently removed from earth at the time of the Rapture. Those who are converted in such great numbers during the Tribulation will be saved by faith in the same way as the New Testament church has always been. They will trust in the same Lord and be indwelt by the same Holy Spirit as we pre-Rapture believers are. Whether they prefer to call themselves messianic Jews rather than "Christians," they are still saved in the same way and belong to the same Lord, and there is no essential difference between the two. While it is perfectly true that an Old Testament pattern will be maintained during the Kingdom Age (according to the indications of Ezekiel 40–48; Psalm 72:8–11; Zechariah 14:9–11, 16–18) with the restoration of specific territories for each of the twelve tribes and the reinstitution of memorial sacrifices offered at a rebuilt temple in Jerusalem, nevertheless the same basic principles will obtain during the Millennium as during the Church Age: salvation by grace through faith, oneness in Christ regardless of racial or cultural background, and an adherence to the standards of Holy Scripture for the maintenance of a holy walk. There will be no essential distinction between the Jewish-Gentile church and the Jewish-Gentile messianic kingdom throughout the Millennial period. And apparently also the saints who have become citizens of heaven prior to the Millennium will have an important part in the administration of the messianic kingdom itself. Just as angels were sent to earth on special missions for the Lord all during the biblical period, so the twelve apostles, the martyred saints of the Tribulation, and doubtless many other Christian believers as well (cf. Rev. 1:6, 20:4), will have a significant role in maintaining the government of the Lord Jesus as He sits upon the throne of David.

THE RAPTURE OF THE CHURCH TO OCCUR IN THE MIDDLE OF THE WEEK

After surveying the difficulties involved with the posttribulation theory and those of the pre-seventieth-week, we come to the most viable option of all, the mid-seventieth-week theory of the Rapture. This is popularly known as the midtribulation theory, but such a term gives rise to a possible misunderstanding. If the Great Tribulation is to be identified with the second half of the final seven years prior to Armageddon, during which the bowls of divine wrath will be poured out upon the earth, then the view we are about to advocate is really a form of pretribulation Rapture. It simply regards the first three and a half years, during which the Antichrist will increase his power and mount his persecution against the church, as a lesser tribulation, not nearly as terrifying or destructive of life as those fearsome plagues that will dominate the last three and a half years. In other words, this interpretation makes a clear division between the first half as the period of the wrath of man, and the second half as the period of the wrath of God. For the reasons adduced on pages 117–18 of this chapter, we understand that the final generation of the pre-Rapture church will be subjected to the wrath of man, but spared from the wrath of God. We will now proceed to a discussion of the more specific evidences from Scripture that support this interpretation.

The Emphasis on Three-and-a-Half Months in Daniel and Revelation

In Daniel 9:27 (NASB) we read concerning the antitype of the prince who will come to destroy the city and the sanc-

tuary: "And he will make a firm covenant with the many for
one week [i.e., a heptad of years], but in the middle of the
week he will put a stop to sacrifice and grain offering; and on
the wing of abominations will come one who makes deso-
late." In other words, the Antichrist will for strategic reasons
allay apprehensions concerning his future tyranny by entering
into a solemn pact with the believing community (here referred to as הָרַבִּים, "the many," a term derived from Isaiah
53:11). The pact guarantees freedom of religion for the next
seven years. But after three and a half years have elapsed, the
Antichrist will feel confident enough of his dictatorial power
to abrogate this covenant and to terminate the worship services being carried on by the believing Jewish community in
their newly rebuilt temple. At this point he involves himself
in a heinous breach of faith which is soon followed by sacrilege. Presumably this sacrilege is the same as that foretold in
2 Thessalonians 2:4 (as discussed above), which states that he
will enthrone himself as the incarnate God right in the temple
itself. Very much like Adolph Hitler, he will attempt to coerce
all of his subjects to worship himself alone as the embodiment
of the divine upon earth.

An earlier passage, Daniel 7:25, gives more details as to
the *program* of the Antichrist as he attempts to remake the
world to suit himself. It reads: "He will speak against the
Most High and oppress his saints and try to change the set
times and the laws. The saints will be handed over to him for
a time, times and half a time." This term for "time," the
Aramaic *'iddān,* is used to mean "year," as in the account of
Nebuchadnezzar's madness recorded in Daniel 4:16. If the plural, "times" (*'iddanīn*) is meant to indicate two years, then we
have here again a mention of an interval of three and a half
years—presumably the second half of the seventieth week
(although the first half might also be a possible alternative).
Whether this indicates that the saints have been removed from
the domain of the Beast through the Rapture, or whether this
phase of this tyrannical rule will prevail during the second half
of the week, affecting the Jewish community until the Second

Advent, the midway point in the seventieth week is given great prominence.

In Daniel 12:7 the angel explains to Daniel the Lord's plan for the end time in the following terms: "It will be for a time, times and half a time. When the power of the holy people has been finally broken, all these things will be completed." In other words, in the three-and-a-half-year period the power of the saints will be completely shattered by the forces of the Antichrist, and he will at the midpoint of the seventieth week succeed in attaining absolute dictatorship over the world—at which point he will reveal himself to be God in the flesh, sitting enthroned as such in the temple of the Lord.

Daniel 12:11 reveals the timetable of events as follows: "From the time that the daily sacrifice is abolished and the abomination that causes desolation is set up, there will be 1,290 days"—or a total of twelve days more than three and a half years. This seems to indicate that the second half of the seventieth week will be devoted to the cult of the Beast, the worship of the Lord having been completely suspended.

Passing now to the Book of Revelation, we find that in 12:14 "The woman was given the wings of a great eagle, so that she might fly to the place prepared for her in the desert, where she would be taken care of for a time, times and half a time, out of the serpent's reach." The "woman" in this case seems to be the faithful community of Israel, from which (racially speaking) the "son" (Jesus Christ) was born (12:5). After this Son, who was destined to rule over all the nations with an iron scepter, "was snatched up to God and to his throne" (at His ascension), it is stated that the "woman"—the faithful, believing community of Israel (rather than the nation of Israel as a whole)—will flee for refuge to the desert, "to a place prepared for her by God." And now we are told that she will be taken care of there for a period of "1,260 days"—approximately three and a half years. This would seem to refer to the final half of the seventieth week, during which the Tribulation saints (many of whom will be Jews who have turned to the Lord after the Rapture) will hide from the Anti-christ's persecution by taking refuge in the desert.

Revelation 14 More Satisfactory Than Revelation 4 as the Time of the Rapture

The usual point in the Book of Revelation that is assigned to the Rapture by pre–seventieth-week rapturists is Revelation 4:1, where John records hearing a command from heaven, "Come up here, and I will show you what must take place after this." This is identified with the gathering of all the saints, both the living and the resurrected, to meet the Lord Jesus in the clouds as He is descending from heaven to earth (1 Thess. 4:16–17). But in Revelation 4:2 we are told that John himself personally and alone is lifted up in the Spirit to behold the glorious throne room of God in heaven, surrounded by the angels and the twenty-four elders. There is no mention whatever of Christ's earthward descent as a prelude to John's translation to heaven, and there is no suggestion that anyone else accompanied John, any more than was true of Ezekiel when he was transported in the Spirit to view what was going on in the Jerusalem temple (Ezek. 8:3; 11:1). Therefore we must conclude that Revelation 4:1 has no relationship to the Rapture of the church.

A far more likely point of identification is found in Revelation 14:14: "I looked, and before me was a white cloud, and seated on the cloud was one 'like a son of man' with a crown of gold on his head and a sharp sickle in his hand." As we look back to 14:1–5 we find that the Lord Jesus is accompanied by 144,000 of His saints who appear with Him on Mt. Zion (which probably is the heavenly counterpart of Mt. Zion as the celestial temple of the Lord). Verse 13 records the declaration of a "voice from heaven," saying, "Write: Blessed are the dead who die in the Lord from now on. 'Yes,' says the Spirit, 'they will rest from their labor, for their deeds will follow them.' " Although there is no explicit mention of their being resurrected from their graves, the mention of the blessed condition of deceased believers suggests the immediate fulfillment of that blessing by the event of the Rapture. Moreover

(v. 6) Jesus is represented here as sending forth His angels to notify true believers in every kindred, nation, and tribe to give God glory and praise, for He is very shortly going to impose His righteous judgment upon the wicked world. That judgment is then described by way of anticipation in the closing verses (16–20), which point to the final conflict of Armageddon. In this connection it is important to note that John here anticipates the descent of Christ to earth, riding upon a white horse and followed by the heavenly hosts, which is recorded in Revelation 19:11–21. This should alert us to the fact that John does not follow a neatly segmented chronological sequence in the series of visions revealed to him, but rather, there is occasional overlap or preliminary anticipation from time to time, which is taken up again and brought to its conclusion later in the book. But in regard to the earlier part of Revelation 14, which can be tied in with the Rapture more easily than Revelation 4:1 can be, it should be pointed out that the "144,000 who had been redeemed *from the earth*" may be the company of true believers translated from earth to meet the Lord in the clouds. Other interpretations of the 144,000, both here and in Revelation 7:4–8 have been advanced, and a more thorough discussion of this identification is warranted than the limits of this chapter will permit. It should be added in this connection that Revelation 14 cannot be taken as representing the *first* mention of the events of the second half of the seventieth week, for the breaking of the sixth seal described in 6:14 introduces episodes that surely belong to the last three and a half years rather than to the earlier half of the week. These include the great earthquake (cf. Zech. 14:4), the meteoric manifestations of Joel 2:30–31 and Matthew 24:29, and the complete shattering of the power and the courage of the rulers and denizens of earth in the day of Jehovah's wrath. Here again the apostle John records a weaving pattern in the successive visions which were given to him, and so it is only by careful comparison of one Scripture with another that we can discover a sequential, chronological pattern.

J. Oliver Buswell, Jr., identifies the mid–seventieth-week Rapture with the seventh trumpet referred to in Revelation 11:15–19 (*A Systematic Theology of the Christian Religion* [Grand

Rapids: Zondervan, 1962], 2:397). This passage announces rewards for the righteous dead (v. 18) as well as the approach of the wrath of Almighty God, which is about to be visited upon the earth. This occurs after the episode of the trampling of the city of Jerusalem for forty-two months (three and a half years) and the earnest testimony of the two witnesses sent from heaven, who warn and exhort the disobedient world for a period of 1,260 days before they are slain by the power of Satan and of the Antichrist. But after their corpses have been exposed to public view and jeered at for three and a half days (v. 9), they are brought to life once more (v. 11), and are raised to heaven again by God's command (v. 12). It goes without saying, that the two witnesses (who probably are to be identified with Moses and Elijah), can hardly be representative of the saints who are taken up at the Rapture (as Buswell suggests). But the events following after the sounding of the seventh trumpet might conceivably be understood as relating to that translation of the church, especially if the flight of Israel into the desert (12:13–17) is brought into correlation with the climax of the middle of the week. But in my opinion there are too many obscurities and difficulties to make out a convincing case for this identification, and it is better to abandon it altogether.

Concluding Observations Concerning the Timing of the Rapture

As we draw this whole discussion to a close, we must confess that the data of Scripture do not lend themselves to any clear and unambiguous pattern which is completely free of difficulties. The most we can say is that the problems attending the mid–seventieth-week position are on the whole less serious than those connected with the posttribulational theory and those that the pre–seventieth-week interpretation encounters. It seems to this writer that either of those approaches involve basic violations of hermeneutical principle, and entail the surrender of the perspicuity of Scripture to a degree that is quite unacceptable. The midweek-Rapture view clearly affords a solution far more compatible with the plain and ordinary sense of the terms employed by the biblical text than can be maintained with either of the other alternatives. We therefore offer this position for favorable consideration, not as a matter of settled dogma, binding upon the consciences of all premillennial Evangelicals, but as the best available solution to a difficult and highly involved matter of controversy. May the Lord give us all the grace to live and labor in the vineyard of Christ as workmen who do not need to be ashamed. And as His servants who love Him with all our heart, let us look eagerly and expectantly for His soon return, at whatever point of the final seven years He may make His appearance. Thank God for the clear assurance of all Scripture, that our Redeemer will surely return to this sin-cursed earth as complete Victor and absolute Sovereign over the whole earth. Then every knee will bow to Him and every tongue will confess that Jesus Christ is Lord, to the glory of God the Father. Then every other song will be drowned out by the mighty hallelujah chorus from all the choirs of earth and heaven. And we who are raised from earth to meet our Lord in the sky will have a very special section assigned to us in that celestial choir. Of this much we can be absolutely certain. Thank God for that!

RESPONSE: PAUL D. FEINBERG

Archer's defense of a mid–seventieth-week Rapture raises two questions for a pretribulationist. First, has he presented a convincing case for placing the Rapture in the middle of Daniel's seventieth week? Second, are his criticisms of pretribulationism fatal to that view? In the response that follows I shall examine each of these questions.

First, is there a convincing case for placing the Rapture at the middle of Daniel's seventieth week? Archer thinks that neither pretribulationists or posttribulationists explain adequately the scriptural emphasis on the middle of the week and its bifurcation. I think that Archer is correct in noting that Scripture emphasizes the middle of the seventieth week, but doubt that it is due to the Rapture of the church.

Let us examine the passages that Archer cites that deal with the middle of the seventieth week. He begins with Daniel 9:27. He notes that the middle of the week is important. Indeed it is, but is its importance related to the Rapture? Daniel says that a future leader will make a covenant with many in the nation of Israel for seven years. It seems that the primary result of this agreement is that the nation will be free to practice their own form of religious worship. In the middle of the week this freedom will be taken away. The middle of the week is significant because this covenant will be broken. The Jews will no longer be free to sacrifice, because an idolatrous system of worship will be set up. Daniel 7:25 and 12:7, 11 deal with the last three and a half years of this seventieth week, or seven years. Daniel 12:11 confirms the teaching of the latter part of 9:27. The daily sacrifice will be taken away, and idolatry will be established. On the other hand, Daniel 7:25 and 12:7 tell of one who will persecute the *saints* and break up their power. So rather than the saints being raptured into heaven, we see that they will be persecuted on the earth. While it is true that the Rapture might occur at the middle of the week and explain the importance given to the last three and a half years, these Old Testament passages give no indication of the Rapture.

Possibly the New Testament sets the Rapture of the church at the middle of the seventieth week. Archer suggests three passages from Revelation that might support his view: Revelation 11:15–19; 12:14; 14:14. Revelation 11 is often taken as the point in the book where the Rapture of the church occurs. Two reasons are usually cited either separately or in conjunction with one another. First, the Rapture is seen as symbolically taught in the resurrection of the two witnesses (11:13). The two witnesses are symbolic of a larger group of witnesses. Their resurrection and ascension into heaven, then, is symbolic of the church. Second, the "seventh trumpet" of 11:15 is identified with the "trumpet of God" (1 Thess. 4:16) and the "last trump" (1 Cor. 15:52). This is further supported by the fact that 11:18 associates the seventh trumpet with rewards for the righteous and the announcement of God's wrath for unbelievers. This trumpet sounds after the city of Jerusalem has been given over to the Gentiles for three and a half years (11:1, 2).[1]

While one cannot rule out the possibility that such an interpretation is correct, there are some reasons for rejecting it. The two witnesses appear to be individuals rather than representatives of all living and dead saints. The witnesses perform miracles; they testify. These actions are usually done by individuals, not groups. Moreover, both witnesses are killed by the Beast. If they are symbolic of *all* saints, then it seems as if all saints will be martyred before the Rapture. Further, it also appears that all saints will have men gaze at their dead bodies and desecrate them.

The identification of the "last trumpet" and the "seventh trumpet" is also tenuous. If the identification rests on the bare fact that in both passages we have last trumpets, then there is a problem. Gundry points out that if the seventh trumpet comes at the middle of the seventieth week, there is still another trumpet. It is the trumpet with which the angels call

God's elect from the four winds after Christ's return (Matt. 24:31).[2] On the other hand, if the identification is based on the fact that both trumpets are the last trumpet for the church, then I think the argument is dubious. There is no question that 1 Corinthians 15:52 and 1 Thessalonians 4:16 deal with the church. The problem relates to the seventh trumpet of Revelation 11:15. Here you have the final trumpet in a series of judgments. On what ground should this trumpet be taken as identical with the last trumpet of 1 Corinthians 15:52?

For the sake of argument, however, let us assume that the trumpets mentioned in the three passages above are the same. Would that show that a mid–seventieth-week Rapture was correct? I do not think so. We must further show that the seventh trumpet of Revelation 11:15 comes in the middle of the week. Robert Gundry thinks that the last of each series of judgments takes one to the end of the week.[3] Therefore, the identification of the trumpets with one another could support a posttribulation Rapture equally as well. In fairness to Archer, he does not advance this argument because he thinks that there are problems with it.

Archer does cite Revelation 12:14. Here again one finds the occurrence of the three and a half years or 1,260 days. However, as he notes the subject under discussion is the protection of a righteous Jewish remnant from the wrath of this satanic masterpiece. Could the Rapture of the church occur before this flight by believing Jews? Surely. The problem again is that there is no statement of such a fact here.

Finally, we come to Revelation 14 where Archer thinks the Rapture is more likely to occur than anywhere else in the book. In verses 1–5 we have 144,000 in the heavenly Zion. Revelation 14:13 pronounces a blessing on those who are dead. Archer thinks that this blessing suggests the immediacy of the Rapture, and 14:14–20 pictures the Son of Man as prepared to impose His righteous judgment in the final conflict of Armageddon.

The heart of Archer's argument rests with the identification of the 144,000 with raptured saints. He says that the argumentation for this position is beyond the limits of his presentation, so it is impossible to know why he thinks as he does. However, I do think that there are good reasons for rejecting his view. The first mention of the 144,000 in the Book of Revelation is found in 7:4–8. There they are explicitly said to be 12,000 from each of the twelve tribes of Israel. Moreover, there is also no clue as to whether they have been resurrected or await glorification. Further, they are contrasted with a Gentile multitude in 7:9–12, leading me to think that they are a part of the Jewish multitude. While the beatitude may be pronounced on those who are dead because the Rapture is about to occur, as Archer thinks, it is at least as possible that they are blessed because they will miss the last woe (the final and most severe of the divine judgments).

In sum, I am in hearty agreement with Archer over the importance of the middle of the seventieth week. However, I see no convincing text that places the Rapture at that point and makes it a part of that importance.

I would now like to turn to some of Archer's criticisms of pretribulationism. I would like to say something about the Olivet Discourse, and then treat in some detail the question of imminency.

Archer objects to the pretribulation understanding of the Olivet Discourse because it violates an important hermeneutical principle, the perspicuity or intelligibility of Scripture. The problem is this. Jesus spoke of signs. However, if these signs applied to the Jewish age, then the disciples would not be alive. Thus, Jesus is saying something like, look for these signs, but you will never see them. Such is a serious charge.

First, I think it is helpful to see that these are not signs that will characterize the whole age, whether it be Jewish or Christian, but that precede the coming of Christ. If these eight signs are true of the *whole* 1,900 plus years that have elapsed since Christ revealed them, it is difficult for me to see how they are *signs* in the biblical sense of the term.

Second, if, on the other hand, the sign character of these events is in the fact that they will increase in number as we near the coming of the Lord, then only the final generation will see the *signs* spoken of in the text. If this is so, then whatever interpretation one takes, the generation that will see the signs is not the generation that hears Jesus' discourse.

Thus, the problem, if decisive, is the same for any interpretation, Archer's included.

Third, there is at least one sign that no one there saw on any interpretation. In Matthew 24:15 our Lord spoke of the abomination of desolation. This was a reference to Daniel (9:27 and 12:11). While the destruction of the temple and the fall of Jerusalem in A.D. 70 may have been a prefiguring of what would come, this passage finds its fulfillment in eschatological times. No one saw its fulfillment, yet Christ predicted it to them.

Let me put the matter in this way. The New Testament commands the believer to look for Christ's coming. For these many years saints have watched, but He has not returned. Only one generation will look and see Him. Does this call into question the perspicuity of Scripture? I do not think so. The problem arises if we are told to look because *we* will see Him come, and He does not. Neither in the case of the Second Coming nor in the case of the Olivet Discourse do I see a promise that the events spoken of will transpire in the lifetime of the hearers.

I now turn to the question of imminency. Both Archer and Moo criticize the pretribulationist view, and I should like to examine their objections. Pretribulationists argue that the coming of Christ at the Rapture may occur at *any moment*. This means that there are no prophesied events that *must* take place before Christ can come. In its strongest form, pretribulationists claim that this has been true all along. Others simply would hold that this is true now without reference to the past, particularly the distant past.

Let me summarize the arguments of Archer and Moo against the any-moment Rapture. First, none of the words used to indicate the nearness of Christ's return and the believer's attitude requires an any-moment imminency. Second, the contexts in which these terms are used do not demand the any-moment Rapture. Thirdly, there are a number of prophecies that require a delay before our Lord's return. There are passages of a general nature that suggest a delay in His return (Matt. 24:45–51; 25:5, 19; Luke 19:11–27). More importantly, there are *specific* predictions that make an any moment return impossible. There are passages that teach the preaching of the gospel to the ends of the earth (Matt. 24:14; Acts 1:8). Moreover, there are predictions about events in the life of Peter (death at an old age, John 21:18–19), and Paul (proclamation of the gospel in Rome and Corinth, Acts 23:11, 27:24, 18:10). Finally, there are the prophecies about the fall of Jerusalem in A.D. 70, and the completion of the times of the Gentiles with the return of the city of Jerusalem to Jewish control in 1967.

Two preliminary remarks are in order. First, it should be noted that the word *imminency* is a theological word rather than a biblical word. This simply means that there is no Hebrew, Aramaic, or Greek word translated "imminent." One can look in a concordance and not find it. "Imminent" is a word that theologians use to express the teaching of Scripture about the believer's expectation concerning the nearness of Christ's coming. This does not mean that the word is a bad one. Theologians use words that do not appear in the text of Scripture such as "inerrant," "trinity," or "substance." What is distinctive about a theological term in contrast with a biblical word is that one cannot establish its meaning through word studies. The justification for using a theological term, then, will be its adequacy in expressing the biblical data.[4]

A second remark has to do with the relationship between the doctrine of imminency and pretribulationism. There is no question that pretribulationists have and do make a great deal of an any-moment imminency and its practical consequences. Nevertheless, I think it is important to see that an any-moment imminency could be wrong and pretribulationism could still be right. The minimum requirement for the truth of pretribulationism is simply that the Rapture of the church must *precede* the Tribulation. That is all. Thus, problems with an any-moment Rapture *alone* are not sufficient grounds for rejecting pretribulationism.

Now let me take up the objections mentioned above. The first argument relates to the New Testament terminology for expectancy. I find the statement of the issue a bit curious. Gundry argues that imminence of a pretribulation type is only established if these terms show that Christ *must* come without some intervening event or time delay.[5] Moo puts the point in a slightly different way. He asks if these words *require* an any-moment Rapture. Both men then go on to show that in at least some cases the words used to indicate expectancy can be shown to require an intervening event or a time delay. I think that what has been said to this point is true. But it would be an invalid inference to conclude from what has been shown that *no* occurrence of the terms *could* be without intervening events or time delay. Furthermore, what makes the discussion more perplexing is that as a pretribulationist I want to see an occurrence of one of the terms in a passage that I understand as relating to the Rapture (e.g., John 14:1–3 or 1 Thess. 4:13–18) that requires intervening events or time delay. Simply to appeal to passages that are noneschatological or relate to the Second Coming will not convince me. I agree with both midtribulationists and posttribulationists that signs and time precede the Second Advent, *but* I do not think the Rapture and the Second Coming are the same event.

Is the context any more decisive on this issue? Gundry's argument from the contexts of eschatological passages is as follows. First, some passages dealing with the Second Coming do have a mention of signs (e.g., Matt. 24:32–25:13; Luke 21:28). This also shows that signs are not inconsistent with watching for Christ, as Tribulation saints are exhorted to look for Him *through* signs. Second, some passages lack a reference to signs, but this absence is explainable on one of these grounds: (1) The text is not an exhortation to watch (e.g., 1 Thess. 4:13–18). However, in the more general context there are signs that are given for the commencement of the Day of the Lord (1 Thess. 5; 2 Thess. 2:2–4). (2) Signs are not absent outside the Gospels in the New Testament (e.g., 1 Tim. 4:1–2; 2 Tim. 3:1–7; Jude 17, 18). (3) Often the references to the Second Coming outside the Gospels are isolated verses or clauses within a verse where brevity or the surrounding material makes a reference to signs inappropriate (e.g., 1 Thess. 1:10; Titus 2:13). (4) Some passages that make no mention of signs also make imminency impossible (e.g., Rom. 8:18–25; 1 Cor. 1:7).[6]

My response to Gundry's treatment of the contexts is as follows. Those passages that teach that signs precede Christ's coming deal with the return of Christ at the end of the Tribulation; they do *not* refer to the Rapture of the church. I have tried to argue elsewhere that there is a difference between these two events. I do think that those passages that lack signs are significant. If Gundry means to show only that there are alternative explanations *possible* for the lack of signs, then I agree but this is hardly surprising. It does seem significant that in the vast majority of the passages dealing with the Second Coming signs are present. Why then is it the case that there are no signs in any passage that deals with the Rapture in the opinion of all? If there were such signs, that would be a decisive argument against an any-moment Rapture.

In the cases where there are signs in the more general context, the topic under discussion has changed from the Rapture (1 Thess. 4:13–18) to the Second Coming (1 Thess. 5; 2 Thess. 2:2–4). While this point is not argued here, it is elsewhere. But let it be further noted here that, while 1 Thessalonians 5:6 does exhort the believer to watch, there is no object for the verb. It does not say, for instance, watch for the Day of the Lord. As a matter of fact, it does say that the Day will overtake the unbeliever by surprise, but the believer is distinguished from the unbeliever, raising at least the possibility that the believer is not there.

Finally, I do not think the "signs" that Gundry cites in the Epistles (1 Tim. 4:1–3; 2 Tim. 3:1–7; Jude 17, 18) are really signs; nowhere are they called signs. They are simply conditions that will prevail as the end of the church age approaches. Further, nowhere are we told that when we see these conditions obtaining, we can know that Christ's coming is near, even at the door (Matt. 24:33). For me at least, these are not insignificant differences. Thus, I find myself unconvinced by Gundry's claim.

The final line of argument against an any-moment imminency is related to predictions Jesus made, which would have had to occur before the Rapture could have taken place. Any response to this point should begin by pointing out that not all of the predictions constitute a problem. For instance, most pretribulationists, myself included, would hold that the prophecy in Matthew 24:14 that the gospel would be preached to all nations before the end, relates to the Tribulation, when the church is gone. Yet Acts 1:8 is applicable and could be taken to make a very similar point; it must be dealt with.

The prophecies that Archer brings up relating to the nation of Israel, the destruction of the temple in A.D. 70 and the end of the times of the Gentiles in 1967 (if one accepts his interpretation on this matter), have nothing to do with the question of imminency. While these events are predicted in Scripture as *occurring, no* date is given for their occurrence. Moreover, they are events that are related to the nation of *Israel,* not the church. Let us assume that the Rapture had occurred in A.D. 40. The temple could have fallen in A.D. 40 or 41, and the times of the Gentiles would have been completed in A.D. 47 or 48 without any prophecy being falsified.

What is puzzling about Archer's argument against imminency is this. He argues that the apostles thought they might see the Lord's return in their lifetime. He says such expectancy is compatible with a three-and-a-half-year Tribulation, but not with a seven-year Tribulation. And yet he criticizes pretribulationists for their belief in an any-moment Rapture because the Rapture could not have happened until 1967. One wonders how such an argument is compatible with any understanding of imminence (even a view that holds that Christ can come at any time though some events need to transpire first). If one wants to hold to imminency in any meaningful sense (and I gather that both Archer and Moo do), one cannot hold that events that occurred a hundred or even a thousand years after the time of Christ, required fulfillment before He could return. If one does, then these predictions become a problem for imminency in a midtribulational or posttribulational eschatology as well.

Having made the point that not all the predictions are problematic, or if they are, they are problems for other positions as well, we have not dismissed all the difficulties. We have simply reduced the problems to those general statements about delay in Christ's return, and specific predictions that relate to the church (e.g., Acts 1:8) or individual members in it (e.g., John 21:18–19). I shall now try to answer these difficulties for an any-moment Rapture.

I think that the belief in an any-moment imminency grows

out of these three lines of argumentation: Paul's inclusion of himself and his readers among the potential participants in the Rapture, passages in the Epistles that teach the nearness of Christ's return and the absence of any signs in any undisputed Rapture text.

First, in a number of places Paul writes as though he and his readers might participate in the Rapture. In 1 Corinthians 15:51–53 he uses the first person plural pronoun as he relates a mystery. He says that *we* shall not all sleep, but some shall be translated at the coming of Christ. Not only will the dead be raised but those who are alive shall be given their glorified bodies in a moment, in the twinkling of an eye. A similar use of the first person can be found in 1 Thessalonians when Paul talks of Christ's return. In 1 Thessalonians 1 Paul is characterizing the exemplary conduct of this church. They were an expectant church waiting "for his Son from heaven, whom he raised from the dead—Jesus, who rescues us from the coming wrath" (1:10). If the wrath spoken of is not simply eternal damnation (a point argued in "The Case for the Pretribulation Position"), then Paul seems to raise the possibility that Christ might come and take them from the world, saving them from the approaching wrath of the Day of the Lord. In another central Rapture passage, 1 Thessalonians 4:13–14, Paul not only teaches the resurrection of those who have died, but says, "*We* who are alive, and remain until the coming of the Lord . . . shall be caught up to be with the Lord" (vv. 15–17). The use of the first person plural pronouns may simply be Paul's way of identifying with the church as a whole, but one cannot escape the impression that Paul thought that he and the Thessalonians might be participants in the Rapture. This impression is further substantiated by certain of the problems that prompt the writing of the Epistle itself.

Second, there are a number of texts that teach that Christ's coming is at hand. Passages that make up this line of evidence may be further divided. There are those verses that state explicitly that Christ's return is at hand. Romans 13:12 says that "the night is nearly over; the day is almost here." James teaches that the "Lord's coming is near" (5:8–9). John agrees as he writes, "This is the last hour" (1 John 2:18) and "The time is near" (Rev. 22:18). Moreover, as we come to the last chapter of the Bible, three times there is the promise, "I am coming soon" (Rev. 22:7, 12, 20). Further, there is a group of passages that exhort the believer in New Testament times to wait eagerly for or look for Christ's return (1 Cor. 1:7–8; Phil. 3:20; Titus 2:13). Then John twice uses ἐάν with the subjunctive to express the unpredictability of Christ's appearance (1 John 2:28; 3:2). Finally, the nearness of the Rapture is implied by the nearness of events that are to occur after the church is gone. The end of all things is near (1 Peter 4:7), and judgment is about to begin (1 Peter 4:5, 17).

Moo and Gundry object to the use of many of the passages just cited (e.g., "wait eagerly" does not *require* an any-moment Rapture, and ἐάν with the subjunctive does not *require* uncertainty); nevertheless I see nothing that precludes imminency in these texts. Imminency is not required, but it is also not precluded by anything they have said.

We are now ready to return to the predictions that raised problems for the doctrine of imminency. What about preaching the gospel to the end of the earth, and the death of Peter as an old man? The difficulties cease to exist when one realizes that the doctrine of imminency rests not on the teachings of Jesus, but on the Epistles. The Epistles began to be written in the late 40s and early 50s. By that time the preaching of the gospel throughout the then-known world was imminent, as was Peter's death. The doctrine of an any-moment return of Christ began to be taught somewhere during the apostolic period of the church's history. The problems for an any-moment Rapture only arise if one makes Jesus' teachings the bases of the doctrine. However, what sense can be made of an imminent Rapture of the church *before* it is even formed? The point being made is extremely important, but should not surprise us.

Third, there is an absence of signs or intervening events in any undisputed Rapture passage. In each of the central Second Advent texts, Zechariah 14:1–5; Matthew 24:29–31; and Revelation 19:11–21, the return of Christ is preceded by great upheaval, distress, and signs that alert one to its occurrence. Neither the trial nor the signs are to be found in the Rapture texts, John 14:1–3; 1 Corinthians 15:51–58; and 1 Thessalonians 4:13–18. It may at first appear that this third line of argument is an example of the notorious argument from silence. However, careful reflection will convince one that this is not the case. I am not arguing to some positive conclusion because of the lack of some data. Rather, I am *comparing* two groups of texts. In one group there are signs and an Advent that occurs in the context of tribulation; in the other group neither signs nor distress are found. I am arguing that the presence of certain data in one group and the lack of it in another are significant facts.

While it is true that events could precede Christ's coming and that coming could be pretribulational, I see nothing that prevents and much that commends an any-moment Rapture.

RESPONSE: DOUGLAS J. MOO

GLEASON ARCHER PRESENTS his case for a mid–seventieth-week Rapture by means of three arguments, two negative and one positive. Negatively, against a posttribulational view, he argues that a significant interval of time must separate the Rapture and the Parousia. Against a pretribulational approach, on the other hand, he finds reason to think that the church will be on earth during at least part of Daniel's seventieth week. In the concluding positive argument, Archer claims that only the mid–seventieth-week Rapture position is able to integrate these two lines of evidence.

Not surprisingly, I have a decidedly mixed reaction to Archer's position. His arguments against the pretribulational view seem to me to be sound, and I make some of the same points. But I do think his objections to the posttribulational view are answerable. I will explain why I feel this way by responding in turn to each of the five points he raises. Then, after pointing out some implications of Archer's own case against pretribulationism, I will examine his argument *for* a mid–seventieth-week Rapture.

In his first argument against posttribulationism, Archer claims that the New Testament attitude of expectancy is difficult to understand if a seven-year period of Tribulation was believed to precede the Rapture. Now it is important to note that Archer's objection is not based on the belief that the Rapture must be an "any-instant" event, unheralded by signs—he himself points to New Testament texts that clearly indicate that certain events must precede the Rapture. Rather, his point is that a *seven-year* interval is more difficult to reconcile with expectancy than a *three-and-a-half-year* interval. But is this really true? Whether the early church believed that three and a half years or seven years of tribulation were to precede the Rapture would seem to me to make little difference with respect to their attitude of expectancy. And it must be remembered that New Testament expectancy was *always* qualified by the belief that tribulation would precede deliverance. As Paul warned his new converts in Asia Minor, "Through many tribulations we must enter the kingdom of God" (Acts 14:22). Thus, the New Testament believers' conviction that the entire period between Christ's resurrection and coming in glory was to be characterized by tribulation would have rendered relatively insignificant the exact length of time they expected to spend in the final climactic tribulation.

Archer's second objection to the posttribulational view is that it ignores the "significant interval" between the depiction of the Rapture in 1 Thessalonians 4:13–18 and the judgmental wrath associated with the Day of the Lord in 1 Thessalonians 5:1–10. But the evidence for inserting a temporal interval between 1 Thessalonians 4 and 5 is quite inadequate. The δέ that begins chapter five need not, in the first place, connote a contrast[1] and, secondly, need not indicate a *temporal* contrast even if it does have adversative force. The construction περὶ δὲ, used nine times by Paul in 1 Thessalonians and 1 Corinthians, denotes a change in subject matter, but the nature of that change must be inferred from the context.[2] In the case of 1 Thessalonians 5:1 the transition from the topic of the believers' hope of chapter 4 to the times and dates of the eschatological events in chapter 5 suffices to explain the construction. Indeed, the manner in which the phrase "times and dates" is introduced, without qualification ("times and dates" of what?) suggests that the time of the Rapture just discussed is the topic.

Since I have already dealt at length with Revelation 3:10 in my response to Paul Feinberg, we can turn directly to Archer's fourth point, that the presence of white-clad figures with Jesus as He descends in glory (Rev. 19:11–15) can only be explained if Christians had been previously raptured. As a matter of fact, I agree with him on this point. While it is sometimes claimed that these individuals who accompany Christ at His return are angels, the association of white clothing with saints in Revelation strongly implies that Christians are present. But the question that must be asked is: how long before the scene depicted in Revelation 19:11–15 need the Rapture be? Can it not be a few moments rather than three and a half years or seven years? Archer gives no reason to reject the posttribulational interpretation according to which the saints who are raptured as Christ descends (1 Thess. 4:17) accompany Him back to earth (Rev. 19:11–15). Nowhere does the text imply that these individuals have come from heaven. And, as a matter of fact, Revelation provides positive support for the view that they have come from the earth, since those who are awarded white robes in 7:14 are those who have come out of the "Great Tribulation."

The claim that a posttribulational scheme cannot explain how nonglorified individuals enter the Millennium, Archer's fifth and final objection to that view, is also made by Feinberg. I find this argument the most difficult to handle—not only because the argument presents a difficulty for the posttribulational view, but also because the relevant evidence is both sparse and complex. Thus, I offer the following suggestions.

That the existence of natural processes, evil, and rebellion against God in the Millennium (Rev. 20:7–10) constitutes a difficulty for all premillennialists is suggested by Arthur Lewis's attempt to refute premillennialism on this basis.[3] He suggests that it is far easier to account for these factors if the Millennium is regarded as a description of the present age. But if, as I think, the amillennial alternative is unacceptable because of its inability to provide a satisfactory exegesis of Revelation 20:1–6, the problem remains a real one. However, Feinberg and Archer maintain that their views have a signal advantage over the posttribulational approach in handling this problem, since their schemes allow for a period of time between the Rapture and the Parousia during which individuals will be converted and so enter the Millennium in natural bodies. These people will, of course, be subject to natural processes and some of their descendants will be unbelievers and will make up the great army that gathers against God at the end of the Millennium. A posttribulational scenario, it is argued on the other hand, cannot account for the origin of these people, since on this view, all living men are either raptured or destroyed immediately prior to the inauguration of the Millennium.

Before involving ourselves in a discussion of this problem, the scriptural basis for the problem itself should be examined. That is, how strong is the evidence that saints in natural bodies and evil will exist during the Millennium? The fact of evil in the Millennium is impossible to contest; Revelation 20:7–10 can only be so interpreted. But the presence of saints in natural bodies finds much weaker support. The key text is Isaiah 65:20, which appears to imply the existence of physical death. However, some, noting that this verse is a description of the "new heaven and new earth" (v. 17) and that there will be no more weeping at this time (v. 19) argue that all that is indicated by the prophet is that believers will live "incalculably long lives."[4] Revelation gives some support to this view because parallels to Isaiah 65 are found in the description of the new Jerusalem rather than the Millennium: "new heaven and new earth" (Rev. 21:1) and the absence of mourning (21:4). Nevertheless, Archer and Feinberg are probably correct in refusing this identification since it is only with difficulty that the implication of physical death can be removed from Isaiah 65:20. Perhaps, with Delitzsch, we should think of a combination of descriptions of the Millennium and the eternal state.[5]

Thus the problem cannot be avoided; a premillennial scheme must provide an explanation for the presence of nonglorified saints and unbelievers in the Millennium. Is it possible for a posttribulational premillennialism to do this? I think that two suggestions will show that it is.

First, it is entirely possible that some unbelievers will enter the Millennium in their natural bodies. Both Feinberg and Archer contest this, so it will be necessary to give some justification for this possibility. Feinberg notes a number of texts in which the judgment upon unbelievers at Christ's return appears to be universal. But these references do not clearly specify that the judgment involved transpires at the beginning of the Millennium. All premillennialists recognize that Scripture often blends together events that precede and follow the Millennium (cf. John 5:29; Jude 14–15). I would suggest that verses specifying the universality of judgment also involve such a "telescoping" of events. That this is a plausible approach is suggested by the problem of the unbelievers in the Millennium if these texts are viewed as speaking of the judgment of *all* the wicked before the Millennium. It would seem that, in order to include these millennial unbelievers, descriptions of universal judgment in the New Testament would *have* to include both premillennial and postmillennial judgments. It is in this light that Matthew 25:31–46 should be viewed. Feinberg argues, against Gundry, that this judgment must precede the Millennium because of the explicit statement in verse 31 to the effect that it will occur "when the Son of Man comes in his glory." Nevertheless, Gundry's reason for supporting a reference to the final judgment is also valid: the issue of the judgment is "eternal life" and "eternal punishment."[6] Therefore this passage, like the others mentioned above, should be understood as featuring a merging of the premillennial judgment (at Christ's coming) and the postmillennial judgment (the final judgment). Thus passages that describe a universal judgment along with Christ's return have as their purpose to specify the ultimately universal effects of Christ's victory; they do not require that *all* are judged *at the same time* (at the Parousia). Therefore these texts constitute no difficulty for the view that some unbelievers will enter the Millennium.

Nor does Revelation 19 necessarily imply that all unbelievers will be annihilated at the Parousia. The seer in this text concentrates on the ultimate defeat of the antigodly coalition of nations; his purpose is not to include every single living human in the destruction of that battle.[7] Therefore, since nothing in Scripture contradicts such a view, it can plausibly be suggested that some of the wicked in the Millennium come from unbelievers who survive Armageddon to enter the Millennium in natural bodies.

But what can be said from a posttribulational perspective about millennial saints who live in natural bodies? While the evidence is far from conclusive, it seems to me probable that the conversion of the Jewish nation will not take place until the Parousia. These Jewish saints, who would of course not have participated in the Rapture, would then enter the Millennium in their natural bodies. The evidence for thinking that this national conversion takes place at the time of the Parousia comes from several texts. First, Zechariah 12:10 predicts that the Lord will "pour out the Spirit of grace and supplication" on the Jewish nation when "they look on me whom they have pierced." This verse is quoted in Revelation 1:7 and also in Matthew 24:30, with clear reference to the posttribulational Parousia. Thus the divine gift of grace that stimulates conversion comes only at the end of the Tribulation. The text just alluded to, Matthew 24:30, provides further evidence for the view that Israel's conversion occurs only after the Tribulation. After the depiction of the glorious return of Christ in verse 20, it is said in verse 31 that the Son of Man "will send His angels with a loud trumpet call, and they will gather his elect from the four winds, from one end of the heavens to the other." I would contend that this is a reference to the ingathering of *all* the elect at the time of the Parousia: the dead through resurrection, the living through the Rapture, and the nation of Israel through conversion. The inclusion of Israel is suggested by the resemblance of this verse to Isaiah 11:12, which depicts the "gathering of the dispersed of Judah from the four corners of the earth." Thirdly, Paul links the salvation of "all Israel" with the coming of the deliverer from Zion in Romans 11:25–26 (quoting Isa. 59:20). Other texts could be cited, but these seem to be the clearest.

It must be admitted, however, that other verses have been understood to imply that Israel's conversion will *precede* the Parousia. Feinberg, for instance, appeals to Hosea 5:15–6:3 and Zechariah 13:8–9, but the former probably refers to the events of the Exile rather than the last days and nothing is said in Zechariah 13 about *Gentiles* warring against Israel; it seems more natural to find in these verses a reference to God's elective decision that discriminates among the people. In any event, the fact of Gentile oppression of Israel (Zech. 12:1–5; 14:1–3) implies nothing about the conversion of the nation. Nor does Revelation 12:13–17 clearly show that Israel is the subject of satanic oppression, since it is at least equally probable that the reference there is to the church. On balance, therefore, the position that holds that Israel as a nation is converted only at the Parousia has the best support in the most directly relevant texts.

We conclude, then, by asserting that the posttribulational scheme *can* satisfactorily explain the existence of nonglorified saints and wicked men in the Millennium. Jews converted at the time of the Parousia would be included among the saints, and there would be unbelievers left alive after the Battle of Armageddon.[8] We said at the outset, and say here again, that these options can be advanced only as suggestions. Scripture is by no means clear on these matters and it is probably best not to base too much on such problematic considerations— either for *or against* a posttribulational position.

Having concluded that none of the arguments brought against the posttribulational position by Archer is convincing, we can turn our attention to the positive case for the mid–seventieth-week position. But before doing this, some comments on his response to the pretribulational position are called for.

Of course, I agree with the points Archer makes against the pretribulational view, but an implication of one of these points for his own view must be spelled out. He maintains, correctly in my opinion, that the church must be included among those addressed in the Olivet Discourse. But if this is so, it becomes difficult to keep the church out of the whole of the seventieth week. This is so because Matthew 24:15–28 clearly describes the *second* half of Daniel's week: the Antichrist has set himself up in the temple, (v. 15) the greatest distress in world history is being experienced (v. 21) and Christ's coming is to take place suddenly (vv. 26–28). But the second person plural ("you") continues to be used throughout these verses. In other words, if the church must be included in the first part of the discourse because of the second person plural pronoun, it can hardly be excluded from the second part.

We turn, finally, to the positive points made by Archer in favor of his position.

I can agree with Archer that it is necessary to distinguish the wrath of man and the wrath of God during the Tribulation. But I do not believe that it is possible to separate the two into neat temporal periods in the way Archer suggests. Indeed, the evidence he himself adduces demonstrates how difficult it is to view the first half of the Tribulation as the time of "man's wrath." For Daniel 9:27, the text that most clearly delineates the sequence of events in the seventieth week, explicitly states that it is only at the mid-point of the week that the Antichrist begins his persecution of the saints—during the first half of the week, he is in covenant relationship with Israel. Similarly, Paul indicates that the evil of the Antichrist is restrained at the present time but that that restraint will one day be lifted, at which time the Antichrist will exalt himself above God and demand worship in the temple (2 Thess. 2:1–10). A comparison of the texts reveals clearly that this is the same event predicted by Daniel for the mid-point of the seventieth week. With this picture the Revelation is in complete agreement; the thirteenth chapter portrays the Antichrist as the active initiator of persecution against the saints. Even the Olivet Discourse hints at this by commanding the saints to flee from Jerusalem only after "the abomination of desolation" is set up in the temple. The point, then, is that Scripture consistently portrays the first part of Daniel's seventieth week as a time of relative tranquility for the saints; it is only at the midpoint of the week when the Antichrist asserts his authority that the "wrath of man" against the saints becomes evident. It is this outbreak of satanic activity that makes the midpoint of the seventieth week significant.

Again, I can agree with Archer in finding a reference to the Rapture in Revelation 14:14–16. But while he would locate this scene at the midpoint of Daniel's seventieth week, I would argue that it should be located at the end of that week. This is suggested by the fact that the immediately following verses (17–20) appear to depict the Battle of Armageddon. Archer suggests that this is an anticipatory vision, but it seems easier to think that it takes place at the same time as the scene described in verses 14–16. Likewise, I can agree that the Rapture takes place between the fifth and sixth seals. But the sixth seal clearly describes events that *follow* the Tribulation, as a comparison of Revelation 6:12–17 and Matthew 24:29 shows.

In sum, then, I am not convinced by Archer's presentation of the mid–seventieth-week position: his arguments against the posttribulational position are answerable; at least one of his arguments against the pretribulational view undermines his own position; and the positive evidence for his own approach is indecisive. Indeed, it is important to note that little *positive* support for the mid–seventieth-week view is given by Archer. While it is not wrong to supply evidence for one's view by pointing to the difficulties faced by other views, such negative argumentation never constitutes a logically compelling testimony for the alternative. The simple fact is that each of the views possesses some problems—what will be ultimately decisive is the question as to which view can most satisfactorily handle the most directly relevant texts.

4

THE CASE FOR THE POSTTRIBULATION RAPTURE POSITION

Douglas J. Moo

Douglas J. Moo is Assistant Professor of New Testament at Trinity Evangelical Divinity School. He holds the M. Div. degree from Trinity Evangelical Divinity School and the Ph.D. from the University of St. Andrews. He has written *The Old Testament in the Gospel Passion Narratives* and contributed articles to *Trinity Journal, Westminster Theological Journal, Journal for the Study of the New Testament,* and *Journal of the Evangelical Theological Society.* He is a member of the Evangelical Theological Society, the Institute for Biblical Research, the Chicago Society for Biblical Research, and the Society of Biblical Literature.

PURPOSE, ASSUMPTIONS, AND APPROACH

It is my purpose to present an exegetical and theological argument for the view that the church, or the saints of the present dispensation, will be raptured *after* the Great Tribulation. This argument makes several assumptions. First, the argument assumes, although it is not necessarily predicated upon, the view that the return of Christ in glory will occur before the Millennium (Rev. 20:4–6). A second assumption is that the Scriptures predict a period of unparalleled distress, called in Revelation 7:14 "the great tribulation," which will immediately precede the Second Advent. Third, it is accepted that the seventieth week of Daniel (cf. Dan. 9:24–27) has not yet found complete fulfillment and that it is related to the time of unprecedented tribulation.[1]

In approaching the topic under consideration, it is especially important that the bearing of ecclesiology on the investigation be made clear. If a radical disjunction between Israel and the church is assumed, a certain presumption against the posttribulational position exists, since it would be inconsistent for the church to be involved in a period of time that, according to the Old Testament, has to do with Israel. However, it is important at the outset to note that a posttribulational Rapture is *not* necessarily excluded by a view that keeps Israel and the church separate. Thus, if Scripture indicates that *both* Israel and the church are to experience the Great Tribulation, each could remain on earth during that time as separate entities. Even if it be concluded that the Great Tribulation is for Israel *only,* is it not a priori impossible to think that the church will remain on earth during that period without undergoing this climactic affliction.[2]

In other words, a total and consistent separation of Israel and the church does not *necessarily* entail *any* specific view of the time of the Rapture. Since this is the case, an approach to the topic that assumes no particular view on this ecclesiological question cannot be deemed illegitimate. Furthermore, such an approach is to be preferred because it paves the way for more objective exegesis of the relevant texts. To begin with a particular view of the relationship of Israel and the church can too easily lead to circular reasoning. One argues that such and such a text cannot refer to the church because it describes the Great Tribulation, which is only for Israel— but one can know that it is exclusively for Israel only on the basis of an exegetical treatment of every relevant passage including the one under scrutiny! Certainly it is preferable to draw tentative conclusions on the larger theological issue (Israel and the church) only after the exegesis has been carried out.

Inasmuch as the Rapture is clearly revealed only in the New Testament, the decisive evidence for its timing with respect to the Tribulation must come from the New Testament also. Furthermore, it is sound hermeneutical procedure to establish a doctrine on the basis of the texts that speak most directly to the issue. Thus, the major part of the paper will be devoted to an exegesis of these texts. However, some foundational issues must be addressed before this important task is begun.

THE TRIBULATION AND THE SECOND ADVENT

The Nature of the Tribulation

While it is the message of both the Old and the New Testaments that the saints experience tribulation throughout history, both also clearly speak of a climactic time of tribulation that will immediately precede the Second Advent. To define the nature of this period, particularly with respect to

God's wrath, is the purpose of this section. When we turn to the Old Testament, the situation is complicated by the fact that it is often difficult to discern whether a particular description of "tribulation" relates to the Exile, the final judgment, or the "Great Tribulation" as such. The distinction between the latter two is not always recognized, but it would seem to be an important one in discussing Old Testament prophetic texts. For passages that describe the horror of the end itself (e.g., what the New Testament describes as the Battle of Armageddon, etc.), which, according to all three views, *follows* the Tribulation, cannot be used as evidence for the nature of the Great Tribulation, which *precedes* the end. Since many of the relevant prophetic texts involve descriptions of the "Day of the Lord," and do not indicate clearly whether the Tribulation or the end itself is envisaged, the problem is a real one. Caution is called for, then, in applying these descriptions to the Tribulation.[3]

With this in mind, it must be concluded that only in Daniel do we find passages that *must* refer to the Great Tribulation (cf. especially 7:7–8, 23–25; 8:9–12, 23–25; 9:26–27; 11:36–12:1). Certainly others *may* describe the Tribulation—Deuteronomy 4:29–30; Isaiah 26:20–21; Jeremiah 30:4–9; Joel 2:30–31; and Zephaniah 1–2, to name a few. But none of the depictions of distress in these passages is clearly distinct from the final outpouring of God's judgmental wrath that occurs only *after* the Tribulation. In the interests of accuracy, then, it is important to use the texts in Daniel as primary evidence in constructing the Old Testament concept of the Tribulation and employ the other texts only as they corroborate the picture in Daniel.

Two points of relevance for our topic emerge from the texts in Daniel. First, the sufferings of the saints during this period are uniformly attributed to an ultimate opposer and usurper of God (7:7–8, 20–25; 11:35–48). It is "the little horn" who "wages war against the saints and overpowers them" (7:21; cf. 8:25).

Second, Daniel 11:36 and (probably) 8:19 attest to the existence of divine wrath (זַעַם) during this period of intense persecution. But nothing is said about the extent or duration

173

of this wrath nor is it stated that the wrath falls upon the *saints*. But while Daniel is silent about the extent and objects of this Tribulation wrath, it is significant that a related text, Isaiah 26:20–21, specifically depicts the *selective* nature of God's wrath: "Come, my people, enter into your rooms, and close your doors behind you; hide for a little while, until indignation [זעם] runs its course. For behold, the Lord is about to come out from His place to punish the inhabitants of the earth for their iniquity. . . ."

If this passage refers to the Tribulation, we possess clear evidence that saints *on earth* are protected from the divine wrath. Even if one argues that this situation obtains *only* for Israel, it is still important to recognize that God's people can remain on earth while escaping the wrath. On the other hand, this text may not relate to the Tribulation at all—in which case the *principle* of selectivity in the exercise of God's wrath remains. At the least, then, Isaiah 26:20–21 establishes the *possibility* that God's people can escape divine wrath though present during its outpouring.

We conclude that the depiction of the Tribulation in the Old Testament includes severe persecution of saints at the instigation of a powerful leader along with a revelation of divine wrath, undetermined in its extent and objects.

Of the forty-five occurrences of the noun θλιψις ("tribulation") in the New Testament, only five are probably related to the final period of distress (Mark 13:19, 24; Matthew 24:21, 29 and Rev. 7:14), while two others *may* refer to it (Rom. 2:9 and 2 Thess. 1:6). Rather full descriptions of the Tribulation occur in Mark 13:14–23 and parallels, 2 Thessalonians 2:3–8, and in Revelation 6–16. Before examining these passages in order to delineate the New Testament concept of the Great Tribulation, it is worth observing that the normal usage of "tribulation" occurs in descriptions of the distresses and sufferings that the church experiences in the present age. If it is held that the church is to be exempted from the *Great* Tribulation, it must be shown that there is something *distinctive* in *quality* (not just in quantity) about that period in comparison with the present age.

In keeping with the Old Testament evidence, there is

emphasis in the New Testament portrayal of the Great Tribulation on the persecution of saints by a great antigodly leader, variously characterized as "the desolating sacrilege" (Mark 13:14),[4] "the man of lawlessness" (2 Thess. 2:3), and the "beast" (Rev. 13:1–8).[4] The Revelation also pictures the Tribulation as a time during which God is judging unbelievers and pouring out His wrath upon them. Two aspects of this presentation in Revelation merit our attention. First, the wrath appears to be concentrated in the last part of the Tribulation period. It is mentioned in Revelation 6:16–17, where the context (cosmic disasters elsewhere said by Jesus to occur *"after that tribulation"*—(Mark 13:24) plainly indicates that the end has been reached; in 11:18, which again occurs in a context portraying the end; in 14:7, 10, 19, which describe the coming judgment; three times in conjunction with the bowls, which immediately precede the Advent (15:1, 7; 16:1) and twice in descriptions of the Parousia itself (16:19; 19:15). Then, second, the judgments and wrath of God are clearly selective. The demonic locusts of the fifth trumpet are ordered to harm "only those people who did not have the seal of God on their foreheads" (Rev. 9:4), while the first bowl is poured out only on "the people who had the mark of the beast and worshiped his image" (Rev. 16:2). And the recipients of a number of the plagues are said to refuse to repent (9:20–21; 16:9, 11)—an indication that only unbelievers are affected by them. In other words, there is no place in which the judgment or wrath of God is presented as afflicting saints, and there are indications on the contrary that God is purposefully exempting the saints from their force.

Thus, the New Testament picture is similar to that of the Old Testament. The Great Tribulation is presented as a period of severe persecution of saints then on earth and a time of God's wrathful judgment. But the New Testament is clearer in suggesting that the wrath is confined to the last part of the Tribulation and in specifically indicating the protection from God's wrath afforded to the people of God who live through that time. But, it must be asked, how can they be protected from such universal judgments as, for instance, the death of every sea creature (16:3)? In response, two points can be made.

First, this constitutes a problem for *all* interpreters because everyone agrees that saints of some sort will be divinely protected and preserved alive until the Parousia—whether they be part of the church or the Jewish remnant represented by the 144,000 (Rev. 7). Second, the history of Old Testament Israel would suggest that, although God's judgments are never directed toward those who truly belong to Him, the judgments can indirectly affect them. Thus Noah and his family were, to say the least, inconvenienced by the flood. And did not Jeremiah and other true servants of God experience suffering, even death, as a result of God's wrathful judgment upon Judah through the Babylonians?

An important conclusion emerges from this discussion of the nature of the Great Tribulation: there is nothing inherent in it that makes it impossible for the church to be present during it. All agree that no true believer will experience the wrath of God (1 Thess. 5:9), but no description of the Tribulation presents it as a time of wrath upon God's people. All agree that the church experiences tribulation—at times severe tribulation—throughout its existence; but no description of the Tribulation indicates that it will involve greater suffering than many believers have already experienced.

The Vocabulary of the Second Advent

Three words are frequently used in the New Testament to describe the return of Christ: ἀποκάλυψις ("revelation"), ἐπιφανεία ("manifestation"), and παρουσία ("coming" or "presence"). Παρουσία, which occurs most frequently (15 times), should probably be translated "coming," but its associations with the concept of "presence" are probably not lost sight of. Its appropriateness as a characterization of the Lord's return is evident from the fact that it is used in the papyri to designate the special visits of kings. Ἐπιφανεία (5 times with reference to the Second Coming) connotes a decisive divine appearance for the benefit of God's people, while an allusion to the completion of God's purposes is suggested by the term ἀποκάλυψις (5 times).[5]

What is important to note about these terms is, first, that

each is clearly used to describe the *posttribulational* return of Christ and, second, that all three also designate an object of the believer's hope and expectation. The Parousia is indisputably posttribulational in Matthew 24:3, 27, 37, 39 and in 2 Thessalonians 2:8; ἀποκάλυψις has the same time frame in 2 Thessalonians 1:7, as does ἐπιφανεία in 2 Thessalonians 2:8. On the other hand, the Parousia of Christ is explicitly stated to be an object of the believer's expectation in 1 Thessalonians 2:19; 3:13; James 5:7–8; and 1 John 2:28. The word ἀποκάλυψις is presented as an expectation in 1 Corinthians 1:7; 1 Peter 1:7, 13; 4:13, while all four references to the ἐπιφανεία in the Pastorals (1 Tim. 6:14; 2 Tim. 4:1; 4:8; Titus 2:13) bear this significance. If, then, believers are exhorted to look forward to this coming of Christ, and this coming is presented as posttribulational, it is natural to conclude that believers will be present through the Tribulation.[6]

However, this would be to proceed far too quickly. It *may* be that the Second Coming must be divided into two stages: a "coming" of Christ *for* His church before or sometime during the Tribulation and a "coming" *with* His church after it. Such a two-stage coming cannot be ruled out a priori, but on the other hand it cannot be accepted unless there is clear evidence for such a division. We have seen that such evidence is not available in the terms used to depict the Second Advent—each of them includes *both* the Rapture *and* the posttribulational descent of Christ from heaven. The analogy of the Old Testament hope of the coming of Messiah, which in the light of fulfillment can be seen to have two stages, is hardly appropriate. For these two separate stages were only obvious *after the fact*. Likewise, it is difficult to find evidence for a "two-stage Parousia" in descriptions of Christ's coming "*with* His saints." For in only three texts is mention made of Jesus coming with His saints—Revelation 19:14; 1 Thessalonians 3:13; 4:14–15. In the former two, it is not clear whether those who accompany Christ are angels or believers,[7] in either case, it is important to note that 1 Thessalonians 4:14–15 presents saints as coming "with Jesus" *at the time of the Rapture*.

Therefore, a study of the vocabulary employed in describing the return of Christ paints a uniform picture: believers are exhorted to look for and to live in the light of this glorious event. And, while some texts obviously place this coming *after* the Tribulation, there are *none* which equally obviously place it before the Tribulation. However, it may be that a closer look at the contexts in which these terms occur will reveal that there is, in fact, a pretribulational aspect to the Second Coming. It is to these texts that we now turn.

THE RAPTURE—THREE BASIC PASSAGES

It will be appropriate to begin our study of these texts with what are claimed to be ". . . the three principal Scriptures revealing the rapture— John 14:3; 1 Corinthians 15:51, 52; and 1 Thessalonians 4:13–18."[8] Since our study of the nature of the Tribulation has revealed nothing that would necessitate the removal of the church during that period and the important terms used to describe the Second Advent give no indication that anything other than a posttribulational event is envisaged, we would expect to find in these texts clear indications of a pretribulational aspect of the Advent, if such an aspect exists.

In the farewell discourse of John's gospel (14–17), Jesus seeks to prepare His disciples for the time of His physical absence from them. In 14:1–4, Jesus encourages them by asserting that His "going" to the Father is for the purpose of preparing a "place" for them in the Father's many "dwelling places" (v. 2), and that He will come again and "receive" them to Himself, "in order that where I am there you also may be" (v. 3). It is almost certain that the latter verse describes the Second Advent and Rapture. But there is no indication in the text that any "coming" other than the posttribulational one described elsewhere in the New Testament, is in Jesus' mind. The fact that believers at a posttribulational Rapture would rise to meet the Lord in the air only to return immediately to earth with Him creates no difficulty, for the text does *not* state that believers will go directly to Heaven,[9] but only that they will always be with the Lord. If it be argued that this is the inference of the text, it is hard to see how any other view can offer a more reasonable scenario. As Gundry says, "The pretribulational interpretation would require us to believe that the

Church will occupy heavenly mansions for a short period of seven years, only to vacate them for a thousand years . . . ."[10] Neither is it true that a promise of deliverance only after the severe distress of the Tribulation could not be a "comfort" to the disciples. The "blessed hope" of being reunited with the risen Lord is surely a comfort, no matter what believers have previously experienced. Thus, John 14:1–4 offers no indication at all of the time of the Rapture.

In 1 Corinthians 15:51–52, it is Paul's purpose to indicate how living saints can enter the kingdom at the last day even though "flesh and blood cannot inherit the kingdom of God" (v. 50). To do so, he affirms that, while "we" (believers in general) will not all die, we will all be "changed"—whether living or dead.[11] That Paul calls this transformation a "mystery" indicates nothing about *who* will participate in it; only that it was not clearly revealed previously.[12] And in quoting an Old Testament verse (Isa. 25:8) with reference to the resurrection of *church* saints in this context (vv. 54–55), Paul may be indicating his belief that Old Testament saints participate in this "change."[13] Further indication that this transformation involves Old Testament saints (and cannot thereby be limited to a separate event for *church* saints) is found in the reference to "the last trumpet." As the commentators note, this does not refer to the last in a series, necessarily, but to the trumpet that ushers in the "last day."[14] And this trumpet is a feature of the Old Testament Day of the Lord at which time the Jewish nation experiences final salvation and judgment (cf. Isa. 27:13; Joel 2:1; Zeph. 1:16; Zech. 9:14). The Isaianic reference is particularly suggestive inasmuch as the sounding of the "great trumpet" is associated with "the gathering up of the Israelites one by one." This is probably a description of the gathering of Israel in preparation for entrance into the millennial kingdom—an event that is always posttribulational. Furthermore, it is probable that the trumpet here in 1 Corinthians 15:52 is the same as the one mentioned in Matthew 24:31. For when one finds only *one* reference throughout Jesus' teaching to a trumpet, and it is associated with the gathering of the elect into the kingdom, and further finds Paul making reference to the transformation of saints in preparation for the kingdom when *he* mentions a trumpet, the parallel can hardly be ignored. But the trumpet sound in Matthew 24:31 is manifestly posttribulational. Thus, while dogmatism is unwarranted, the reference to "the last trumpet" in 1 Corinthians 15:52 would suggest that the "transformation" Paul describes takes place at the time when the Jewish nation experiences its eschatological salvation (Isa. 27:12–13) *after* the Tribulation (Matt. 24:31).

The third principal text relating to the Rapture is 1 Thessalonians 4:13–18. Clearly, Paul is here seeking to comfort the Thessalonian believers over the death of believers. Why were they concerned? Certainly it could not be because they did not know of the resurrection of the dead—this doctrine was central to Paul's preaching (1 Cor. 15:3–7), and he assumes it in his discussion here.[15] Since Paul's emphasis in the passage is on the fact that the dead in Christ will fully participate in the blessing of the Parousia, it is probable that the Thessalonians ". . . feared that their dead would not have the same advantages as the survivors when the Lord came."[16] It is important to note that the comfort Paul offers does not have to do primarily with the position of *living* believers, nor does he suggest that exemption from the Tribulation is a source of this comfort.[17] His encouragement lies *solely* in the fact that *all* believers, living or dead, will participate in the glorious events of the Parousia and that they will as a result "always be with the Lord."[18] That such a hope, if it included a previous experience in the Great Tribulation, would not be a comfort to believers is manifestly untrue. For, in fact, these Thessalonians had already experienced very difficult times—they had been converted "in great tribulation" (1:6) and were still undergoing such tribulation (3:3,7). Nowhere does Paul seek to comfort Christians by promising them exemption from tribulation.

Are there any indications in this description of the Rapture and accompanying resurrection as to when it takes place with reference to the Tribulation? The failure of Paul to mention preliminary signs is hardly relevant for there is no reason for him to include them here—in the light of the extreme sufferings that the Thessalonians were *already* experiencing, he hardly needed to warn them of this. He focuses exclusively on the great hope lying at the end of all earthly distresses. On the other hand, there are four indications that favor a posttribulational setting. First, while little can be definitely concluded from Paul's reference to "a word of the Lord" in verse 15,[19] there are suggestive parallels between the Parousia of 1 Thessalonians 4 and the Parousia described by Jesus in the Olivet Discourse. Both refer to a heavenly event with angels (archangel in 1 Thess. 4), clouds, a trumpet, and the gathering of believers.[20] And while each of these texts mentions details not found in the other, none of the details are contradictory. However, the Parousia of the Olivet Discourse is, as we have already noted, posttribulational.

A second indication that the Rapture of 1 Thessalonians 4 may be posttribulational is found in the reference to the trumpet, which, as we saw in discussing 1 Corinthians 15, is an established symbol for the ushering in of the time of Israel's salvation and judgment. (And, in keeping with Paul's allusion to the trumpet *of God,* it should be noted that Zechariah 9:14 specifically says that the Lord will sound the trumpet.)

Third, 1 Thessalonians 4:13–16 features a number of elements closely parallel to Daniel 12:1–2: the description of the dead as "sleepers"; the presence of Michael, the archangel (cf. Jude 9); and, of course, a resurrection and deliverance of God's people.[21] But the Daniel passage definitely places the resurrection *after* the Tribulation.

Fourth, the word used by Paul to describe the "meeting" between the living saints and their Lord in the air (ἀπάντησις) occurs in references to the visit of dignitaries, and generally implies that the "delegation" accompanies the dignitary *back to* the delegation's point of origin.[22] The two other occurrences of this term in the New Testament seem to bear this meaning (Matt. 15:6; Acts 28:15). This would suggest that the saints, after meeting the Lord in the air, accompany Him back to earth, instead of going with Him to Heaven. However, this argument can be given little weight—the word does not *have* to bear this technical meaning, nor is it certain that the return to the point of origin must be *immediate.*[23]

It may be concluded that the details of the description of

the Parousia and Rapture in 1 Thessalonians 4:13–18 do not allow a *certain* conclusion as to when these take place with reference to the Tribulation. Such indications as there are, however, favor a posttribulational setting. This we have found to be the case also in 1 Corinthians 15:51–52, while John 14:1–4 sheds no light on the question either way. The implications of this must not be overlooked. We have discovered that the terms used to describe the Second Advent are all applied to a posttribulational coming and that believers are exhorted to look forward to that coming. Any indication that this coming is to be a two-stage event, in which the Rapture is separated from the final manifestation, would have to come from passages describing that event. *We can now conclude that no evidence for such a separation is found in any of the three principal texts on the Rapture.* On the contrary, such evidence as exists is in favor of locating the Rapture *after* the Tribulation, at the same time as the final Parousia. But there are other important passages related to the Parousia yet to be examined before final conclusions can be drawn.

1 THESSALONIANS 5:1–11

After the depiction of the Rapture and Parousia in chapter 4, Paul turns to the subject of the "day of the Lord" in chapter 5. He introduces this topic with the phrase: "Now [δέ], brothers, about times and dates we do not need to write to you" (v. 1). Since this "day" includes the destruction of unbelievers (v. 3), it is clear that a posttribulational event is described. The question to be asked, then, is this: does Paul intimate that the Thessalonian Christians to whom he writes may be still on earth when the Day comes? Three considerations are relevant: the relationship between chapter 4 and chapter 5, the meaning of "day of the Lord," and the nature and basis of Paul's exhortations in 5:1–11.

It is sometimes claimed that the δέ introducing chapter 5 demonstrates a transition to a wholly new topic and that it is therefore inappropriate to include the Rapture (4:13–18) as part of the "day" in 5:1–11. Three considerations cast doubt on this conclusion. First, while δέ generally denotes a mild contrast, it also occurs frequently "as a transitional particle pure and simple, without any contrast intended . . ."[24] (note the NIV translation quoted above). Second, even if a contrast is intended by Paul, one must determine the *nature* of that contrast. Rather than distinguishing two separate events, Paul may be contrasting the effect of the same events on two different groups—believers and unbelievers. Third, observe how Paul speaks of "times and dates" in verse 1 without specifying the time or date of *what*. The omission of any specific event here could indicate that the previous topic is still in Paul's mind.

Next, then, we must seek to determine what Paul includes in the "day of the Lord." Can the Rapture be part of that Day?

In the Old Testament, the Day of the Lord (also "that day," etc.) denotes a decisive intervention of God for judgment and deliverance.[25] It can refer to a relatively *near* event or to the *final* climactic event—it is not always clear that the prophets clearly distinguished the two. Although the Day is frequently described as one of *judgment,* deliverance for the people of God is often involved also (cf. Isa. 27; Jer. 30:8–9; Joel 2:32; 3:18; Obad. 15–17; etc.). In the New Testament, the term is almost universally related to the end. From the great variety of expressions which are used in the New Testament, it is clear that there is no fixed terminology[26] and that distinctions on that basis cannot be drawn.[27]

All agree that the final judgment is included, but is the Tribulation period also part of the Day of the Lord? Several factors suggest that it is not. First, no reference to the eschatological "day" in the New Testament clearly includes a description of the Tribulation. In fact, it is interesting that the only two occurrences in the Revelation (6:17; 16:14) refer to the final judgment brought through the Parousia. Second, Malachi 4:5 (the coming of Elijah) and Joel 2:30–31 (cosmic portents) place what are generally agreed to be Tribulational events *before* the Day (cf. Acts 2:20). Third, Paul seems to suggest in 2 Thessalonians 2 that the Day cannot come *until* certain, clearly tribulational, events transpire. While these points carry considerable weight, it must be said that the evidence is not entirely clear, and it will be best not to base too much on the exclusion of the Tribulation from the Day.

However, while there is some indication that the Tribulation should not be regarded as an element of the Day, it would seem that the resurrection of the saints *is* included. Five times in John's Gospel Jesus proclaims that He will raise those who believe in Him on "the last day" (6:39, 40, 44, 55; 11:54). And since the Rapture occurs at the same time as the resurrection of believers, the Rapture, too, must be part of that Day. That this is so finds confirmation in the fact that Paul frequently describes the Day as an event to which believers in this life look forward (1 Cor. 1:8; Phil. 1:6, 10; 2:16; 2 Tim. 4:8; cf. also Heb. 11:25)—it is a "day of redemption" (Eph. 4:30).

Thus in the New Testament, the Day includes the destruction of the ungodly at the Parousia of Christ, along with the Rapture and the resurrection of the righteous dead. That is, for Paul as for the other New Testament writers, the "Day" is "a general denotation of the great future that dawns with Christ's coming."[28] The fact that the Tribulation seems *not* to be part of that Day suggests that it precedes all these events, but this is not certain. What is certain is that believers cannot be excluded from involvement in the events of 1 Thessalonians 5 simply because the Day of the Lord is the topic.

In this passage, the emphasis is undoubtedly on judgment, which comes suddenly and certainly on those not expecting it (v. 3). Does Paul suggest that the Thessalonian believers may have a relationship to this judgment? If so, this would constitute strong support for the posttribulational position because either (1) believers will be alive during the Tribulation (if this is the judgment Paul thinks of), or (2) believers will be on earth when the posttribulational Parousia occurs (if the judgment occurs then). (The fact that people are saying "peace and security" does not mean that the Tribulation period cannot be indicated—such people were doing the same thing during Old Testament calamities, and Revelation 13:16–17 indicates a high degree of normality for those following the Beast.)[29]

That Christians *are* associated with the Day is the clear inference of verse 4. Here Paul tells the Thessalonian believers; "You are not in darkness, that the day should overtake you as a thief." *Why,* if believers are raptured *before* the Tribulation, would Paul have qualified his assertion with "as a thief"? Much more appropriate would have been the simple statement "that the day not overtake you." If you had a friend visiting from another country who was worried about becoming involved in a war you both knew would soon break out, and *if* you knew that he would, in fact, be safely out of the country before it started, you would assure him by telling him; "Don't worry—this war will not affect you." Only if you knew he would be present during it would you say, "Don't worry—this war will not affect you as the kind of disaster it will be for citizens of this country." In other words, what Paul rather clearly suggests is that the Day overtakes both believers and unbelievers—but only for the latter does it come "as a thief"—unexpected and harmful.[30]

A second reason for thinking that in 1 Thessalonians 5 Paul associates believers with the Day in a setting after the Tribulation has begun, is found in his close dependence on two gospel passages in which Jesus encourages watchfulness in view of the *posttribulational* Parousia—Matthew 24:42–44 and Luke 21:34–36. The parallels between the latter text and 1 Thessalonians 5:2–6 are particularly compelling—both have as their subject the Day, which, it is warned, will come upon those unprepared suddenly and unexpectedly ("as a trap," Luke 21:34); both emphasize that there will be no escape (cf. Luke 21:35); both encourage believers to watch in light of that coming "Day"; both use the same verb (ἐφίστημι) and the same adjective, αἰφνίδιος ("suddenly") of the "Day"—and the latter is used only in these two places in biblical Greek.[31] There is every reason for thinking that the same event is depicted in both and, in fact, strong indications that one is dependent on the other. But if Luke 21:34–36 encourages watchfulness in light of the posttribulational coming (as both, e.g., Pentecost and Walvoord argue[32]), there is every reason to think that 1 Thessalonians 5:2–6 does also.

Finally, the logical connection between Paul's assertion

in verses 4–5 and the following exhortations is also better explained if the Thessalonians are to experience the Day. It is not Paul's point to encourage the believers to "watch" for the Day so that they might *escape* it entirely. For the verbs Paul employs in his commands (vv. 6, 8) do not connote watching *for* something, but faithfulness to Christ, as incumbent upon those who belong to the "light" and to the Day.[33] Nor can 1 Thessalonians 5:9 be used to argue that Paul promises believers such an escape—since Paul never uses *wrath* without qualifiers to denote a period of time, and in view of its contrast with "salvation" here, it must indicate the condemning judgment of God associated with the Day, not the Day itself.[34]

To summarize Paul's argument: the salvation to which God has destined the Thessalonians (v. 9), and which they already experience (v. 5), should act as a stimulus to holy living—holy living that will enable them to avoid experiencing the Day in its unexpected and destructive features. In other words, Paul exhorts the Thessalonians to live godly lives in order that they might avoid the judgmental aspect of that Day—not that they might avoid the Day itself. Whether this Day includes the Tribulation or, as is more probable, the climactic return of Christ at the end of the Tribulation, believers *on earth* are clearly involved in it; and only a posttribulational Rapture allows for this. Finally, this interpretation provides a coherent explanation of the transition from chapter 4 to chapter 5—whereas Paul has comforted believers about the position of the *dead* at the Parousia in chapter 4, he turns to exhort the *living* about their responsibilities in light of that Parousia in chapter 5.

2 THESSALONIANS 1–2

Second Thessalonians was written by Paul shortly after 1 Thessalonians in order to correct some misapprehensions about eschatology, particularly with respect to the erroneous belief that the end had to occur almost immediately. Thus, Paul in chapter 1 assures the Thessalonians of the certainty of the end, with the judgment it will bring on those who are now "distressing" them. Then he seeks to calm their excitement over the nearness of the end in chapter 2.[35]

In 2 Thessalonians 1:5–7 Paul appears to provide strong support for the view that believers will not be raptured until the Parousia of Christ at the end of the Tribulation. For there can be no doubt that in verses 7–8 Paul depicts this coming in glory, which he characterizes as "the revelation of the Lord Jesus from Heaven in blazing fire with His powerful angels." Yet it is *at* (ἐv) this time that the believers who are suffering tribulation are given "rest." In other words, it is only at the posttribulational Advent that believers experience deliverance from the sufferings of this age. Attempts to avoid this conclusion take two forms.

First, it is argued that since the Thessalonians were *not* in fact delivered at the time of Christ's return (they died long before it) and their persecutors will likewise *not* be destroyed at the return (being dead, they will not experience judgment until the conclusion of the Millennium), Paul must be saying that "God in His own time will destroy their persecutors."[36] But not only does this interpretation fail to explain the fact that Paul obviously links both the "rest" and the destruction to "the Revelation of the Lord Jesus" (How can this mean "in God's own time"?), it overlooks the fact that everywhere in Paul's letters he speaks as if the generation in which he lived *might* be the last. Thus in both 1 Corinthians 15:51 and 1 Thessalonians 4:15, he indicates that the participants in the Rapture are "*we* who don't sleep/are alive." Does this mean that Paul cannot be describing the Rapture in these texts? Moreover, the eschatological "rest" Paul describes here *does* come to all believers at the time of Christ's revelation—for dead saints (including the Thessalonians) through resurrection; for living saints through the Rapture. And that Paul associates the destruction of unbelievers with the "revelation" of Christ is likewise no difficulty: Scripture often associates events that will, in fact, be separated by the Millennium—see John 5:29.

A second way of avoiding a posttribulational interpretation of these verses is to claim that the "rest" promised to the Thessalonians need not occur at the Rapture.[37] While this point must be appreciated—believers who die before the Lord's return are certainly delivered from earthly trials before the Rapture—the clear temporal link between the rest and the "revelation" of Christ cannot be severed. The only satisfactory way of explaining this text is to assume that Paul addresses the Thessalonians as if they would be alive at the Parousia— and he states that they experience "rest" only at the posttribulational revelation of Christ.

Paul's purpose in chapter 2 is to calm the Thessalonians with reference to "the Parousia of our Lord Jesus Christ and our being gathered to him." The emotional state of the Thessalonians suggested by the prohibitions in verse 2 is not clearly one of fear or disappointment such as could be induced by the belief that they had missed the Rapture; the verbs suggest rather that they were agitated and unsettled—abandoning their normal common sense and daily pursuits in nervous excitement over the nearness of the end.[38] This improper excitement was caused specifically by the belief that the Day of the Lord had come, a belief that is not easy to explain. Although we have suggested that the Day includes the Parousia and the Rapture, it must have been obvious even to the excitable Thessalonians that *these* events had not occurred. Perhaps then the Tribulation *should* be included in the Day, and the Thessalonians regarded their extreme sufferings as evidence that they were in it.[39] But a better interpretation is to regard this excitement as caused by their conviction that the dawning of that Day was regarded as even then occurring, with the other events associated with it just around the corner.[40] However we explain this statement, one thing is clear—the Thessalonians had *not* experienced the Rapture, yet they thought themselves to be in the Day. How does Paul disabuse them of this notion?

He does so by citing events that *must* occur *before* that Day comes.[41] According to the apostle, there are two of these: the ἀποστάσια and the revelation of "the man of lawlessness, . . . the man doomed to destruction" (v. 3). The latter is probably to be identified as the eschatological Antichrist, described also in Mark 13:14 and parallels and in Revelation 13:1–8—all these descriptions depend on the characterization of this figure in Daniel 7:8, 20–25; 11:36–39.[42] And it is improbable that this "revelation" can indicate anything other than the actions enumerated in verse 4. The other necessary antecedent to the Day, the ἀποστάσια, is best understood as a *religious* rebellion against God.[43] Although some have argued that it should be translated "departure" and have seen in it a reference to the Rapture,[44] such a translation is most improbable in light of the meaning of the term in biblical Greek.[45]

What is crucial to notice in Paul's response to the Thessalonians' unrest is that he does *not* say anything about the Rapture as a necessary antecedent to the Day. *If* the Thessalonians were to be raptured *before* the Day, we would expect Paul to say something like, "You know that your present sufferings cannot represent the final Tribulation because you will be taken to heaven before then."[46] To use the illustration introduced earlier, if you *knew* that your foreign friend was to be safely out of the country by the time the war broke out, and he, in seeing great unrest beginning to happen, thought he was becoming involved in it, would you calm him by telling him that certain events had to happen before the war *without* reminding him that he would be safely out of the country when it actually occurred? The fact that Paul points to the nonpresence of an indisputably tribulational event, the revelation of the Antichrist, as evidence that the "Day" has not come, surely implies that believers *will* see it when it does occur. Furthermore, it cannot be argued in reply that Paul simply assumes the Thessalonians know that the Rapture will occur before that Day; the fact that the Thessalonians believed themselves to be in the Day shows either that they had forgotten or were never taught that the Rapture preceded it. In either case, it is difficult to see why Paul would not mention it.

Before leaving this text, one final argument brought against a posttribulational interpretation must be dealt with. It is often argued that the tribulational events described here by Paul cannot transpire until the church is physically removed, because it is the Holy Spirit through the church who *now* "restrains" the Antichrist (vv. 6–7). Three points need to be made with reference to this argument. *First,* it is unlikely that the Holy Spirit is the One whom Paul describes in these verses. There seems to be no reason for using such mysterious language if the Holy Spirit is intended, nor is it probable that Paul would have spoken of the Spirit as being "taken out of the way."[47] Neither does the fact that Paul uses both a *masculine* participle ("He who restrains") and a *neuter* participle ("That which restrains"), sometimes adduced in support of this interpretation, favor it. I can find no place in Paul's writings where he uses a neuter term to designate the Holy Spirit except where it is directly dependent on the term πνεῦμα ("Spirit"). *Second,* even if the Holy Spirit is intended, there is nothing in the passage that would indicate that His restraining activity must be carried out through the church.[48] *Third,* whatever one's view, it is improper to base very much on a text that is so notoriously obscure—the verb κατέχω can be translated "hold back" or "hold fast," "occupy,"[49] and has been understood as signifying Rome/the emperor,[50] civil government,[51] God and His power,[52] Michael the archangel,[53] the preaching of the Gospel/Paul,[54] Satan,[55] general evil forces,[56] a combination of benevolent forces,[57] the Jewish state, and James,[58] or a mythic symbol with no particular content.

THE OLIVET DISCOURSE

Many scholars have claimed that this discourse is the most difficult portion of the Gospels to interpret. In investigating this address, it will be necessary to confine ourselves to those questions that are of relevance for this present topic. These would appear to be: (1) What did the disciples ask? (2) Does the "abomination of desolation" and tribulation mentioned in conjunction with it refer to end-time events? (3) Is Jesus' end-of-the-age Parousia described in Mark 13:24–27/Matthew 24:29–31? (4) Does Mark 13:27/Matthew 24:31 refer to the Rapture? (5) To whom is the discourse addressed?

Jesus has just shocked the disciples by predicting the complete destruction of the temple, which they have just been admiring (Mark 13:1–2). In response to this, the disciples ask, "When will this be, and what will be the sign when these things are all to be accomplished?" Matthew makes it clear that their question is essentially twofold: "Tell us, when will these things [the destruction of the temple and associated events] be, and what will be the sign of your coming and of the close of the age?" It is probable that the disciples, in keeping with much Jewish eschatological expectation, believed that the close of the age would include the destruction of the temple.[59] The relationship between these two events in Jesus' answer constitutes one of the great difficulties in the discourse.

The focus of this difficulty, to take up our second question, is the reference to the "abomination of desolation" in Mark 13:14; Matthew 24:15.[60] Is Jesus envisaging an event that transpired in A.D. 70, when Jerusalem was destroyed by the armies of Rome, or an end-time event? In favor of the former is the parallel passage in Luke's gospel, which substitutes "Jerusalem surrounded by armies" for the "abomination of desolation" and records as a consequence of this event the scattering of the Jewish people among the Gentiles (21:20–24). Moreover, warnings associated with the "abomination" in Mark and Matthew seem to envisage a *local* situation ("Let those in Judaea flee," "pray that it might not be on a Sabbath"). On the other hand, a number of indications that Jesus thinks of an event at the end of the age are present. The phrase "abomination of desolation" clearly alludes to several verses of Daniel's prophecy. These verses cannot properly be interpreted as having their fulfillment until the end of the age. Mark (13:14) clearly indicates, by using a *masculine* participle after the neuter "abomination" that he is thinking of a person—and the similarities to the Antichrist described in 2 Thessalonians 2 are clear. Clear temporal links in the text also demonstrate that this is the case. The "abomination" occurs in the days of a tribulation "as has not been from the beginning of the creation which God created until now, and never will be" (Mark 13:19)—a probable reference to the final, Great Tribulation.[61] But this Tribulation, in turn, is said to precede *immediately* the Parousia (Matt. 24:29; although Mark 13:24 does not have "immediately," this seems to be implied).[62]

This latter point involves us necessarily in our third question—does Matthew 24:29ff. really depict the end-of-the-age Parousia? This is disputed by some who find in this language a metaphorical description of God's judgment on Jerusalem in A.D. 70.[63] But this view is very difficult—two crucial objections can be cited. First, the association of Jesus' "coming" with clouds (dependent on Dan. 7:13) always has reference to the Parousia in the New Testament. Second, the cosmic signs of Mark 13:24–25 are held by the author of Revelation to be future (6:14–17)—and he is probably writing *after* A.D. 70.

Thus, to return to our initial point, the structure of the text itself demonstrates that the "abomination of desolation" probably refers to an event at the end of the age—almost certainly the usurpation of God's position by the Antichrist. However, there is much to be said for the view that finds a reference also to A.D. 70 here. Luke 21:20–24 *does* appear to be parallel to the reference in Mark and Matthew—it comes at the same point in the structure of the discourse and shows verbal similarity (cf. "devastation" in v. 20). But if, as it appears, Luke gives a historical application of this portion, there would seem to be a need to find this in Matthew and Mark also.[64] Furthermore, it is hard to see how Jesus could have ignored in His answer the destruction of the then existing temple about which the disciples asked Him. Probably, then, Jesus "telescopes" A.D. 70 and the end of the age in a manner reminiscent of the prophets, who frequently looked at the end of the age through more immediate historical events.[65]

What relevance does this discussion have for the question of the relationship between the Tribulation and the Rapture? Much. For Jesus clearly asserts that the disciples standing before Him will see the "abomination of desolation," which, we have seen, comes in the midst of the Great Tribulation. But it is obvious that the disciples did *not,* in fact, see the eschatological "abomination." Thus, the crucial question becomes: *Whom* do the disciples represent in this passage—Israel or the church? In order to approach this question properly, it is important to keep in mind a fundamental consideration. No one doubts that the disciples in most contexts of the gospels stand for Christians of all ages—or else why do we take Jesus' teaching as our own instruction? *Only if the context clearly necessitates a restriction should any narrowing of the audience be suggested.*

Are there clear indications in the Olivet Discourse that

Jesus did not intend His words to apply to all the people of God, including the church? Walvoord argues that the nature of the question in Matthew 24 excludes a reference to the church because the disciples were asking about the coming of the millennial kingdom.[66] There are some real difficulties with this argument, however. First, it apparently demands that Jesus answered a *different* question in Mark and Luke than He did in Matthew. But where is the indication in the text of such a difference? The question relating to the temple is identical—word for word—in Matthew, Mark, and Luke. Second, this view assumes that Jesus answered the question about the destruction of the temple and the question about the coming of the kingdom in virtually identical discourses. Doesn't this degree of resemblance indicate that it is improper to separate them in the way Walvoord suggests? Third, Walvoord claims that the disciples asked about the coming of the millennial kingdom, which has no relevance for the church. Not only is there no indication in the disciples' question or in Jesus' answer that the millennial kingdom is the topic, but Jesus in Matthew 28:20 promises the disciples, that as representative of the church He will be with them "to the close of the Age"—and this is the same phrase used in the disciples' question in Matthew 24:3. It is difficult to see why the Parousia of Christ and the consummation of the age would not be relevant to the church.

On the other hand, there are a number of indications which, taken together, make it clear that Jesus addressed the disciples as representative of *all* believers (we do not want to *exclude* Israel, but to *include* the church). First, the depiction of the end-time events in Matthew 24–25 is clearly parallel to the description of the Parousia found in Paul's epistles, directed to the *church*. Some of these have already been noted, but it will be helpful to set them out in parallel columns. See the chart on page 194.

Particular attention should be directed to the obvious parallels between the Olivet Discourse and *both* 1 Thessalonians 4:13–18 (the Parousia and the Rapture) and 2 Thessalonians 2:1–12 (the Parousia and the judgment on the wicked)—in fact there are closer parallels to the former than to the latter.

OLIVET DISCOURSE (Matthew)	EVENT	PAUL
24:5	warning about deception	2 Thess. 2:2
24:5, 11, 24	lawlessness, delusion of the nonelect, signs and wonders	2 Thess. 2:6-11
24:12	apostasy	2 Thess. 2:3
24:15	Antichrist in the temple	2 Thess. 2:4
24:21-22	tribulation preceding the end	2 Thess. 1:6-10
24:30-31	Parousia of Christ, on clouds, at the time of a trumpet blast, with angelic accompaniment	1 Thess. 4:14-16
24:30-31	in power	2 Thess. 2:8
24:31	gathering of believers	1 Thess. 4:16; 2 Thess. 2:1
24:36, 42, 44, 50; 25:13	unexpected and uncertain	1 Thess. 5:1-4
24:42–25:13	exhortation to watch!	1 Thess. 5:6-8

Paul clearly describes in these two passages what Jesus depicts as *one event*[67]—showing that it is illegitimate to separate the Parousia of 1 Thessalonians 4 and the Parousia of 2 Thessalonians 2 in time *and* making it overwhelmingly probable that Jesus addresses the *church* in the Olivet Discourse. For surely, if Paul addresses the church in the Thessalonian epistles, it is obvious that Jesus, who says virtually the same thing, is also addressing the church.

A second reason for thinking that the Olivet Discourse is directed to the church is the use of the term "elect." The word is used to describe those who are on the earth during the events portrayed in the Discourse and therefore presumably denotes those addressed (Matt. 24:22, 24, 31). Yet this word, denoting one graciously chosen by God, is consistently used in the New Testament to refer to members of the *church*; there is no verse in which there is indication that any restriction is in mind. Nor is there any hint of such a restriction in meaning in the Olivet Discourse. Moreover, Jesus has not many days previously pronounced this judgment upon Israel: "Therefore I tell you that the kingdom of God will be taken away from you and given to a people who will produce its fruit" (Matt. 21:43). Could Jesus, after this, think that the disciples would have understood Israel to be the elect to whom He refers in Matthew 24?[68]

A third reason for thinking that the church cannot be excluded from that group represented by the disciples has to do with the nature of the exhortations addressed to the disciples at the end of the discourse. Matthew 24:36–25:13 describes the situation that will exist at the same time of the Parousia of the Son of Man—certainly the Parousia (posttribulational) that has just been described. Yet, these same exhortations appear in other contexts in the Gospels where it seems obvious that the disciples as representatives of the church are addressed (cf. Luke 12:39–46; 19:11–27). Furthermore, the same command addressed to the disciples in Matthew 24–25, "Watch!" (γρηγορέω), is addressed to Christians elsewhere in the New Testament.

That the church is involved in the end events depicted in the Olivet Discourse would be conclusively proven if a reference to the Rapture were found in it. There is some reason for finding such a reference in two places. As an event which transpires at the time of the Parousia, Jesus describes a gathering of the saints "from the four winds, from one end of heaven to the other" (Matt. 24:31; cf. Mark 13:27). It is to be observed, first, that this "gathering" takes place at the sounding of "a great trumpet"—a feature that Paul mentions in both of his presentations of the Rapture (1 Cor. 15:51–52; 1 Thess. 4:16–17). Second, it should be noted that the verb used here, ἐπισυνάγω ("gather together"), is employed in its noun form, ἐπισυναγωγή, to depict the Rapture in 2 Thessalonians 2:1. Since the verb and noun *together* occur only nine times in the New Testament and there are so many other parallels between 2 Thessalonians 2 and the Olivet Discourse, there is good reason to accord significance to this verbal contact. But it is probable that the "gathering" includes more than the Rapture—inasmuch as the description seems to envision a great coming together of *all* God's saints, one would be well-advised to think that the resurrection of the righteous is included also. Thus, Jesus would be depicting the great, final gathering of all saints—the dead through resurrection, the living through the Rapture.[69] In a manner typical of the

New Testament, Jesus takes the prophetic depiction of the posttribulational regathering of Israel (cf. Deut. 30:4; Isa. 27:12–13; 43:5–7; Zech. 2:6–13) and applies it to *all* the people of God.[70]

A second text that *may* refer to the Rapture is the reference in Matthew 24:40–41 (parallel in Luke 17:34–35) to the "taking" of one who is contrasted with another who is "left." It may be that the one "taken" is taken *in judgment* while the one left is allowed to enter the kingdom.[71] But the verb for "taking" is used of the Rapture in John 14:3 (although, to be sure, it is also used in other ways) and it is significant that the verb for "take" *in judgment* in verse 39 is different than the one used in verses 40–41. And the analogy to the flood may suggest that just as Noah was saved by being taken away from the scene of judgment, so believers at the Parousia will be taken away, through the Rapture, from the scene of judgment.[72]

For the reasons cited above, we conclude that Jesus in the Olivet Discourse is addressing His disciples as representatives of *all* believers. This leads necessarily to a posttribulational location of the Rapture, since those addressed in the Discourse are indisputably said to be on the earth until the posttribulational Parousia.

REVELATION

With the concentration on the events of the end found in Revelation, we would expect that here, if anywhere, we could find clear evidence for the relationship of the Tribulation to the Rapture. Unfortunately, this is not the case. Many would argue, in fact, that the Rapture is never even mentioned in Revelation; all would agree that it is not described in direct temporal association with the Tribulation. Therefore, evidence for the topic before us comes from three sources: promises and warnings made to the seven churches; specific texts in which the Rapture may be indicated; and the descriptions of the saints who experience the Tribulation.

Although attention is often given exclusively to Christ's promise to the Philadelphian church in 3:10, there are, in fact, three other texts in Revelation 2–3 in which related promises and warnings are given. In the letter to the church at Smyrna, Christ warns the believers that they can expect tribulation (θλιψις) for ten days (2:10). While it is probable that this is not referring to the climactic, end-of-history Tribulation, it should be noted that believers (and they are clearly regenerate—cf. v. 10) are promised persecution and possible death. Similar to this verse is 2:22, only in this case those who engage in Jezebel's sin are promised "great tribulation"—the lack of article suggests that this refers to suffering in a general sense. Thirdly, Christ exhorts the church at Sardis to repent and warns: "If you do not wake up, I will come like a thief, and you will not know at what time I will come to you" (3:3). The close similarity between this language and that used in 1 Thessalonians 5 and in Jesus' warnings about His *posttribulational* coming in Matthew 24:42–44—all three passages have "as a thief," "watch" (γρηγορέω), and the note of uncertainty—suggests that the church at Smyrna has exactly the same need as those addressed in Jesus' parable and in Paul's letter: to watch lest the coming of Christ in glory take them by surprise.[73] But this, of course, assumes that the church will not be raptured previously.

Finally, we must consider that much-debated promise of Christ in Revelation 3:10: "I will also keep you from the hour of trial which is coming on the whole world to test them who live on the earth." It is probable that the reference is to the Great Tribulation,[74] and all agree that the Philadelphian church is promised protection from it. The question is how: through physical removal in a pretribulational or midtribulational Rapture or through divine safekeeping during the period of distress? Attention is focused on the construction τηρήσω ἐκ ("keep from").

The nearest parallel to this phraseology (and the only other place in biblical Greek where τηρέω and ἐκ are used together) is John 17:15—"I do not ask that you take them out of the world, but that you *keep them from* the evil one." Here it seems clear that Jesus prays for the disciples' preservation from the power of Satan, even though they would remain *in* the "world," the sphere of Satan's activity (cf. 1 John 5:19).[75] Furthermore, it is helpful to note that in only three other verses in the New Testament does τηρέω ("keep") have God or Christ as its subject and believers as its object—John 17:11, 12, 15. In each case, *spiritual preservation* is clearly intended. With these parallels in mind, it seems best to think that in Revelation 3:10 Christ promises the church at Philadelphia that it will be *spiritually protected* from "the hour of trial." In this interpretation, ἐκ, "out of," would denote, as it seems to in John 17:15, *separation*. That this spiritual preservation is to be accomplished through *physical removal* is not indicated, and had John intended physical removal there were other ways of saying so that would have made it more obvious.[76] It is perhaps more likely that, as in John 17:15, believers are physically in the sphere of that from which they are protected.[77] But it must be said that neither view, nor any other that has been proposed, can be conclusively established. We must conclude that Revelation 3:10 neither offers clear-cut evidence for or against a posttribulational Rapture.

Turning now to texts that *may* indicate the time of the Rapture, we can rather quickly dismiss 4:1. The command to John to "come up here" (to heaven) is manifestly intended to suggest a visionary experience that John has while still in the body on the island of Patmos. As Walvoord rightly says, "There is no authority for connecting the rapture with this expression."[78]

Of more significance is the depiction of events in chapter 11. Although there are many details that are obscure in this chapter it seems reasonably clear that 11:11–12 describes a resurrection of the two witnesses. Does this resurrection have anything to do with the Rapture? The fact that the two are said to go up "in a cloud" may suggest this, for clouds are consistently mentioned in descriptions of the Rapture (cf. Matt. 24:30; Acts 1:9; 1 Thess. 4:17; Rev. 14:14). And, as elsewhere when the Rapture is mentioned, a trumpet is found in this text (11:15). While these indications can certainly not be regarded as conclusive, the determination of the *time* of this event may shed more light on the question. There are many indications that strongly suggest that the very end of the Tribulation is reached in 11:11–19. The "great earthquake" that is said to take place immediately after the resurrection of the witnesses (11:13) is mentioned in only two other verses in Revelation, both of which describe the end—6:12 and 16:18. No one doubts that 16:18 occurs in a posttribulational setting, but it may be necessary to point out that 6:12–17, the sixth seal, also almost certainly depicts the end. For unless one attempts to avoid the literal meaning of the language, it is hard to avoid the conclusion that history as we know it cannot go on after the stars have fallen to the earth, the sky has been rolled up, and every mountain and island has been removed from its place. As Beasley-Murray says, "This language permits one interpretation alone: the last day has come."[79] But the decisive consideration is that Jesus refers to these events as taking place *after* the Tribulation and immediately in conjunction with His Parousia (Matt. 24:29–30).

If the "great earthquake" points to a time at the end of the Tribulation, there are other factors that suggest the same. The witnesses are said to prophesy for forty-two months (11:2) and then to lie in death for "three and a half days" (11:9). If the former reference is to the first half of the Tribulation period, the second reference *could* indicate the second half. But it must be admitted that this is far from certain. At the blowing of the seventh trumpet, there can be little doubt that the end is reached; the kingdom of the world becomes the kingdom of Christ (11:15), the Lord begins His reign (11:17), the time for His wrath and for judging and rewarding comes (11:18), and the heavenly temple is opened (11:19). If the seventh trumpet is chronologically related to the resurrection of the witnesses, then we have a rather clear indication that the resurrection is posttribulational.

While it is therefore probable that the resurrection of the two witnesses is posttribulational, this would have decisive bearing on the question of the time of the Rapture only if it could be shown that the witnesses represent the church.[80] But this is not clear, and the most that can be said is that this verse could be suggestive if other similar indications are found.

In one of a series of visions that occur between the depiction of the trumpets and the bowls, John sees "one like a Son of Man" seated on a cloud. He descends to "harvest the earth" (14:14–16). That the Parousia is portrayed here is probable in light of the references to "Son of Man" and "clouds."[81] But can the harvesting of the earth in verses 15–16 include the Rapture? This may be the case—Jesus uses the image of harvesting to describe the gathering of God's people into the kingdom (Matt. 13:30). Verses 17–20 would then be a description of the judgment of God on unbelievers. The precise reference in the imagery of the harvest is not altogether clear, however. Scholars debate over whether the first harvest is solely for the righteous,[82] solely for the wicked,[83] or includes both.[84] However, it seems difficult to *exclude* the saints from this first harvesting, which, unlike the second, has no reference to God's wrath. Therefore, *if* one holds that the church is addressed in these chapters of Revelation, the Rapture would almost certainly be included as an aspect of this great ingathering of the saints at the end.

A final text that may indicate the time of the Rapture is Revelation 20:4, in which John describes the "first resurrection." The participants in this resurrection are not specifically named—there is no expressed subject of the third person plural verb ἔζησαν ("they come to life"). While some would want to confine the participants to the martyrs specifically mentioned in verse 4,[85] there are good reasons for including more than the martyrs in this resurrection. First, in addition to the martyrs, verse 4 also describes those who sit on the thrones and to whom judgment is given—the syntax clearly suggests that this is a group different from the martyrs.[86] Secondly, those who come to life are "priests of God and reign with Him" (v. 6) and Revelation 5:9–10 stresses the fact that this group will include people "from every tribe and language and people and nation." If, as is clear, the group in 5:9–10 includes the church, it is probably not legitimate to exclude the church in 20:4. Thirdly, John describes only two resurrections in Revelation—the "first," in verse 4 and the "second," in which the wicked take part. The first resurrection in verse 4 must certainly have a *temporal* force, since it is used in conjunction with "second,"[87] and it is not easy to think that John's language allows for any resurrection preceding this one. Observe also that those who do not participate in the first resurrection are labeled "the *rest* of the dead"—indication that John includes in his two resurrections *all* the dead. Finally, it is inherently unlikely that John, writing to churches (1:4; 22:16), would omit in his grand portrait of the end one of the most blessed and anticipated aspects of that period—the resurrection of believers.

For these reasons, it is probable that Revelation 20:4 depicts the resurrection of *all* the righteous dead—including church saints. Since the Rapture occurs at the same time as this resurrection, and the first resurrection is clearly posttribulational, the Rapture must also be considered posttribulational.

The third main line of investigation to be pursued in Revelation relates to the identity of the saints whom John sees participating in the tribulational events. Are believers of *this* dispensation, church saints, included in this group? A negative answer to this question is often given because the word ἐκκλησία ("church") does not occur in Revelation 4–19. But this is hardly conclusive—John plainly has in mind the worldwide body of saints in these chapters, and ἐκκλησία is only rarely used in the New Testament to indicate such a universal group. John, himself, *never* uses ἐκκλησία other than as a designation of a local body of believers.[88] Moreover, it is important to note that John never in chapters 4–19 calls any group in *heaven* the church.[89] Thus the lack of reference to ἐκκλησία as such cannot decide this issue.

Nor does the structure of Revelation shed light on the question. Revelations 1:19 suggests that the book unfolds in three major sections: "the things you have seen" (= chapter 1); "the things which are" (=Rev. 2–3); and "the things which are about to happen after these things" (4–22). But while the events of chapters 4–22 are probably regarded as *future* from John's perspective, there is nothing to suggest that this must be after the "church age."

Therefore, it becomes necessary to ask whether we can identify any *particular* group in Revelation 4–19 with the church so as to enable us to determine its location during these events. In the heavenly throne room scene of chapter 4, a group of twenty-four "elders" is described, who are grouped around God's throne and wear white robes and crowns of gold (v. 4). Most commentators think a superior order of angels is depicted here,[90] but there is some reason to think rather that the "elders" are glorified men.[91] However, there are sound reasons for refusing to confine the group to church saints alone. In Revelation 5:10 the "elders" address a group that includes the church in the third person—"them."[92] The wearing of gold crowns is certainly not restricted to the church—in Revelation 9:7 the demonic locusts wear "something like crowns of gold." Neither do the white robes necessarily suggest a raptured church since the Laodiceans are told to wear them *on earth* (3:18). If John's own symbolism is to be followed, it would seem that the reference to "twenty-four" most naturally suggests the whole people of God, Israel *and* the church. Thus, in Revelation 21:12–14, the New Jerusalem is pictured as having twelve gates with the names of the twelve tribes of Israel and twelve foundations with the names of "the twelve apostles of the Lamb." But since Daniel 12 clearly shows that Israel is not raptured until *after* the Tribulation, the presence of the "elders" in Heaven in Revelation 4 cannot be used to refute a posttribulational Rapture. In this respect, it is significant that the "twenty-four elders" are always portrayed in visions of heaven which bear no clear temporal relationship to *any* earthly event—in a sense it is asking the wrong question to enquire about *when* these scenes take place.

It does not seem that it can be definitely concluded *what* group of saints is depicted in the 144,000 of Revelation 7:2–8, but it does seem that the "bride" of the wedding supper in Revelation 19:7–9 must include the church. But this does not indicate that the Rapture must have *preceded* the Parousia of 19:11ff., for the visions of 17:1–19:10 appear to give *proleptic* views of the effects of the Parousia.

Finally, there are some general indications that taken together provide good reason for thinking that the church cannot be eliminated from the body of saints pictured on the earth during the Tribulation. One must take note of the promises and warnings given church saints in Revelation 2–3 that are found also in chapters 4–20. Thus, for example, the church at Smyrna is promised that believers will be spared from "the second death" if they "overcome." But it is rescue from this "second death" that the first resurrection of Revelation 20:4–6 provides (cf. v. 6). A continual theme in the letters to the churches is the need to "triumph" (7 times); Revelation 18:2 pictures "those who triumphed over the beast and his image." Four times in the letters the need for "endurance" is stressed; the same quality is demanded of the tribulation saints (13:10; 14:12). Other such parallels could be mentioned,[93] and whereas they cannot be considered decisive evidence (the same characteristics can be ascribed to two different groups), they do seem suggestive.

The reference to the Parousia in 1:7 is also suggestive. If the church is not to take part in the events of Revelation 4–19 it seems incongruous that John should highlight this Parousia, the great climax of these chapters, in the address to the *churches* (cf. 1:4). In 22:16, Jesus claims that He has sent His angel "to give you (plural!) *this testimony for the churches.*" It is difficult to see how the chapters on the Tribulation could be a "testimony for the churches" if they are not involved in it.[94] Finally, it simply appears improbable that the event described at greatest length in Revelation (the Tribulation) would have no *direct* relevance for those to whom the book is addressed.

We would conclude our discussion of the Revelation by attempting to indicate how our understanding of particular events in the Revelation fits into the overall structure of the book. It seems clear that the seventh in each series of seals, trumpets, and bowls brings us to the time of the Parousia. Interspersed among these series are visions of the heavenly warfare that is manifested in the tribulational distress (chap. 12), of the satanic power of that time (13) and of the protection and ultimate vindication of God's people (7, 14). Immediately before the Parousia is given a proleptic vision of the judgment and salvation that the heavenly intervention brings (17:1–18:10). Following the Parousia are portrayed the events that flow from it. In other words, it is the Parousia of Christ that is the focal point of Revelation 6–20—all other events lead up to or follow from it, while periodic visions reveal different aspects of these events. It might be helpful to set out this structure in a rough diagram (the rectangular border encloses events associated with the Parousia):

STRUCTURE OF REVELATION

Seals	Trumpets	12-14	Bowls	17-19:10
1				
2				
	1			
3				
	2			
		(12-13)		
4	3			
			1	
	4		2	
5			3	
	5		4	
			5	
6	6		6	

Vision of Redeemed (7:9-17)	Resurrection (11:11-12)	14:1-5—Redeemed 14:14-20—Rapture Resurrection, Judgment		Proclamation of Judgment and Salvation
			7	

PAROUSIA
(19:11-21)

7	7			

Binding of Satan

First Resurrection

Millennium

Eternal State

Special attention should be drawn to the way in which the different events that occur at Christ's Parousia are depicted: the deliverance of the saints (7:9–15); the resurrection of the faithful witnesses (11:11–12); the inauguration of the Day of God's judgment and His eternal kingdom (11:15–19); the deliverance of the 144,000 (14:1–5); the final gathering of believers and the judgment (14:14–20); the condemnation of the evil world system (chaps. 17–18); the union of God and His saints (19:8–9); the binding of Satan (20:1–3); the first resurrection (20:4–6). Based on this proposed structure and the underlying exegesis, it can be observed that all these great events are posttribulational.

As a result of our study of key biblical texts, we conclude that the Parousia of Christ is a fundamentally single event at which time both living and dead saints of all dispensations go to be with the Lord and the wrath of God falls on unbelievers. The reconstruction of end events based on this hypothesis demonstrates a remarkable degree of consistency through every important New Testament depiction of the end. (See the chart on p. 206, which includes the major events mentioned in more than one text.) Not every event is included in every text, of course, for the different authors chose to mention only those events which were appropriate for their particular argument.[95] The fact that this reconstruction, founded upon a posttribulational Rapture, fits every passage so naturally is a potent argument in favor of this position.

ISRAEL AND THE CHURCH

Some brief comments must now be made on this issue, which we purposely set to one side in our exegesis of the New Testament texts. In dealing with these texts, we have found places in which language and prophecies that have reference to Israel in the Old Testament (e.g., the eschatological trumpet, Antichrist and, most obviously, the Tribulation itself) are applied to the church. If, of course, it were to be concluded, on the basis of a thorough study of other texts, that a rigid distinction between Israel and the church were necessary, some of our conclusions would have to be reevaluated. However, it seems that the application to the church of the Old Testament prophecies given to Israel is not at all unusual in the New Testament—see, for one of the clearest instances, the use of Jeremiah 31:31ff. in Hebrews 8 and 10. On the other hand, it is important that Israel and the church not be completely merged: Paul clearly expects a future for racial Israel (Rom.

RECONSTRUCTION OF MAJOR END-TIME EVENTS

Event	Matt. 24-25	John 14	1 Cor. 15	1 Thess. 4-5	2 Thess. 2	Seals	Trumpets	Revelation 12-14	Bowls 17-20
wars	6-7a					6:3-4			
famine	7b					6:5-6			
apostasy	13				2:3				
preaching of Gospel	14							14:6-7(?)	
Antichrist (in temple)	15				2:3-7			13:1-8	
Tribulation	16-25				2:9	6:9-11(?)	8:6-9:21		16
false signs	24								
cosmic signs	29					6:12-17			19:11-21
Parousia	30			4:16	2:8				
trumpet	31		51	4:16			11:15	14:15	
angel(s)	31			4:16			11:15		
first resurrection	31	3	51	4:16			11:11-12	14:14-16	20:4-6
Rapture			51	5:3				14:17-20	17:11-19: 3
judgment					2:8	7:9-17	11:18	14:1-5	19:4-9
"with the Lord"		3		4:18			11:18		
"Watch!"	24:36-25:13			5:6-8		throughout Revelation			

9–11). What is important, we would suggest, is to distinguish carefully between prophecies directed to Israel *as a nation* (and which must be fulfilled in a national Israel) and prophecies directed to Israel as *the people of God* (which can be fulfilled in the people of God—*a people that includes the church!*). It should be noted that such an approach is not allegorical or nonliteral; it simply calls upon the interpreter to recognize the intended scope of any specific prophecy. It is our contention, then, that the Great Tribulation predicted for Israel by, e.g., Daniel, is directed to Israel as the people of God. It can therefore be fulfilled in the people of God, which includes the church as well as Israel.

IMMINENCY

There remains to be examined one extremely important aspect of the hope of Christ's return which has great significance for the time of the Rapture: the belief that this event is "imminent." Since a posttribulational view requires that certain events *must* transpire *before* the Parousia, it is often claimed that posttribulationism necessarily involves the denial of imminency.[96] In order to avoid this conclusion, J. B. Payne seeks to explain most events predicted of the Tribulation in such a way that they *could* be present (or past) even now.[97] This attempt must, however, be deemed unsuccessful—the nature of some of these events, which are asserted to be recognizable by the saints when they occur (cf. e.g., 2 Thess. 2), precludes the possibility that they are "potentially present."[98] On the other hand, Gundry, convinced of the posttribulational Rapture position, wants to do away with "imminency" altogether.[99]

However, one very important fact must be recognized: all the views discussed in the previous paragraph assume that *imminent* must mean "any moment." This is simply not the case. The *Oxford English Dictionary* gives as the meaning of *imminent,* "impending threateningly, hanging over one's head; ready to befall or overtake one, close at hand at its incidence; coming on shortly." Clearly this meaning does not require that there be no intervening events before something said to be imminent transpires. It is quite appropriate to speak of the adjournment of Congress, for instance, as being "imminent" even if some event(s) (such as a crucial roll-call vote) *must* elapse before it can occur. In this sense, the term can be applied to an event that is *near* and cannot at *this* point be accurately dated, but that will *not* occur until some necessary preliminary events transpire. Defined in this way, the "imminence" of our Lord's return is a doctrine that should not be jettisoned. It expresses the supremely important conviction that the glorious return of Christ *could* take place within any limited period of time—that the next few years could witness this grand climax to God's dealing with the world. Granted that imminence *can* be defined in this way, is this in fact the manner in which the hope of Christ's return is viewed in the New Testament?

The first point to be made is that none of the many words used to describe the nearness of the Parousia, or the believer's expectation of it, requires an "any moment" sense of imminency. Προσδέχομαι, "wait for" (applied to the Parousia in Luke 12:36; Titus 2:13; Jude 21 [?]), is used of Paul's expectation of the resurrection of the just and the *unjust* (Acts 24:15)—yet the latter does not occur until after the Millennium. Ἀπεκδέχομαι, "await eagerly" (used of the Parousia in 1 Cor. 1:7), can refer to creation's longing for deliverance (Rom. 8:19), which deliverance comes only after the Tribulation. Ἐκδέχομαι, "expect," is used by James of the Parousia in 5:7, but the analogy in the context is with a farmer who waits for his crops—certainly not "any moment!" Προσδοκάω, "look for" (cf. Matt. 24:50; Luke 12:46 with reference to the Second Coming) is the word used by Peter to exhort believers to "look for" the new heavens and earth (2 Peter 3:12–14). Ἐγγίζω, "be near," and the adjectival form, ἐγγύς, applied to the Parousia in numerous texts, are used of Jewish feasts and the seasons of the year (e.g., John 2:13; Matt. 21:34)—and these, obviously, are not "any moment" events. A number of other terms (γρεγορέω, "watch"; ἀγρυπνέω, "be awake"; νήφω, "be sober"; Βλέπω, "look at") are used to exhort believers to an attitude of spiritual alertness and moral uprightness *in the light* of the second return, but imply nothing as to its time.[100]

By themselves, then, these terms do not require that the expectation to which they refer be capable of taking place "at any moment." Crucial will be the context in which they are used. The most important of these contexts have already been examined and it will not be necessary to repeat here the evidence that leads us to believe that a posttribulational Rapture is consistently indicated. But some additional remarks should perhaps be added with respect to the Olivet Discourse.

In the hortatory section following Christ's depiction of the Tribulation and Parousia, Jesus makes three important points: (1) The disciples do not know when the Lord will come (Matt. 24:42, 44; Matt. 25:13); (2) They must therefore watch and be prepared; (3) When they see tribulational events, they can know that Christ is near (Matt. 24:32–33). What is particularly crucial to note is that all *three* statements are made with respect to the *same* event—the posttribulational coming of Christ. There is no basis for any transition from the posttribulational aspect of the Parousia in Matthew 24:32–35 (or –36) to its pretribulational aspect in verses 36ff. Therefore *all* interpreters, whether they believe the discourse is addressed to the church or to Israel, face the difficulty of explaining how an event heralded by specific signs can yet be one of which it said "no one knows the day and hour." One solution may be to understand Jesus' words about the unknown day to apply to every generation *except the last*; *that* generation (γενεά in Matt. 24:34), when it "sees these things happening," knows that Christ is at the very gates.[101] Or, it may be that while the *exact* time cannot be known, one will be able to know the *general* time of the Advent after the Tribulation has begun.[102] And in this regard, the statement about the tribulational days being "shortened" (Matt. 24:22) should be noted; it may be impossible to predict the time of the Parousia even after the Antichrist has been revealed.

Within the New Testament there are indications that suggest that New Testament authors could not have intended to portray the Parousia as an event that could happen "at any moment." For, first of all, Jesus in His teaching rather frequently suggests that there will be a *delay* before His return (Luke 19:11–27; Matt. 24:45–51; 25:5, 19). Second, and more important, are *specific* predictions that could not have been fulfilled if Christ had returned immediately after His ascension. Thus Jesus promises His disciples that they *will* be His witnesses "in Jerusalem, in all of Judea, in Samaria and unto the end of the earth" (Acts 1:8). The gospel *must* be preached to all nations before the end comes (Matt. 24:14); Peter will die a martyr's death *as an old man* (John 21:18–19); Paul *will* preach the Gospel in Rome (Acts 23:11; 27:24). It is not sufficient to say that all these *could* have been fulfilled in the first century and therefore represent no barrier to an "any moment" Rapture *now*. [103] For the point is to determine what the statements about the nearness of the Parousia would have meant to those who first heard them. If the original speakers did not intend and the original hearers did not understand a particular statement to require an "any-moment" interpretation, that statement can hardly have such a meaning *now*. [104]

Therefore, it does not appear that the imminence of the return of Christ can be understood in an "any-moment" sense. (The apostolic Fathers also believed in a posttribulational Rapture *and* expected to participate in tribulation events.) [105] It is better to define *imminency* as the possibility of Jesus' coming for His people *at any time*—"time" being understood broadly as a short *period* of time. It is in light of that "any-time" coming that the church is called upon to live out its calling. But, it is objected, doesn't the denial of the any-moment coming of Christ for His church take away the force of those exhortations to right conduct? In *negative* applications of the return (as when people are warned to be careful lest Christ "surprise" them), an "any-moment" Rapture adds nothing to the associated exhortations, for it is precisely and *only* those who do not heed the warnings who will be surprised (cf. 1 Thess. 5:2–4; Luke 21:34). And the exhortations to "watch," because the time is not known require only that the *exact* moment is unknown for the force of the warning to be maintained. But the stimulus to holy living provided by the expectation of Christ's return is based *primarily* on a *positive* application of the return in the New Testament. Believers are to remain spiritually alert and morally sober because they recognize that they will stand before their Redeemer to answer for their conduct. And the force of *this* appeal surely does not depend on the "any-moment" possibility of such an encounter.

CONCLUSION

The truth of the imminent coming of our Lord Jesus Christ is an important and indispensable element of biblical truth. That this coming is to be premillennial the Scriptures plainly state. That a time of unprecedented Tribulation will immediately precede that coming and that living believers will be raptured into the presence of Christ at His coming are also plainly stated. But the *time* of that Rapture with respect to the Tribulation is *nowhere plainly stated*. No Old Testament or New Testament author *directly* addresses that question or states the nature of that relationship as a point of doctrine. What *I* think the Scriptures indicate about this relationship has been stated on the preceding pages. But, because this conviction is founded upon logic, inferences, and legitimately debated points of exegesis, I cannot, indeed *must* not, allow this conviction to represent any kind of barrier to full relationships with others who hold differing convictions on this point. May our discussions on this point enhance, not detract from, our common expectation of "the blessed hope—the glorious appearing of our great God and Savior, Jesus Christ" (Titus 2:13).

RESPONSE: GLEASON L. ARCHER

NEEDLESS TO SAY, those portions of Dr. Moo's discussion directed against the any-moment Rapture theory fall into line with my own remarks and therefore I have little to contribute by way of criticism. The same is true in regard to the closely related matter of the signs, which are declared in the Olivet Discourse and in the Thessalonian Epistles to precede the return of our Lord for His church. But there are two areas in which his discussion seems to fall short of adequate treatment: the question of a two-phase Parousia, and the implications of τηρέω ἐκ in Revelation 3:10.

THE TWO PHASES OF THE PAROUSIA

Dr. Moo regards the Parousia referred to in the Olivet Discourse (Matt. 24:3, 27, 37, 39) as demonstrably subsequent to the Great Tribulation. He feels that 2 Thessalonians 2:8 also demonstrates this. He then points out that the Parousia is presented as an object of the believer's expectation in 1 Thessalonians 2:19; 3:13; James 5:7–8; 1 John 2:28. He then draws the conclusion that is the heart of his entire discussion: "If, then, believers are exhorted to look forward to this coming of Christ, and this coming is presented as posttribulational, it is natural to conclude that believers will be present through the Tribulation." This would of course logically follow if the Parousia is a single event. But if the New Testament indicates that the Parousia will come in two stages, the first of which will be the Rapture of the church from the world scene *before* the final catastrophe of the terrible plagues that will torment and decimate the earth prior to the final dénouement of Armageddon, then the above-stated deduction is invalid.

Considerable discussion has already been devoted to the vital matter of sequential transition between the Rapture of the church in 1 Thessalonians 4 and the final destruction of the forces of evil and rebellion set forth in 1 Thessalonians 5. Both Dr. Feinberg's paper and my own have devoted careful analysis of this important shift in focus and time. We therefore need only to remind the reader of the main points brought out in these discussions.

The setting of the "Rapture passage" (1 Thess. 4:13–18) gives no hint of apocalyptic struggle. This paragraph of re-assurance speaks only of the sequence that will mark the stages of the resurrection of believers in their glorified bodies. Introductory to the actual scene of rising from earth to meet the Lord in the air is the announcement in verse 14, "For if we believe that Jesus died and rose again, even so God will bring with Him those who have fallen asleep through [διά] Jesus." (Or else possibly, "God will bring through Jesus those who have fallen asleep"—which is more difficult to fit in with the following σὺν αὐτῷ, "with Him.") Dr. Moo understands this to mean that Jesus will bring with him from heaven those who have fallen asleep in Jesus. He is therefore surrounded or accompanied by all of the deceased saints in their resurrection bodies as He descends earthward in order to greet those who are still alive on earth at the time of His coming.

This construction of verse 14 seems hard to justify in view of the immediately ensuing verses, 16 and 17. These verses expressly state that those who have died in Christ (οἱ νεκροὶ ἐν Χριστῷ) will *not* be raised from their graves until the Rapture itself. "The dead in Christ shall rise first, and then afterwards [ἔπειτα] we who are alive and remain shall be caught up together with them [ἅμα σὺν αὐτοῖς] in the clouds to meet the Lord in the air." Nothing could be plainer from this description than that the great company of deceased believers will *not* accompany the Lord in His descent from heaven—not in their resurrection-bodies, at least—but will be united with their new and glorious bodies just before the rising of the living survivors of the final generation contemporary with the Rapture.

One of the most striking implausibilities in this interpretation is the accompanying deduction that the just-resurrected saints bob up from the earth to meet the Lord for a brief moment in the clouds, only to return to the earth almost immediately. This appears on page 178 in the following sentence: "The fact that believers at a posttribulational Rapture would rise to meet the Lord in the air only to return immediately to earth with Him creates no difficulty, for the text does *not* state that believers will go directly to heaven, but only that they will always be with the Lord." On the contrary, we maintain that this yo-yo procedure of popping up and down presents a very great difficulty! At one moment the faithful followers of Christ are lifted up out of the revolting scene of the sin-cursed, evil-dominated earth in order to meet with the Lord Jesus in His kingly glory up in the clouds of heaven. But since this descent of Christ is identified by Dr. Moo with the return to earth for judgment described in Revelation 19:11–21, this means that He will descend mounted upon His white horse, followed by the hosts of heaven. If so, he would hardly be apt to check His course for any length of time as He makes His way down to the Mount of Olives (Zech. 14:4) and to the battlefield of Armageddon. If anything, these upward-bobbing saints will only impede the momentum of His earthward charge as He rushes down to crush the rebellious hosts of the Beast and all his minions. The most that can be said of such a "Rapture" is that it is a rather secondary sideshow of minimal importance.

But as we turn back to the actual text of 1 Thessalonians 4:16–18 we receive a far different impression of this marvelous and exalting deliverance of the saints of God. This is surely an event of outstanding importance and tremendous comfort. "Together with them we shall be caught up in clouds to meet the Lord in the air; and thus we shall always be with the Lord. Therefore comfort one another with these words." The overall impression is certainly that the resurrected believers are taken up into glory to be with the Lord Jesus in the realm of heaven, rather than straightway being dropped back on the earth again. The distinction that Dr. Moo tries to draw between mere "clouds" and heaven itself is very difficult to maintain in the light of the usage of Scripture itself. The key verse in Daniel 7:13 that predicts the triumph of the Son of Man represents Him as coming into the presence of the Ancient of Days "with the clouds *of heaven*," a phrase that is repeated in Matthew 26:64; Mark 14:62; Revelation 14:14. Clouds are much more closely associated with the glory and throne of God than they are connected with the earth. It certainly would be difficult to find any other scriptural reference to the clouds as a momentary way-station in the course of a descent to earth. The far greater likelihood, therefore, is that the arrival of the resurrected saints in the glory of the clouds above points to life and activity on a heavenly plane rather than on an earthly plane.

As for the possibility of a two-stage Parousia, we should take careful note of the fact that the Scripture contains many dual fulfillments in regard to eschatology and messianic prophecy. "The day of the Lord" (יוֹם יְהוָה), as is well known and universally acknowledged, refers at times to days of judgment and calamity upon various heathen nations, or even upon Old Testament Israel itself, as well as to the ultimate and climactic day of God's judgment upon the wicked race of men in the end times. There were at least three phases to the Babylonian captivity of Judah predicted in Jeremiah, the first in 605 B.C. (when Daniel was among those deported), the second in 597 (when Jehoiachin and Ezekiel were taken), the third in 587, when all of the survivors of the Jerusalem siege were taken captive to Babylonia. As for the prophetic figure of "the Little Horn" in Daniel 7, 8, and 11, it is perfectly clear that one of these two figures was connected with the Third Kingdom (i.e., Antiochus Epiphanes in 175–164 B.C.), and the other with the Fourth Kingdom (i.e., the Beast of the last days—during the final seven years of this present age before Armageddon). One of the most egregious errors of modern rationalist scholarship is its failure to distinguish properly between these two Little Horns. And as for the Advent of Christ, the chief mistake of official Jewry in Christ's day consisted in their failure to distinguish between His First Advent and His Second Advent. It was because He did not come in great power and glory for the purpose of delivering Israel from the yoke of Rome and establishing her as supreme among the nations (achievements reserved for the Second Advent alone) that the majority of His countrymen rejected Him—even though He perfectly fulfilled the prophecies of His first advent. All of these analogies furnish a firm basis for distinguishing between a Parousia that precedes the Great Tribulation (especially the last three and a half years of the outpouring of the wrath of God upon earth), and a Parousia that features the return of Christ as Conqueror and Judge.

Much has been made of similar features which will be manifest at the Rapture (according to 1 Thess. 4) and the Second Coming in final judgment (according to the Olivet Discourse and the Book of Revelation). Page 206 presents a list of phenomena common to both that includes at least three items: a trumpet, angel(s), first resurrection, with sundry other resemblances in Revelation 6, 11, 14, etc. "With the Lord" is found in five Second Advent passages in Revelation, as well as in 2 Thessalonians 4:17. The list takes up a whole page and looks very impressive at first. But a closer examination will show that as between the classic passage on the Rapture (1 Thess. 4) and the other passages referring to the Second Parousia in judgment there are really only four (if we include the mention of clouds). A systematic survey of all other theophanies described in Scripture will show similar phenomena, both in the Pentateuch and in the Prophets, as well as in various passages of Job and Psalms. A celestial trumpet blew at the summit of Mt. Sinai in Exodus 20, angels flew about the throne of Yahweh in Isaiah 6, and various clouds, bright and dark and fiery, accompanied the manifested presence of the Lord all during the wilderness wanderings. But the contrasts between the scene of 2 Thessalonians 4 and the apocalyptic terror and overwhelmingly destructive force that characterize the various descriptions of the Second Coming clearly outweigh these alleged similarities. All that is necessary is to read all of the passages cited on page 204 of Moo's presentation and then reread 2 Thessalonians 4; the differences in atmosphere, mood, and setting are so obvious as to discourage all hope of identifying the two as pointing to the one and same transaction. References to the bodily resurrection that occur in connection with both Parousias should occasion little surprise. It is quite obvious from the scriptural record that a first resurrection of Old Testament saints took place very soon after the Crucifixion (Matt. 27:52), perhaps even before Easter morning. The second resurrection was that of Christ Himself. The third resurrection of the dead will occur at the Rapture; the fourth will take place at the Second Coming (Dan. 12:2, John 5:28–29), and the fifth at the end of the Millennium, the judgment of the Great White Throne (Rev. 20:11–15). If, then, there are no less than five bodily resurrections, the mention of this in connection with both Parousias falls far short of proving that they are one and the same!

Before leaving this subject, it would be helpful to recapitulate the contextual evidence pointing to the fact that the Day of the Lord in 1 Thessalonians 5 is by no means identical with the Rapture in 1 Thessalonians 4. First Thessalonians 5:1 brings in a consideration of times and seasons (χρόνοι and καιροί) in such a manner as to suggest that there may be a significant time interval between the two events. The Day of the Lord will fall unexpectedly upon the unbelieving world like a thief in the night (v. 2)—whereas the Rapture passage contains not the slightest hint of anything sinister and dangerous. Verse 3 speaks of the blind optimism of the deluded world culture, completely unprepared for the overwhelming destruction that comes upon them. In other words, the evidence of the context compels us to regard these two episodes as being in complete contrast to each other, and the most that can be said is that there is an interval of time between them, which may not be greatly extended but is nevertheless quite significant. An interval of three and a half years accords perfectly with these specifications. The reassuring comment contained in 5:4–5 concerning the safety of true believers as "children of light" can certainly be applied both to the saints who are taken up at the Rapture and (so far as their eternal fate is concerned) also the new converts who bear the brunt of the fury of the Antichrist during the final three and a half years.

THE PRESERVATION OF BELIEVERS FROM THE GREAT TRIBULATION

We now pass on to a short discussion of another key point in Dr. Moo's argument, the statement that the promise

of preservation in Revelation 3:10 means only a successful
endurance of affliction rather than an exemption from it. Much
depends on the implications of the phrase τηρήσω ἐκ τῆς ὅρας
τοῦ πειρασμοῦ ("I will keep you from the hour of temptation"). In support of his interpretation Moo cites John 17:15,
where our Lord in His high-priestly prayer petitions the Father
that He may keep (τηρήσῃς) them (the disciples) from (ἐκ) the
Evil One. Moo feels that this does not imply that believers are
to be exempt from attack by Satan, but rather that they may
be kept from succumbing to it through bitterness and despair.
He admits that this is the only other occurrence of the verb
τηρεῖν with ἐκ to be found in the New Testament. If so, this
certainly furnishes a weak statistical base on which to make
a ruling on the force of ἐκ in Revelation 3:10. Let us examine
this combination in the Septuagint, however, that we may
gain a clearer perspective. In Proverbs 7:4–5 we read: "I have
told wisdom to be your sister, and acquire prudence as an
acquaintance for you, in order that she might keep (τηρήσῃ)
you from (ἀπό) a woman who is a stranger and a wicked
person, if she should assail you with words of blandishment."
This falls short of being a conclusive parallel, for there is some
distinction between ἐκ ("out of") and ἀπό ("from") even
though they overlap. But in all three passages the clear purpose
of τηρεῖν is to guard the potential victim from harm by the
menacing force that threatens his safety. To argue that one
cannot be preserved out of (from) something unless he has
first gotten into it is highly questionable. Does Christ presup-
pose in John 17:15 that His disciples will get into the devil
before God intervenes to keep them out of him again? Hardly.
His obvious desire is that they may not fall into Satan's fellowship and power. How then can this be taken as proof that
the Philadelphian church in Revelation 3:10 must become en-
meshed in the toils of the Tribulation before God is expected
to keep them from it? The same thing is true of the instructed
son in Proverbs 7; he is hardly expected to become guiltily
involved with the harlot before God will keep him out of her
clutches. Therefore there is little force to the position that the
believers must be brought into the severe testing of the Tribulation before they may be "kept" out of it. Actually the most

important factor here is the true significance of τηϱεῖν itself; rather than treating it as if it meant "deliver," it rather signifies "keep, guard, preserve." It is hard to see how "preserve from" can be construed as necessarily implying partial involvement in the evil from which one is to be preserved. It would normally be taken to mean escaping from contact with it altogether. To be preserved from the Tribulation is surely a different thing from being saved out of it. The most likely implication of Revelation 3:10 is therefore that those who faithfully keep Christ's word will themselves be kept from the severe testing (πειϱασμός) of the Tribulation itself. This blessed assurance is held forth as a special reward by the Savior, rather than a general promise of divine protection from succumbing to the horrors of the Antichrist's rule any time through the seven years of his supremacy. Sustaining grace through hardships and trials is always available even today for the believer who practices the means of grace. But surely something more distinctive in the way of divine favor is implied by these glowing words than simply making it through without serious spiritual loss throughout a period of grave danger and sore affliction. In other words, to keep them out of the Tribulation can only mean that they do not get into the Tribulation period at all. This furnishes an admirable reason for Christ's planning the Rapture as a deliverance of all the already-converted believers just on the threshold of the second half of the "seventieth week" (Dan. 9)—the period of the outpoured wrath of God— before they get into that dreadful period at all. Definite confirmation of this understanding of Revelation 3:10 is furnished by Romans 5:8–9: "But God commends His own love toward us because while we were yet sinners Christ died for us. Much more, therefore, having now been justified by His blood, we shall be saved from wrath [ἀπὸ τῆς ὀϱγῆς] through him." In this particular context it seems all but certain that this particular wrath of God referred to is the wrath of God poured out on the wicked world of unbelievers during the last three-and-a-half years before Armageddon. That is to say, verse 8 makes it clear that those who are to be saved from ὀϱγή are those who have already been justified and are therefore quite secure from experiencing the final, judicial wrath of God. But verse 9 goes on to introduce this deliverance from divine wrath by the words "much more, then" (πολλῷ οὖν μᾶλλον). This strongly suggests that in addition to salvation from eternal judgment and condemnation to hell there is to be a still further benefit: deliverance from "the wrath." This ὀργή cannot be equated with the general judicial wrath of God on the unbelieving world of all ages (that use of ὀργή appears, for example, in Rom. 1:18).

To sum it all up, then, I feel that posttribulationism fails to account for the tremendous importance attached to the division of the final seven years into two halves. Second, it fails to account adequately for the great contrasts presented by the Bible description of the Rapture in 1 Thessalonians 4 and the fearsome and turbulent atmosphere that always characterizes the onset of the frightful destruction connected with the coming of Christ for judgment. In other words, the strong evidences of a two-phase Parousia have been ignored. Third, it fails to do justice to the assurances of preservation from the "hour of testing which is coming upon the whole world to try those who live upon it"—promises contained in Revelation 3:10; 1 Thessalonians 5:9; Romans 5:8–9, and other passages. If indeed this "hour of testing" refers to the Great Tribulation, and the Great Tribulation is appointed for the last three-and-a-half years, then the Rapture itself will certainly take place just before God begins to pour out the bowls of His wrath on a world ripe for final judgment.

RESPONSE: PAUL D. FEINBERG

IN RESPONSE TO Moo's presentation of posttribulationism I would like to discuss three matters: the concept of divine wrath, the Thessalonian epistles, and the Olivet Discourse.

The issue of divine wrath has been discussed at length in the position chapters, but it is still worth some attention. It should be clear that the question of divine wrath is a fundamental one for the Rapture positions. The difference of opinion centers about the *commencement* of divine wrath and the *nature* of divine protection from that wrath. For Moo the wrath of God is concentrated toward the end of the Tribulation period and at the Battle of Armageddon. Further, he defends the principle of selectivity as God's means of protecting His saints. God makes a distinction between believers and unbelievers. His wrath falls on the unbeliever. Thus, Moo sees no reason for the church to be taken out of the world before the Second Advent. On the other hand, I have argued that the entire Tribulation period is a time of God's wrath, from the first seal to the last bowl. The judgments of God fall universally upon all on the earth. John says that they come upon the *whole* earth (Rev. 3:10). Further, the nature of divine protection is by the Rapture of the church prior to the time of trouble.

I remain unconvinced by Moo's presentation on this matter. I think that he is wrong on the commencement of divine wrath as he fails to see the judgments of Revelation 6–19 as related to Revelation 5 and the scroll given to the Lamb. Each of the seals is broken, and judgment proceeds, showing that it is divine in character. While the principle of selectivity is not without some support, I fail to see any indication that at least some of the judgments are not universal in character. The hour of trial is to come and test the whole world. Furthermore, the whole question of selectivity is moot, if Revelation 3:10 promises protection from *outside* the period of time. For me it seems that the evidence best supports this view.

These are two portions of Scripture that have not been discussed, but that deserve careful and complete discussion. The first is the Thessalonian epistles and the Second Coming. The place to begin our discussion is with 1 Thessalonians 4:13–18, since this is a central passage for the pretribulation position. Let me begin by summarizing my understanding of Moo's argument. The concern of the Thessalonian believers was over their dead loved ones. They feared that those who had died would not have some of the advantages of those who lived to the coming of the Lord. Paul's encouragement is that all will participate in the glorious events of the Parousia and be with the Christ.

Further, there are four indications that the hope under discussion was posttribulational: (1) suggestive parallels between 1 Thessalonians 4 and the Olivet Discourse (both events are associated with angels, clouds, a trumpet, and the gathering of believers); (2) the use of the trumpet is an established symbol for the ushering in of the time of Israel's salvation and judgment; (3) 1 Thessalonians 4 is similar to Daniel 12:1–2 (the dead being called "sleepers," the presence of Michael, and the resurrection of God's people); (4) ἀπάντησις usually implies that the delegation accompanies the dignitary back to the delegation's point of origin. These considerations lead Moo to think that the passage favors a posttribulation Rapture.

I think that closer examination of 1 Thessalonians 4 shows that it does not favor a posttribulational Rapture. Moo has not really given an adequate explanation for the Thessalonians' concern or sorrow. If Paul had preached the truth of the resurrection, what possible advantage could the survivors have over those believers who had died? I cannot see any. Let me suggest a more likely explanation. Paul, while he was in Thessalonica, taught the new converts about the hope of the resurrection and about a pretribulation Rapture. After he left, some believers died. The only text the church would have had available to them to set the time of the resurrection was Daniel 12:1–2. This put the resurrection *after* the Tribulation. The

Thessalonian Christians were concerned that their deceased loved ones would not be raised until after the Tribulation, missing out on the the Rapture of church.[1] This explains why Paul says that those of us who are alive and remain to the coming of the Lord will not *precede* those who have died. Gundry's view[2] that they thought that the resurrection would not occur until the end of the Millennium, causing those who had died to miss out on the blessings of the kingdom age, is without scriptural support. There is not a text anywhere in Scripture that speaks of a resurrection at the end of the Millennium until Revelation 20. The Thessalonians would not have had access to this passage.

Furthermore, I do not find the parallels convincing. First, that there should be similarities between passages dealing with the posttribulation return of Christ and a pretribulation Rapture of the church should not surprise us. While the two events are different, they are not entirely dissimilar. The two events may be similar, but they are not the same. For me the fact that there are differences, even if they are not contradictory, is more significant than the similarities. Second, the similarities can be maintained only if we understand the passages in their most general sense. Take the supposed similarities between 1 Thessalonians 4 and the Olivet Discourse. There are angels, clouds, trumpets, and the gathering of believers in both texts. Notice what happens when you examine both passages carefully. In Matthew the Son of Man comes on the clouds, while in 1 Thessalonians 4 the ascending believers are in them. In Matthew the angels gather the elect; in 1 Thessalonians the Lord Himself (note the emphasis) gathers the believers. Thessalonians only speaks of the *voice* of the archangel. In the Olivet Discourse nothing is said about a resurrection, while in the latter text it is the central point. In the two passages the differences in what will take place prior to the appearance of Christ is striking. Moreover, the order of ascent is absent from Matthew in spite of the fact that it is the central point of the epistle. Similar points could be made about the parallel between 1 Thessalonians 4 and Daniel 12. While it may be true that the trumpet is an established symbol for the ushering in of the time of Israel's salvation and judgment, it surely has many other functions in eschatological literature. This can easily be seen from the Book of Revelation. Finally, does the occurrence of ἀπάντησις favor the posttribulation view? Even Moo is cautious here. Three occurrences in the New Testament hardly give you enough of a sample to conclude anything about the usage of the word. Moreover, there is lively debate over whether the term always has that significance outside the New Testament. But even if it could be shown that it did, there are enough differences from the normal usage of this word that any conclusion should be called into question. Here believers are snatched away to meet the Lord; they are not coming on their own to meet a visitor.[3]

1 Thessalonians 5 is another area of significant dispute. Again, let me summarize Moo's argument. He begins with a discussion of the particle δέ that connects chapters 4 and 5. This particle generally denotes a mild contrast, but there are cases where no contrast is intended. Moo thinks that even if a contrast is in Paul's mind, there is still the question about the nature of the contrast. Paul talks of the "times and events" (5:1), but does not give a date or a time, indicating that the previous topic is still in view. The key point that Moo wants to make, however, is that the Rapture can be a part of the Day of the Lord. He sees the believer as being in the period because, while it will not overtake him like a thief in the night, it will overtake him. The contrast is not between inclusion and exclusion, but between surprise and preparedness. What the believer escapes is not the Day, but the condemnation or judgmental aspect of it.

This is an important passage. Does a posttribulation interpretation fare any better here? I do not think so. First, the connective is not simply δέ but περὶ δὲ. The subjects need not be so different that they are in contrast, but there is not simply the continuation of the same subject. This is Paul's typical way of introducing a new topic (e.g., 1 Thess. 4:9, 13). Paul clearly intends some kind of distinction here.

As Moo says, the issue becomes the nature of the comparison. The contrast is not between attitudes of surprise and expectation, but between no escape and escape. Paul says that the unbelievers will be surprised by the coming of the Day, and for him or her there is *no* escape (5:3). In 5:4–11 the believer's position to the Day is contrasted. Whereas the unbeliever will not escape, the believer has been appointed to salvation. This ties this verse with 1 Thessalonians 1:10 where the coming of Jesus rescues the believer from the coming wrath. Because of the believer's different position in relation to the Day (note the emphatic use of different pronouns), the believer is to act differently now (5:4–8).[4]

Second Thessalonians 1:5–7 is next cited by Moo as strong support for his position. There is the promise that God will bring vengeance upon those who persecute the Thessalonians and give rest to those oppressed when He is revealed from heaven in blazing fire with His powerful angels. Thus, the rest for these persecuted believers will come at the posttribulational revelation of Christ. Admittedly, this is a difficult passage for the pretribulation position. However, the problem is insoluable only if either of these is true. First, that the revelation of Christ with His powerful angels cannot be at the Rapture. Moo has said that angels are mentioned in connection with the Rapture. Thus, it is not absolutely necessary on the basis either of the mention of ἀποκάλυψις or the powerful angels to immediately assign this passage to the posttribulational return of Christ. Second, that the revelation of Christ cannot be understood as the whole complex of events, beginning with the Rapture and ending with the Second Advent. Ἀποκάλυψις would then refer to various phases of end-time happenings. This association of events is not uncommon in prophetic portions. Moo himself says that the combining of the destruction of unbelievers at the end of the Millennium with the revelation of Christ is no difficulty since Scripture often relates two events separated by a millennium. If this is so, and it is, what prevents a similar association of two events separated by only seven years? The point being made is that in the whole eschatological complex of events, God is both going to bring rest for the Thessalonians and retribution on their persecutors.

There is one final passage in the Thessalonian epistles, 2 Thessalonians 2, that must be discussed. Paul writes to calm the Thessalonians' agitations concerning the Day of the Lord. They thought that it had come. He tells them that two events

227

must occur before the Day of the Lord will come: the apostasy must come and the Man of Lawlessness must be revealed. The point that Moo draws from this for a posttribulational Rapture is this: Had the Thessalonians been taught a pretribulation Rapture in the first epistle, then the most decisive answer that Paul could have given them against their belief that they were in the Day of the Lord would be that the Rapture had not taken place. Yet he does not, leading us to question the truth of a pretribulation Rapture.

I think that this passage is a difficult one for any interpretation. Moo says it is hard to know what gave rise to their problem relating to their belief that they were in the Day of the Lord. Why should they be agitated and unsettled (two very strong words) about being in the Day of the Lord, if the Rapture was to be included in that period of time? One would expect that the Thessalonians should have rejoiced that the Rapture was nearing.

Why did not Paul calm their fears by reminding them that the Rapture had to occur before the Day of the Lord could have begun? There are some pretribulationists who believe that he did. They see in the word ἀποστασία a reference to the Rapture. They take that word to mean a departure. On this point I think that Moo is right in saying that such a translation is unlikely. What about Moo's point? I think that it is fair to say that one could wish that Paul had answered in the way that Moo suggests. It would have settled the matter. However, there is a more pertinent question to ask here. Is Paul's answer a legitimate answer to the problem raised by the Thessalonians? On this count I think that his answer is a good one. The Thessalonians were concerned that they were in the Day of the Lord. Paul responds by telling them that they are not because two important events had not transpired yet. The apostasy had not come, and the Man of Lawlessness had not been revealed. Why Paul did not cite the Rapture as a reason is only speculation. However, it well could be that the Holy Spirit was desirous to give *new* revelation rather than just confirm old revelation.

One last point before I leave the Thessalonian Epistles. It has to do with the restrainer of 2 Thessalonians 2:6, 7. Unlike Moo, I am more confident that the reference is to the Holy Spirit. Whether one thinks that it signifies the emperor, civil government, or any of the other suggestions, ultimately the One in Scripture that restrains evil is the Holy Spirit. However, I am also in agreement with Moo that this text is compatible with either posttribulation or pretribulation views of the Rapture. The passage nowhere requires that the restrainer be removed from the world, only that he cease his restraining ministry so that evil can run its course. That is possible on any Rapture position.

We now must turn to the Olivet Discourse and the Second Coming. There is much in Moo's discussion of this passage that I agree with. However, there are two crucial points at which we disagree. First, Moo thinks that the Olivet Discourse is addressed to the church. His arguments are as follows. The disciples in most contexts in the Gospels stand for Christians of all ages or we would not take the teachings of Jesus as our instruction. Thus, we need some clear *restriction* to narrow the audience. The teaching of Jesus about eschatological events parallels that of Paul. The term "elect" used in the discourse is used consistently throughout the New Testament to refer to members of the church. Finally, the exhortations found in the Olivet Discourse are not unlike others addressed to the church elsewhere in the New Testament.

It seems to me that each of these points is open to question. Must it be true that the disciples stand for Christians of all ages in order to apply Jesus' teaching to our own lives? I do not think so. This claim overlooks the distinction between those addressed and those to whom the teaching may be applied. The disciples may represent the believing remnant in the nation of Israel, and the teaching of Jesus may still have application to us. If this is the case, the church would not be in the Tribulation, and yet the truth of Jesus' teaching would have application to Christians today. Is there any indication that the disciples represent the believing remnant in Israel? I think there is. The topic under discussion is Jewish eschatological expectations. Jesus and the disciples are discussing the destruction of the temple, the abomination of desolation (clearly related to the nation of Israel in Daniel 9 and 11) and

Sabbath restrictions. Thus, I think that a careful examination of the context shows that there is clear restriction of the audience addressed. The parallel that Moo cites between the teachings of Jesus and Paul rests upon the assumption that 1 Thessalonians 4, 5 and 2 Thessalonians 2 speak of the same event. If my arguments hold, that is not true. The fact that there are parallels between 1 Thessalonians 5 and 2 Thessalonians 2 should not be surprising since they speak of the same events; *but* the church is not there. The attempt to relate Matthew 24 and 1 Thessalonians 4 fails as I shall try to argue below. The argument from the New Testament usage of "elect" is misguided. If something happened that was unique on the Day of Pentecost, then the Gospels may bear a closer resemblance to the Old Testament than to the rest of the New Testament. I think Moo's position fails to take account of progress in salvation history. At any rate, those to whom the Olivet Discourse was given would have understood the term "elect" in the context of the Old Testament, not the New Testament, which had not yet been given. Finally, the fact that there should be exhortations directed to the church that are similar to those found in the Olivet Discourse rests simply on the general character of those exhortations and the similarities between the Rapture and the Second Advent.

The second point that Moo makes about the Olivet Discourse that demands comment, is his contention that the Rapture is found in the passage. His reasons for that contention are as follows. 1 Corinthians 15:51–52 and 1 Thessalonians 4:16–17 as well as Matthew 24:31 (cf. Mark 13:27) all mention a great trumpet. The verb ἐπισυνάγω is used in 24:31 and it is found in its noun form (ἐπισυναγωγή) in 2 Thessalonians to refer to the Rapture. These two considerations lead Moo to think that the Rapture is found in Matthew 24:31.

There is also the possibility that there is a reference to the Rapture in Matthew 24:40–41. There is the contrast between the one taken and the one left. The verb "take" is the same one that is found in John 14:3.

Let me comment on these arguments in reverse order. It seems to me that Moo gives us sufficient reasons in his discussion of Matthew 24:40–41 to reject any identification with the Rapture. First, he says that it may be that the one taken goes to judgment and not to the kingdom. This is clear, I think, from the parallel in Luke 17:34–35. Second, he points out that "taken" is used in many ways, and is not a technical term. As a matter of fact, it is quite a common word.

Of the two possibilities, Matthew 24:31 is the formidable one. However, it should not go unnoticed that the identification rests on only two matters. As I have already said, the great trumpet is an eschatological symbol. But it has many uses. There are seven trumpet judgments in the Revelation. There are trumpets that gather the elect. This point of similarity is not a strong one in my judgment.

The other issue revolves around the verb and noun forms of "gather together" that are found in Matthew 24:31 and 2 Thessalonians 2:1. There are, however, only nine occurrences of the word in the New Testament. Of these nine references, only three have eschatological significance: Matthew 24:31; its synoptic parallel, Mark 13:27; and 2 Thessalonians 2:1. The other six uses are quite general. It seems clear that any identification based on this word rests on the slightest of evidence.

Again, let me repeat that in contrast to these few similarities there are many significant differences. Matthew says that the angels gather the elect; 1 Thessalonians says that the Lord Himself does it. Matthew uses the great trumpet to call the elect from the four winds; 1 Thessalonians teaches that it announces the descent of our Lord. Matthew makes no mention of either a resurrection or translation of saints. These are important points in the Rapture passages. In Matthew the gathering appears to be on earth (Matt. 24:31–32), while it is in the air in 1 Thessalonians. First Thessalonians 4 makes no mention of the effects on the sun, moon, and stars, yet this is an important part of Matthew 24. First Thessalonians gives the order of ascent; it is not clear there is any ascent in Matthew 24:31.

While there may be some general similarities, the differences are far greater in both number and importance. Thus, for me at least, I see no mention of the Rapture in the Olivet Discourse. This is quite in keeping with a pretribulation Rapture.

NOTES

Chapter 1

[1]Helpful historical studies on this era are increasing. See George M. Marsden, *Fundamentalism and American Culture. The Shaping of Twentieth-Century Evangelicalism: 1870–1925* (New York: Oxford University Press, 1980); Larry Dean Pettegrew, "The Historical and Theological Contributions of the Niagara Bible Conference to American Fundamentalism" (Th.D. dissertation, Dallas Theological Seminary, 1976); Ernest R. Sandeen, *The Roots of Fundamentalism: British and American Millenarianism 1800–1930* (Chicago: University of Chicago Press, 1970); Timothy P. Weber, *Living in the Shadow of the Second Coming: American Premillennialism, 1875–1925* (New York: Oxford University Press, 1979). Additional material for this essay comes from my own uncompleted manuscript on the Niagara Bible Conference intended for a Ph.D. dissertation at New York University.

[2]Dennis L. Reiter, "Historicism and Futurism in Historic Premillennialism: 1878–1975" (M.A. thesis, Trinity Evangelical Divinity School, 1975). The gratitude I owe my brother Dennis for his help in organizing and evaluating this essay far exceeds mere mention in a note.

[3]Sandeen, *Roots of Fundamentalism,* 276–77.

[4]Nathaniel West, "Introduction," *Premillennial Essays of the Prophetic Conference Held in the Church of the Holy Trinity, New York City, Oct. 30–Nov. 1, 1878,* ed. Nathaniel West (Chicago: Revell, 1879), 8.

[5]Daniel Payton Fuller, "The Hermeneutics of Dispensationalism" (Th.D. dissertation, Northern Baptist Theological Seminary, 1957), 92; C. Norman Kraus, *Dispensationalism in America: Its Rise and Development* (Richmond, Va.: Knox, 1958), 89–91; Sandeen, *Roots of Fundamentalism,* 150–51, 158. Niagara leaders certainly studied Brethren literature, but my evidence accords with the view of Charles Caldwell Ryrie (*Dispensationalism Today* [Chicago: Moody, 1965], 81–82). Ryrie summarizes the distinctives of dispensational theology as (1) a clear distinction between Israel and the church, (2) consistent literal Bible interpretation, and (3) the glory of God worked out in several different ways as the unifying principle of the Bible (ibid., pp. 211-12).

[6]West, "Introduction," 8. The resolutions committee was listed, with Lord at the top, in "The Prophetic Conference at the Church of the Holy Trinity, New York. Closing Session," *The Christian Herald and Signs of Our Times* 13 (January 16, 1879):205, and James H. Brookes, "Prophetic Conference in New York," *The*

Truth 5 (1879): 29-30. The previous year Lord had written *The Blessed Hope: or, The Glorious Coming of the Lord* (Chicago: W. G. Holmes, 1877). For a study of Lord and the generation of historic premillennialists who preceded the Niagara era see Robert Kieran Whalen, "Millenarianism and Millennialism in America, 1790–1880" (Ph.D. dissertation, State University of New York at Stony Brook, 1972).

[7] Stanley N. Gundry, *Love Them In: The Proclamation Theology of D. L. Moody* (Chicago: Moody, 1976), 188.

[8] Charles Hodge, *Systematic Theology,* 3 vols. (New York: Scribner, Armstrong, 1872–1873)2:373–77.

[9] B. B. Leacock, "Any-Moment Theory," *The Episcopal Recorder* 70 (January 12, 1893):1–2.

[10] Adoniram J. Gordon, *Ecce Venit: Behold He Cometh* (New York: Revell, 1889), 29, 33.

[11] Ibid., 23–24, 66; cf. vii, where he says both historicists and futurists hold to imminency.

[12] Samuel H. Kellogg, "Christ's Coming—Is It Premillennial?" in *Premillennial Essays,* 57.

[13] William J. Erdman, *The Parousia of Christ a Period of Time; or, When Will the Church be Translated?* (Chicago: Gospel Publishing House, n.d.), 126. Probably written between 1886 and 1895.

[14] Reiter, "Historicism and Futurism," 124–26.

[15] *Scriptural Truth About the Lord's Return* (New York: Revell, 1922), 146. But the date of 1884 given by Cameron on p. 145 is in error. Fuller and Sandeen missed this fact, but they were corrected by Pettegrew, "Niagara Bible Conference," 176. Pettegrew then erred himself by saying West was already a posttribulationist by 1880, as shown by *The Thousand Years.* But Cameron's earlier recollection, which placed the time of West's change to posttribulationism between 1880 and 1883, is preferred for several reasons. See [Robert Cameron], " 'Three Mighty Men,' " *Watchword and Truth* 36 (April 1914):104.

[16] A congregational dispute happened in 1886 and 1887 when West was a pastor in St. Paul, Minnesota, and is found in the Presbytery and Synod records for that region. See also a letter from Samuel Huston Thompson to Woodrow Wilson, February 7, 1910 (*The Papers of Woodrow Wilson,* ed. by Arthur S. Link [Princeton: Princeton University Press, 1975] 20:84), and a later postmillennial assessment of West's polemical attitude in James H. Snowdon, *The Coming of the Lord; Will It Be Premillennial?* 2nd ed., rev. (New York: Macmillan, 1919), 11-12, 186, 212, 225-26, 253, 256.

[17] (Chicago: Fleming H. Revell, 1889; reprint ed., Fincastle, Va.: Scripture Truth, n.d.). In a foreword to the reprint edition, Wilbur M. Smith evaluated this as "a very difficult work to read, and at the same time, in many ways, the most learned work on this aspect of Biblical prophecy ever to appear in the English language, i.e., on the subject of the Millennium and the symbolic significance of Biblical numbers" (viii). Many bibliographies have erred in giving the date as 1880, perhaps because of a broken font in the verso of the title page, which made it easy to misread the "9" as "0" in the copyright notice. But 1889 is clearly printed at the end of the author's preface on page xvi and in the text dates between 1880 and 1889 appear on pages 146n, 169n, 173n, 192, 268n, 382n, 395n, 444n, 445n, 446n twice, and 447n.

[18] Ibid., 1–34, 39–47. I differ with H. Philip Hook ("The Doctrine of the Kingdom in Covenant Premillennialism" [Th.D. dissertation, Dallas Theological Seminary, 1959], 10, 52, 54, 64–65, 81, 85, 146, 194–95, 200, 203–4, 222, 226–28) who called West a covenant premillenarian. On *Heilsgeschichte* see Ronald B. Allen,

"The Theology of the Balaam Oracles," in *Tradition and Testament: Essays in Honor of Charles Lee Feinberg,* ed. John S. Feinberg and Paul D. Feinberg (Chicago: Moody, 1981), 83–105, especially 111, n. 9; 116, n. 40; and 117, n. 56.

[19][T. B. Ashton], "Encouraging," a letter to *Watchword and Truth* 36 (October 1914):279. West taught at Moody sometime between the summer of 1889 and November 1891, according to R. A. Torrey, "Home Life," *The Institute Tie* 1 (December 8, 1891):19. Thomas Bert Ashton attended Moody from January 1891 to February 1892 according to the Records Office, Moody Bible Institute, Chicago, Illinois.

[20]Biblical theology was the focus in "Jesus Christ on the 'Any-Moment' Theory," *The Episcopal Recorder* 71 (June 29, 1893):1–3; and "The Apostle Paul and the 'Any-Moment' Theory," ibid., 71 (March 30, 1893):4, 10; and (May 4, 1893):2–3, 14–15; reprint ed. *The Apostle Paul and the "Any-Moment" Theory* (Philadelphia: James M. Armstrong, 1893). Historical theology ranged from "Professor J. C. K. von Hofmann on the 'Any-Moment' Theory," ibid., 71 (February 2, 1893):3–4 to "Cyrill of Jerusalem on the 'Any-Moment' Theory," ibid., 71 (February 9, 1893):1–2. For all concerned a theory was an intellectual scheme (with the negative connotations of scheme) or pattern into which the Scriptures were forced to fit. In the thinking of the Bible conference teachers it was contrasted with the common-sense meaning of the Word of God, so it was always a label used of one's opponents in debate. For the pervasive influence of common-sense philosophy, see Marsden, *Fundamentalism and American Culture,* 55–62, 212–21.

[21]*The Apostle Paul and the 'Any-Moment' Theory,* 24; cf. 3, 12, 22–27.

[22]Ibid., 14; cf. 12, 22–24.

[23]Ibid., 26–27; cf. 28–31.

[24]Ibid., 9.

[25]Ibid., 31.

[26]"Who Shall Be Caught Up," *The Truth* 20 (April 1894):204–7. There is no question mark at the end of the article's title. West replied directly in "The Church and the Tribulation," *The Episcopal Recorder* 72 (May 10, 1894):2–3.

[27]*The Truth* 21 (1895):45–51, 93–101, 148–54, 206–13, 275–81, 338–41.

[28]Ibid., 45.

[29]Ibid., 46–48, 94–96, 209–10, 339.

[30]Ibid., 280; cf. 275–77.

[31]Ibid., 207–13, 277–81.

[32]Ibid., 93–94, 150–51.

[33]Ibid., 340.

[34]Ibid., 47–50.

[35]["Note"], *The Watchword* 10 (June 1888):73.

[36]"The Parousia," *Our Hope* 2 (March and April 1896):213; cited from *Ecce Venit,* 211; cf. 246.

[37]*Maranatha; or, Behold He Cometh* (New York: Revell, 1889 reprint of 1870 ed.), 18–19.

[38]"Important Notice," *The Truth* 21 (October 1895):463.

[39]Gundry, *Love Them In,* 189–93, 220; D. L. Moody, "Letter," *Prophetic Studies of the International Prophetic Conference, Chicago, November, 1886,* ed. by George C. Needham (Chicago: Revell, 1886), 41.

[40]"When Did the Stone Strike? Dan. ii. 34, 35," *The Truth* 21 (1895):175–76. Cf. Lord, *The Blessed Hope,* 89–90.

[41]"Discrediting the Second Advent," *The Truth* 21 (1895):166–71; ibid., *The Watchword* 17 (June 1895):72–75.

[42]"The Turkish Crisis," *Our Hope* 2 (March and April 1896):223–27.

[43]"Our Lord's Second Coming, A Motive to World-Wide Evangelism," in

Prophetic Studies . . . 1886, 27; "The Coming of the Lord—the Practical Center of the Bible," *Addresses in the Second Coming of the Lord Delivered at the Prophetic Conference, Allegheny, Pa., December 3–6, 1895,* ed. by Joseph Kyle and William S. Miller (Pittsburgh: W. W. Waters, n.d.), 104.

[44]"The Final Issue of the Age," *Prophetic Conference . . . 1895,* 15–25. For Moorehead's covenant premillennialism see H. Philip Hook, "Covenant Premillennialism," 79–81; and W. G. Moorehead, "The Two Covenants," *The Truth* 10 (1883):440–44.

[45]W. J. Erdman, "The Oral Teaching of St. Paul at Thessalonica," *Our Hope* 5 (July 1898):19; [Arno C. Gaebelein], " 'Our Blessed Hope,' " *Our Hope* 5 (November 1889):158–60.

[46]*Half a Century: The Autobiography of a Servant* (New York: Publication Office "Our Hope," 1930), 153–63; quote from p. 154. By contrast Gaebelein refused to even name Cameron, characterizing him as "a certain preacher, one of the bitter opponents of the imminent coming of the Lord," in *The History of the Scofield Reference Bible* (New York: Publications Office "Our Hope," 1943), 42.

[47]Nathaniel West, *Daniel's Great Prophecy. The Eastern Question. The Kingdom* (New York: Hope of Israel Movement, 1898). This book was based on West's series "Daniel's Great Prophecy," published monthly in *Our Hope* from March through December 1897.

[48]"The Niagara Conference," *Our Hope* 1 (August 1894):43–44; quote from p. 44.

[49]*Half a Century,* 75–85.

[50]Sandeen, *Roots of Fundamentalism,* 212–13. Also "imminent" was not in the resolutions of the 1901 conference, where Erdman noted "the spirit of charity and unity" prevailed and Cameron published the *Addresses of the International Prophetic Conference Held December 10–15, 1901 in the Clarendon Street Baptist Church, Boston, Mass.* (Boston: Watchword & Truth, n.d.). The resolutions were on page 7, Erdman's remark on page 5.

[51]Sandeen, *Roots of Fundamentalism,* 217–19. Cameron said he traced this important but apparently erroneous view back to S. P. Tregelles, whose account was also accepted by George Eldon Ladd (*The Blessed Hope* [Grand Rapids: Eerdmans, 1956], 40–41). On the pretribulationist side John F. Walvoord called Ladd's reference to Tregelles' account "unfair" ("A Review of *The Blessed Hope* by George Eldon Ladd," *Bibliotheca Sacra,* 113 [October 1956]:293). Later Dave MacPherson argued the pretribulation view developed from statements by Margaret Macdonald, a young girl from Scotland. See *The Unbelievable Pre-Trib Origin* (Kansas City, Mo.: Heart of America Bible Society, 1973), *The Incredible Cover-Up: The True Story on the Pre-Trib Rapture* (rev. and updated ed., Plainfield, N. J.: Logos International, 1975), and *The Great Rapture Hoax* (Fletcher, N.C.: New Puritan Library, 1983). McPherson's evidence led C. S. Lovett to reexamine the issue and change from pretribulationism to posttribulationism ("Time to Settle the Rapture Question!" *Personal Christianity* 21 [September 1981]:1–5). By contrast Brethren scholar F. F. Bruce ("Review of *The Unbelievable Pre-Trib Origin* by Dave McPherson," *The Evangelical Quarterly* 47 [January–March 1975]:58) and historian Ian S. Rennie ("Nineteenth Century Roots," in *Dreams, Visions, and Oracles: The Layman's Guide to Biblical Prophecy* ed. Carl E. Armerding and W. Ward Gasque [Grand Rapids: Baker, 1977], 51–52) regarded McPherson's case as interesting but not conclusive. Bruce's view, which apparently was not changed by McPherson's work, was sketched in *Answers to Questions* (Exeter: Paternoster, 1972), 199,200. More extended reply to MacPherson's was by John F. Walvoord (*The Blessed Hope and the Tribulation* [Grand Rapids: Zondervan, 1976], 42–48).

[52]Gaebelein, *History of the Scofield Reference Bible,* 44.

[53]"Editorial Notes," *Our Hope* 7 (May 1901):381–82 (first quote); "Editorial Notes," *Our Hope* 7 (July 1900):1 (second quote). Similar remarks to the second quote were the climax of Gaebelein's initial Sea Cliff address ("Sea Cliff Bible Conference Addresses," *Our Hope* 8 [September 1901]:96). This was the result of Gaebelein's "new commission" . . . to disseminate especially prophetic truths" which came early in 1899 (*Half a Century,* 81. Cf. 75–85). The third quote is from "The Post-Tribulation Theory," *Our Hope* 7 (February 1901):262. Erdman was speaking at a number of spiritual life conferences of the Keswick type that minimized eschatological issues.

[54]Norman F. Douty, *The Great Tribulation Debate: Has Christ's Return Two Stages?* (Harrison, Ark.: Gibbs Press, 1978), 8–9; *Scofield Reference Bible,* ed. C. I. Scofield (New York: Oxford University Press, 1909), title page, p. [iv]; Ladd, *The Blessed Hope,* 44, 48–52.

[55]Douty, Ibid., 9. The source is otherwise undocumented, but the author knew Scofield personally.

[56]J. Barton Payne, *The Imminent Appearing of Christ* (Grand Rapids: Eerdmans, 1962), 34–35.

[57]Ian S. Rennie, "Nineteenth Century Roots," 59.

[58](London: Marshall, Morgan & Scott, 1937; reprint ed. Grand Rapids: Grand Rapids International Publications, 1975), xii, xv, xvi, 113–15, 130, 146, 228–29, 239, 243–44, 266–74. Gerald B. Stanton regarded Reese "as the leading spokesman for the posttribulational cause" because his work was "no doubt the most voluminous and important posttribulational work to date" (*Kept From the Hour: A Systematic Study of the Rapture in Biblical Prophecy* (Grand Rapids: Zondervan, 1956), 23.

[59]Sandeen, *Roots of Fundamentalism,* 216, 221; R. A. Torrey, "Montrose (Pa.) Bible Conference," *The Institute Tie* 11 (October 1908):149–50; W. J. Erdman, "An Analysis of the Apocalypse," *The Christian Worker's Magazine* 13 (August 1908):767–68. Fuller ("Hermeneutics of Dispensationalism," 117–18) showed how Scofield adapted Erdman's outline for his notes on the Book of the Revelation, changing it from a posttribulation to a pretribulation view.

[60][Robert Cameron], "Another Witness," *Watchword & Truth* 35 (January 1913):2.

[61]"Dr. Erdman's Queries," *The Truth* 21 (1895):300; "The New Hope," *Serving & Waiting* 3 (January 1914):310.

[62]Robert Cameron, "Notes by the Way," *Watchword & Truth* 35 (December 1913):337. In *Fundamentalism and American Culture* Marsden showed that premillenarians engaged in heated controversy with holiness advocates (pp. 94-95, 99-101) and liberal social gospel promoters (p. 91-93, 104-8, 116-23) during this era.

[63]Edward Payson Vining, "Notes by the Way," *Watchword & Truth* 35 (February 1913):35; cf. 34.

[64]"Notes by the Way," *Watchword & Truth* 37 (January 1915):1.

[65]*The Fundamentals: A Testimony to the Truth* 11 (1915?):95; cf. 96–99.

[66]W. B. Riley, "When Will the Lord Come?" in *Christ and Glory,* ed. by Arno C. Gaebelein (New York: Publication Office "Our Hope," 1918), 239; Charles Gallaudet Trumbull and others, "How I Became a Premillennialist: Symposium," in *The Coming and Kingdom of Christ* (Chicago: Bible Institute Colportage Association, 1914), 65–79.

[67]*Watchword & Truth,* passim from 1912 to 1922.

[68]C. L. Heskett, "The Coming of the Lord As In the Thessalonian Epistles," *Watchword & Truth* 38 (December 1916):301–2.

NOTES

[69][Robert Cameron], "Our Critics," *Watchword & Truth* 37 (June–July 1915): 163.

[70]"The C.I.M. in North America," ibid. (August 1915):202; Robert Cameron, "Our Editorial Combination," ibid. (October 1915):270–71, quote from p. 271.

[71]M. A. Matthews, "Christ's Second Coming the Hope of the World," ibid., 38 (March 1916):74–77; quote from M. A. Matthews, "The Church Vs. the Tribulation" *Watchword & Truth* 39 (June 1917):438.

[72]Dwight Wilson, *Armageddon Now! The Premillenarian Response to Russia and Israel Since 1917* (Grand Rapids: Baker, 1977), passim.

[73]Robert Cameron, "Notes by the Way," *Watchword & Truth* 40 (January 1918):8.

[74]Daniel P. Fuller, *Give the Winds a Mighty Voice. The Story of Charles E. Fuller* (Waco: Word, 1972), 64.

[75]William Dryness, "The Age of Aquarius," in *Dreams, Visions, and Oracles,* 16–17; Bernard Ramm, *The Devil, Seven Wormwoods, and God* (Waco: Word, 1977), 120–21 in the context of 105–24; Wilson, *Armageddon Now!* 215–18.

[76]Charles R. Erdman, "The Coming of Christ," 98–99; Weber, *Living in the Shadow,* 65–81; Edwin L. Frizen, Jr., "An Historical Study of the Interdenominational Foreign Mission Association in Relation to Evangelical Unity and Cooperation" (D.Miss. dissertation, Trinity Evangelical Divinity School, 1981), 3–4, 74, 250 quoting the IFMA Confession of Faith. Henry W. Frost elaborated his posttribulationist dispensationalism in *Matthew 24 and the Revelation* (New York: Oxford, 1924) and *The Second Coming of Christ* (Grand Rapids: Eerdmans, 1934). Roland Victor Bingham explained his change of conviction from pretribulationism to posttribulationism in *Matthew the Publican and His Gospel* (Toronto: Evangelical Publishers, n.d.). As a young man Bingham "became infatuated with prophetic study. Had I been warned against systems of prophetic interpretation and directed to the text of Scripture itself, I should have been saved much" (p. 11). This comment is typical of many who change views on eschatology. The word *system* is used similarly in *theory* in note 20.

[77]Frank L. Chapell, "The Holy Spirit in Relation to Our Lord's Return," in *Prophetic Studies . . . 1886,* 24; I. M. Haldeman, *The Coming of Christ Both Premillennial and Imminent* (New York: Charles C. Cook, 1906); Albert Lindsay, "The Two Phases of Christ's Return, the *Parousia* and the *Epiphany,*" in *The Sure Word of Prophecy,* ed. John W. Bradbury (New York: Revell [1942], 268–72; W. H. Rogers, "The Second Coming of Christ," in *Prophetic Messages for Modern Times by Speakers at the Colonial Hills Bible Conference Conducted in the Colonial Hills Baptist Church, Atlanta, Georgia: March 19–26, 1944,* ed. Robert J. Wells (Dallas: Texas Printing, n.d.), 106, cf. 107. Ironically Charles L. Feinberg, who led pretribulationist interpreters to discard this view, also spoke at the Colonial Hills Bible Conference.

[78]Charles Feinberg, *Premillennialism or Amillennialism?* (Grand Rapids: Zondervan, 1936), 205–8; John F. Walvoord, "New Testament Words for the Lord's Coming" *Bibliotheca Sacra* 101 (July–September 1944):283–89; Keith L. Brooks, popular Bible teacher and former editor of *The King's Business* magazine, sensed the turning from the distinction based on the use of terms: "We are fully aware of the discussion that has been going on over the Greek words '*parousia*' (personal presence) and '*apokalupsis*' (unveiling or revelation). Perhaps some excellent teachers have been mistaken in saying that the '*parousia*' always indicates the moment when He comes for His saints and that '*apokalupsis*' is used only for the moment when He comes in power and authority" (Appendix, *The Rapture: Our Lord's Coming for His Church* [Los Angeles: American Prophetic League, 1940], 35).

[79]George C. and Elizabeth A. Needham, *Looking Forward: 1—Will Jesus Come? 2—After the Advent. 3—The New Earth* (3 vols in 1., Narbeth [Philadelphia], Pa.: Albert W. Needham, n.d.) 1:62.

[80]Clarence E. Mason, "The Day of Our Lord Jesus Christ," *Bibliotheca Sacra* 125 (October–December 1968):359.

[81]Norman F. Harrison, *The End: Rethinking the Revelation* (Minneapolis: The Harrison Service, 1941) as cited in Millard J. Erickson, *Contemporary Options in Eschatology. A Study of the Millennium* (Grand Rapids: Baker Book House, 1977), 168. Two noted pretribulationist authors, Herman A. Hoyt (*The End Times* [Chicago: Moody, 1969], 82–83) and John F. Walvoord (*The Rapture Question* [Findlay, Ohio: Dunham, 1957], 171–72) admit Harrison would prefer to be regarded as a pretribulationist; they term him a midtribulationist.

[82]*New Light on the Rapture* (New York: Bible Light, 1980), 8.

[83]E. Schuyler English, "Re-Thinking the Rapture," *Our Hope* 56 (May 1950):650–66, followed by replies of others in "Let the Prophets Speak . . . ," *Our Hope* 56 (July 1950):717–32 and many "Letters" in *Our Hope* 57 (July 1950 through March 1951), passim. The book form was *Re-Thinking the Rapture* (Traveler's Rest, S. C.: Southern Bible, 1951).

[84]Allan A. MacRae, "New Light on the Second Chapter of Second Thessalonians," *The Bible Today* 43 (April 1950):201–10; Kenneth S. Wuest, "The Rapture—Precisely When?" *Bibliotheca Sacra* 114 (January 1957):64–67. Note that MacRae's article actually preceded English's in print, for it was a reply to a letter received from English.

[85]J. S. Mabie, "Will the Church Be in the Tribulation—The Great One?" *Morning Star* 5 (November 1898):123–24. Other Evangelicals who have adopted or defended this interpretation more recently are some faculty of the Grand Rapids Baptist College and Seminary in Leon J. Wood, *Is the Rapture Next?* (Grand Rapids: Zondervan, 1956), 64; Gordon R. Lewis of Conservative Baptist Theological Seminary, Denver, in "Biblical Evidence for Pretribulationism," *Bibliotheca Sacra* 125 (July–September 1968):217–19; and James Montgomery Boice of Philadelphia in *The Last and Future World* (Grand Rapids: Zondervan: 1974), 42–43.

[86]Paul J. Oskarson, "A History of the Doctrinal Emphasis of the Evangelical Free Church of America from 1930 to 1950" (B.D. thesis, Trinity Theological Seminary, 1956), 62 (quoted), 73–74. The Evangelical Free Church of America seems typical of many small North American evangelical denominations in its concern for premillennial doctrine. It is used here because of (1) recent focus on the Rapture issue, (2) professors at its seminary wrote the other essays in this book, and (3) its historical materials document the issue quite well.

[87]Norman F. Douty, *The Great Tribulation Debate. Has Christ's Return Two Stages?* (rev. ed., Harrison, Ark.: Gibbs, 1976), 134. It was formerly titled *Has Christ's Return Two Stages?* (1956).

[88]Ibid., 135–37. For similar sentiments calling for moderation see Ladd, *The Blessed Hope*, 13–14, 58–60, 160–61; Payne, *The Imminent Appearing of Christ*, 1962), 168–69; Ryrie, *Dispensationalism Today*, 1965, 206–12.

[89]Wilbur M. Smith, "Preface" to *Crucial Questions About the Kingdom of God* (Grand Rapids: Eerdmans, 1952), 10–12.

[90]George Eldon Ladd, *Crucial Questions,* 138–41; cf. 97.

[91]*The Greatness of the Kingdom* (Grand Rapids: Zondervan, 1959).

[92]*The Basis of the Premillennial Faith* (New York: Loizeaux, 1953), 70, 144 quoted; cf. 69.

[93]Ibid., 11, 139.

[94]Walvoord, *The Rapture Question,* 50.

[95]Ibid., 148; cf. Ladd, *The Blessed Hope*, 88, 165–67.

[96]Walvoord, *The Rapture Question* (rev. ed., Findlay, Ohio: Dunham, 1957), 148. No revision was indicated by publisher.

[97]Ladd, *The Blessed Hope*, 103–4 and 164–65 quoted.

[98]Walvoord, *The Rapture Question*, 55.

[99]*Kept From the Hour: A Systematic Study of the Rapture in Bible Prophecy* (Grand Rapids: Zondervan, 1957), 4, 30–32, 43 quoted.

[100]J. D. Pentecost, "Review of *Kept From the Hour* by Gerald B. Stanton," *Bibliotheca Sacra* 114 (July 1957):265.

[101]Richard Martin Walston, "A Survey of the Contemporary Views of the Evangelical Free Church of America on the Second Coming of Christ and the Accompanying Events" (B.D. thesis, Trinity Theological Seminary, 1958), 91–94.

[102]Payne, *Imminent Appearing*, 105.

[103]Ibid., 39–40, 157–59, quote from 42.

[104]*Encyclopedia of Biblical Prophecy: The Complete Guide to Scriptural Predictions and Their Fulfillment* (New York: Harper & Row, 1973).

[105]J. Oliver Buswell, Jr., *A Systematic Theology of the Christian Religion*, 2 vols. (Grand Rapids: Zondervan, 1962–63) 2:390, 458–59.

[106]Ryrie, *Dispensationalism Today*, 158–61, quote from 159–60.

[107]Robert H. Gundry, *The Church and the Tribulation* (Grand Rapids: Zondervan, 1973). 9–10 quoted, 29 quoted.

[108]Ibid., 37 quoted.

[109]John A. Sproule, *In Defense of Pretribulationism* (rev. ed., Winona Lake, Ind.: BMH Books, 1980), 10. At the present time Sproule's 1981 Th.D. dissertation, "An Exegetical Defense of Pretribulationism," is awaiting publication. I am pleased Sproule corresponded with Gundry following the first printing of his critical review. The revised edition showed some changes in both content and tone. Compare 6–7, 1974 ed., with 12–13, 1980 ed.; and 12, 1974 ed., with 16, 1980 ed. This interaction clarified Sproule's thought and corrected misunderstandings in several places (p. 8). Perhaps it would behoove more authors engaged in such criticism to follow suit; I think the process strengthened Sproule's work.

[110]Ibid., 43, 47, 52 quoted.

[111]*The Blessed Hope and the Tribulation*, 7–9, quote from 9.

[112]Ibid., 151–58.

[113]Ibid., 166–67, quote from 166. The four pretribulational premises outlined on pp. 159–60 do not seem to be exclusive to pretribulationists (as Walvoord believes) if one considers such scholars mentioned in this essay as Robert Cameron, W. J. Erdman, Henry W. Frost, and Nathaniel West. The premises are probably what Walvoord means when he says, "Pretribulationism . . . is actually the key to an eschatological system." Granted this is his meaning, it would have helped if he had constructed the material quoted so that it did not appear to be circular reasoning.

[114]I recall that Richard Carlson asked the question. The replies were by Paul Feinberg, Gleason Archer, and Douglas Moo in a panel discussion on January 12, 1981, titled "Tribulation: pre-, mid-, or post-?" (Rolfing Memorial Library tape C-754, Trinity Evangelical Divinity School, Deerfield, Illinois). Cf. Allen Beechick, *The Pretribulation Rapture* (Denver: Accent, 1981): 253.

[115]Andrew E. Johnson, *Our Blessed Hope* (Vernon Hills, Ill.: by the author, 1980). As a Trinity board member in 1963, Johnson objected to recruiting seminary faculty who did not interpret EFCA doctrinal statement "in terms of a Pre-tribulational Rapture" (Calvin B. Hanson, *The Trinity Story*, Heritage Series No. 6. [Minneapolis: Free Church Press, 1983], 108).

[116]Arnold T. Olson, "A Perspective From the Retiring President's Viewpoint,"

The *Evangelical Beacon* 50 (October 12, 1976):10; Arnold Theodore Olson, *The Significance of Silence,* Heritage Series No. 2 (Minneapolis: Free Church Press, 1981), 201.

[117]Arnold T. Olson, *This We Believe* (Minneapolis: Free Church Press, 1961), 328.

[118]Payne, *Imminent Appearing*; a short popular presentation was J. Barton Payne, "Jesus is Coming Again: Pasttribulationism," in *When is Jesus Coming Again?* (Wheaton, Ill.: Creation House, 1974).

[119]Edward Kersten, "Ethical Problem?" a letter to *The Evangelical Beacon* 54 (March 15, 1981):19.

[120]Cf. notes 101, 115 above; Hanson, *The Trinity Story,* 108-9.

[121]David J. Hesselgrave, "A Subtle Shift?" a letter to *The Evangelical Beacon* 54 (March 15, 1981):19. Limited space prevented me from elaborating on missions and other practical concerns related to the time of the Rapture. Ample material exists for extended historical study of this area.

[122]Scofield, "Dr. Erdman's Queries," 300; Ladd, *The Blessed Hope,* 146-52. The irony of these accusations within premillennialism is evident to those aware of the 1878 prophetic conference. By spontaneous standing vote the attenders resolved "that the doctrine of our Lord's pre-millennial advent, instead of paralyzing evangelistic and missionary effort [as the postmillennialists contended] is one of the mightiest incentives to earnestness in preaching the Gospel to every creature, until He comes" (West, "Introduction," 9). In this essay I have concentrated on the behavior of premillennialists, not their motivations.

[123]Olson, *The Significance of Silence,* 13-18, 201-2. According to EFCA president Thomas A. McDill, in a conversation with me on June 11, 1982, within the past five years the EFCA Committee on Ministerial Standing issued a letter advising ordination committees to allow candidates for ordination latitude of meaning regarding the term *imminent* in the statement of faith. This recognizes the diversity of views Free Church ministers have held on eschatology, as shown by Walston, "A Survey . . . on the Second Coming," 91-94.

[124]Rennie, "Nineteenth Century Roots," 59.

[125]Robert D. Culver, "The Difficulty of Interpreting Old Testament Prophecy," *Bibliotheca Sacra* 114 (July 1957):205.

Chapter 2

[1]For example see J. D. Pentecost, *Things to Come* (Findlay, Ohio: Dunham, 1958), 164, or John F. Walvoord, *The Rapture Question* (Findlay, Ohio: Dunham, 1957), 15ff.

[2]George A. Ladd, *The Blessed Hope* (Grand Rapids: Eerdmans, 1956), 130-36.

[3]Robert H. Gundry, *The Church and the Tribulation* (Grand Rapids: Zondervan, 1973), 27-28.

[4]See Millard J. Erickson, *Contemporary Options in Eschatology: A Study of the Millennium* (Grand Rapids: Baker, 1977), 125.

[5]For a defense of the futurist interpretation of Daniel's seventieth week see my chapter "An Exegetical and Theological Study of Daniel 9:24-27," in *Tradition and Testament: Essays in Honor of Charles L. Feinberg,* ed. John S. and Paul D. Feinberg (Chicago: Mood, 1982), 189-220.

[6]J. Barton Payne, "Jesus is Coming Again: Pasttribulation," in *When Is Jesus*

Coming Again? Hal Lindsey and others (Carol Stream, Ill.: Creation House, 1974), 72–73.

[7]Ladd, *The Blessed Hope*, 120.

[8]Gundry, *The Church*, 97.

[9]J. Oliver Buswell, Jr., *A Systematic Theology of the Christian Religion* (Grand Rapids: Zondervan, 1962), 2:389.

[10]Walvoord, *Rapture Question*, 69.

[11]Leon J. Wood, *Is the Rapture Next?* (Grand Rapids: Zondervan, 1956), 20.

[12]Gundry, *The Church*, 44–45.

[13]H. C. Hahn, "Anger," in *The New International Dictionary of New Testament Theology*, ed., Colin Brown (Grand Rapids: Zondervan, 1975), 1:110.

[14]G. Kittel and G. Friedrich, eds., *Theological Dictionary of the New Testament*, 10 vols. (Grand Rapids: Eerdmans, 1970), 5:430, s.v. "ὀργή."

[15]Zane C. Hodges, "The Rapture in 1 Thessalonians 5:1–11," in *Walvoord: A Tribute*, ed. Donald K. Campbell (Chicago: Moody, 1982), 68–70. The wrath spoken of in 1 Thessalonians is eschatological, particularly concerned with the Day of the Lord.

[16]Ibid., p. 70. See also Robert L. Thomas, "1 Thessalonians" in *The Expositor's Bible Commentary*, Frank E. Gaebelein, ed. (Grand Rapids: Zondervan, 1978), 11:280–81.

[17]Hodges, "The Rapture," 70–74.

[18]Ibid., 74–78.

[19]Payne, *Jesus Is Coming*, 70–22. Payne's rejection of futurist views of the Olivet Discourse and Revelation make his position a minority view.

[20]Ladd, *The Blessed Hope*, 84–85.

[21]Gundry, *The Church*, 46.

[22]Ibid., 47, 51.

[23]Ibid., 76–77.

[24]Ibid., 46–47.

[25]Ibid., chap 6.

[26]Ibid., 63.

[27]Ibid., 47.

[28]Buswell, *A Systematic Theology*, 2:388–89.

[29]Ibid., 389.

[30]See Walvoord, *Rapture Question*, chaps. 3, 5; Wood, chap. 1; Pentecost, chap. 13; Charles L. Feinberg, *Millennialism: The Two Major Views* (Chicago: Moody, 1980), chaps. 10, 17.

[31]Nigel Turner, in *A Grammar of New Testament Greek* (Edinburgh: T. & T. Clark, 1963), 3:72; or Maximillian Zerwick, *Biblical Greek* (Rome: Scripta Pontificii Instituti Biblici, 1963), 82–83.

[32]Turner, *A Grammar*, 71–72; or Zerwick, *Biblical Greek*, 81–82.

[33]Zerwick, *Biblical Greek*, 84–85.

[34]Gundry, *The Church*, 76.

[35]Alva J. McClain, *The Greatness of the Kingdom* (Grand Rapids: Zondervan, 1959), 465.

[36]Pentecost, *Things to Come*, 230–31; or Charles C. Ryrie, *The Bible and Tomorrow's News* (Wheaton: Victor, 1969), 143.

[37]Gundry, *The Church*, 89–93, 95.

[38]Ibid., 94–95.

[39]A number of posttribulationists do in fact argue this: Ladd, *The Blessed Hope*, 84–85, 120; or Gundry, 50–52.

[40]Jeffery L. Townsend, "The Rapture in Revelation 3:10," *Bibliotheca Sacra* 137:252–66.

[41]Gundry, *The Church,* 54.

[42]Townsend, "The Rapture," 253.

[43]Turner, *A Grammar;* or Zerwick, *Biblical Greek.*

[44]Alexander Reese, *The Approaching Advent of Christ: An Examination of the Teaching of J. N. Darby and His Followers* (London: Marshall, Morgan, & Scott, 1937), 205.

[45]Gundry, *The Church,* 59.

[46]Townsend, "The Rapture," 254.

[47]Henry George Liddell and Robert Scott, *An Intermediate Greek-English Lexicon* (Oxford: Clarendon Press, 1968), 498–99. The example is from *The Iliad* 2.14.130. Two other examples are "out of the smoke," Homer *The Odyssey* 2.19.7; and "stood aside," Herodotus 2.3.83.

[48]Gundry, *The Church,* 59.

[49]Townsend, "The Rapture," 254.

[50]Compare also Ps. 12:8 (LXX, 11:7). Here διατηρέω is used with ἀπό. Thus, even in the LXX ἐκ is capable of the idea of separation usual in ἀπό. See also these uses of ἐκ with ἐκκλίνω in Prov. 1:5 and with ἀνέχω in Amos 4:7.

[51]Townsend, "The Rapture," 254–55.

[52]See Josephus, *Jewish Antiquities* 4.2.1. and ῥύομαι ἐκ in 12.10.5 and 13.6.3.

[53]Townsend, "The Rapture," 255.

[54]A. T. Robertson, *A Grammar of the Greek New Testament in the Light of Historical Research,* 4th ed. (New York: Doran, 1923), 598.

[55]J. B. Smith, *A Revelation of Jesus Christ: A Commentary on the Book of Revelation,* ed J. Otis Yoder (Scottdale, Pa.: Herald Press, 1961), 331–33. This is one of the best treatments of the Revelation from a pretribulation perspective. The appendices are excellent.

[56]Townsend, "The Rapture," 256–57.

[57]Ibid., 257.

[58]Kittel and Friedrich, eds., *Theological Dictionary of the New Testament,* 8:142, s. v. "τηρέω." by Harald Riesenfeld, 8:142.

[59]In my judgment some have not done this, and have conflated the ideas in the two petitions and consequently the two uses of the preposition (cf. Ladd, *The Blessed Hope,* 85).

[60]Townsend, "The Rapture," 258.

[61]The Greek τοῦ πονηροῦ may be either masculine or neuter; it is most likely masculine and a reference to Satan. This is characteristic of John (e.g., John 12:31; 14:30; 16:11; 1 John 2:13–14; 3:12; 5:18–19).

[62]Many examples could be cited. Two are Walvoord, *Rapture Question,* p. 70; and Charles C. Ryrie, "*The Church and the Tribulation*: A Review" *Bibliotheca Sacra* 131:173–79.

[63]Townsend, "The Rapture," p. 258.

[64]Ibid.

[65]Ibid.

[66]Ibid., 259.

[67]Ibid.

[68]Ibid.

[69]Henry C. Thiessen, "Will the Church Pass Through the Tribulation?" *Bibliotheca Sacra* 92:45–50.

[70]Charles C. Ryrie, *A Survey of Bible Doctrine* (Chicago: Moody, 1972), 170.

[71]Gundry, *"The Church,"* 60.

[72]Townsend, "The Rapture," 261. See also George Johnston, "οἰκουμένη and κόσμος in the NT" *New Testament Studies* 10:352–60.

[73]Gundry, 60.

[74]Kittel and Friedrich eds., *Theological Dictionary of the New Testament,* 9:677, s. v. "ὥρα."

[75]Gundry, *The Church,* 60.

[76]Townsend, "The Rapture," 260–61.

[77]Kittel and Friedrich, eds., *Theological Dictionary of the New Testament,* 6:23, s. v. "πεῖρα, κ.τ.λ."

[78]Schuyler Brown, " 'The Hour of Trial' (Rev. 3:10)," *JBL* 85:309.

[79]R. H. Charles, *Revelation,* in the *International Critical Commentary* 7:289.

[80]Townsend, "The Rapture," 261–62.

[81]Walvoord, *Rapture Question,* 92–95; Walvoord, *Blessed Hope,* 53; or Allen Beechick, *The Pretribulation Rapture* (Denver: Accent Books, 1980), 39–57.

[82]William E. Bell, *A Critical Evaluation of the Pretribulation Rapture Doctrine in Christian Eschatology* (Ph. D. dissertation, NYU, 1967), 247–48. See also E. Michael Rusten, *A Critical Evaluation of Dispensational Interpretations of the Book of Revelation* (Ann Arbor, Mich.: University Microfilms International, 1977), 2 vols.

[83]Gundry, *The Church,* 82.

[84]Beechick, *The Pretribulation Rapture,* 48–55.

[85]Charles C. Ryrie, *What You Should Know about the Rapture* (Chicago: Moody Press, 1981), 80–81.

[86]Bell, *A Critical Evaluation,* 247–48.

[87]Ibid.

[88]Ibid., 247.

[89]Gundry, *The Church,* chap. 14.

[90]Ibid., 166.

[91]Ryrie, *Review,* 175ff.

[92]Gundry, *The Church,* 166–67.

[93]George L. Rose, *Tribulation till Translation* (Glendale, Calif.: Rose, 1942).

[94]John F. Walvoord, *The Blessed Hope and the Tribulation* (Grand Rapids: Zondervan, 1976), 88–90.

[95]Ibid., 89.

[96]Gundry, *The Church,* 34, 129.

[97]This point was made to me in a discussion with my colleague, S. Lewis Johnson.

[98]Gundry, *The Church,* 77–81.

[99]In Revelation 6–19 only these passages give glimpses into heaven: 7:9–8:6; 11:15–19; 12:7–8; 12:10–12; 14:1–5; 15:1–8; 19:1–8. It is not my purpose to argue this point, but pretribulationists commonly argue that the twenty-four elders (e.g., Rev. 4–5) and the bride clothed in fine linen (Rev. 19:7–8) represent the church in heaven.

[100]Walvoord, *Blessed Hope,* 51.

Response: Douglas J. Moo

[1]J. D. Pentecost, *Things to Come: A Study in Biblical Eschatology* (1958; reprint ed., Grand Rapids: Zondervan, 1964), 216.

[2]LSJ, 498.

³Gerhard von Rad, *The Theology of Israel's Historical Traditions,* vol. 1 of *Old Testament Theology* (New York: Harper & Row, 1962), 387–88.

⁴J. H. Thayer, *A Greek-English Lexicon of the New Testament* (New York: Harper & Brothers, 1889), 190.

⁵Brooke Foss Westcott, *The Epistle to the Hebrews* (1892; reprint ed., Grand Rapids: Eerdmans, 1973), 126; F. F. Bruce, *The Epistle to the Hebrews* (Grand Rapids: Eerdmans, 1964), 100, n. 51.

⁶Rudolf Schnackenburg, *Commentary on Chapters 5–12,* vol. 1 of *The Gospel According to St. John* (New York: Seabury, 1980), 383.

⁷G. Kittel and G. Friedrich, eds., *Theological Dictionary of the New Testament,* 10 vols. (Grand Rapids: Eerdmans, 1964–1976), 9:677, s. v. "ὥρα." It is curious that Feinberg quotes another statement from this article, though it is not specifically related to Rev. 3:10.

⁸Although his contention that the use of the word (πειράζω, πειρασμός) suggests the restriction of the trial to non-Christians is wrong, this word is consistently employed in Revelation for trials and temptations that *Christians* are subjected to. In fact, the use of this term with reference to the unbelieving world is one of the most curious aspects of this verse (see on this Schuyler Brown, " 'The Hour of Trial' [Rev 3:10]," *JBL* 85 [1966]:308–14).

Chapter 3

Response: Paul D. Feinberg

¹See J. Oliver Buswell, Jr., *A Systematic Theology of the Christian Religion* (Grand Rapids: Zondervan, 1962), 2:389–90.

²Robert H. Gundry, *The Church and the Tribulation* (Grand Rapids: Zondervan, 1973), 200.

³Ibid., 74–77.

⁴See my discussion "The Meaning of Inerrancy," in Norman L. Geisler, ed., *Inerrancy* (Grand Rapids: Zondervan, 1980), 287–89.

⁵Gundry, *The Church,* 29.

⁶Ibid., 36–37.

Response: Douglas J. Moo

¹While *de* most often has an adversative force, its use as a "continuative" particle is well established (BAG 170; Margaret Thrall, *Greek Particles in the New Testament: Linguistic and Exegetical Studies* [New Testament Tools and Studies 3; Grand Rapids: Eerdmans, 1962], 51–52).

²1 Thess. 4:9, 13; 5:1; 1 Cor. 7:1, 25; 8:1; 12:1; 16:1, 12.

³*The Dark Side of the Millennium: The Problem of Evil in Rev. 20:1–10* (Grand Rapids: Baker, 1980).

⁴Anthony A. Hoekema, *The Bible and the Future* (Grand Rapids: Eerdmans, 1979), 202–3; Lewis, *Dark Side of the Millennium,* 37.

[5]F. Delitzsch, *Isaiah,* Commentary on the Old Testament by C. F. Keil and F. Delitzsch (Grand Rapids: Eerdmans, 1969), 2:491–92.

[6]Robert H. Gundry, *The Church and the Tribulation* (Grand Rapids: Zondervan, 1973), 166.

[7]In agreement with this, see George Eldon Ladd, *A Commentary on the Revelation of John* (Grand Rapids: Eerdmans, 1972), 262–63; G. R. Beasley-Murray, *Revelation,* New Century Bible (London: Oliphants, 1976), 282–83.

[8]Nathaniel West pictured the Millennium as populated by three distinct groups: the raptured church, Israel in the flesh, and "favored" nations (*The Thousand Years: Studies in Eschatology in both Testaments* [Fincastle, Va.: Scripture Truth, n.d.], 308–9).

Chapter 4

[1]Jesus' application of the abomination of desolation (Dan. 9:27) to an eschatological event (Mark 13:14) along with numerous allusions to Daniel 9 in Revelation suffice to show that the prophecy did not find complete fulfillment in the first century (cf. Robert D. Culver, *Daniel and the Latter Days* [Chicago: Moody, 1954], 135–60). But there is much to be said for the view that sees the seventieth week as relating to both advents of Christ (cf. Joyce G. Baldwin, *Daniel: An Introduction and Commentary* [Tyndale Old Testament Commentary; Downers Grove, Ill.: InterVarsity, 1978], 168–78).

[2]Cf. Robert H. Gundry, *The Church and the Tribulation* (Grand Rapids: Zondervan, 1973), 25–28.

[3]The doctrine of the Tribulation formulated by, e.g., J. Dwight Pentecost, *Things to Come, A Study in Biblical Eschatology* (Grand Rapids: Zondervan, 1964 [= 1958], 233–35) is largely dependent on texts having to do with the Day of the Lord. Even if the Tribulation is a part of the Day, it is illegitimate to apply to the Tribulation any imagery associated with the Day.

[4]The fact that Mark uses a masculine participle after the neuter *bdelugma* ("abomination") shows that he is thinking of a person.

[5]On the background and meaning of these terms, see B. Rigaux, *Saint Paul: Les Épitres aux Thessaloniciens* (Études Bibliques; Paris: Gabalda, 1956), 196–206; George Milligan, *St. Paul's Epistles to the Thessalonians* (Old Tappan, N. J.: Revell, n.d.), 145–51.

[6]On this point, see: Alexander Reese, *The Approaching Advent of Christ: An Examination of the Teaching of J. N. Darby and His Followers* (London/Edinburgh: Marshall, Morgan and Scott, n.d.), 125–38; Henry W. Frost, *Matthew Twenty-four and the Revelation* (New York: Oxford University Press, 1924), 146–47; J. Barton Payne, *The Imminent Appearing of Christ* (Grand Rapids: Eerdmans, 1962), 47–48; George Eldon Ladd, *The Blessed Hope* (Grand Rapids: Eerdmans, 1956), 63–68.

[7]In favor of the reference being to angels are the parallels in Zech. 14:5, Mark 8:38, and, especially, 2 Thess. 1:7. With respect to 1 Thess. 3:13 it is important to note that angels are called "holy ones" in intertestamental literature. Ernest Best, *The First and Second Epistles to the Thessalonians* (Harper's New Testament Commentaries; New York: Harper & Row, 1972), 152–53; Geerhardus Vos, *The Pauline Eschatology* (Grand Rapids: Eerdmans, 1953), 137; Payne, *Imminent Appearing,* 75–76). On the other hand, Paul consistently uses the term *saints* to denote believers. Milligan (*Thessalonians,* 45) and Leon Morris (*The First and Second Epistles to the Thes-*

salonians [New International Commentary; Grand Rapids: Eerdmans, 1959], 114–15) argue for a reference to both angels and believers.

⁸John F. Walvoord, *The Blessed Hope and the Tribulation: A Biblical and Historical Study of Posttribulationism* (Grand Rapids: Zondervan, 1976), 50.

⁹While Gundry has argued that the *monai* ("dwelling places") are to be regarded as "spiritual abodes in his [Jesus'] own person" (*Church and Tribulation*, 154–55; and in more detail in " 'In my Father's House are many *Monai*' (John 14, 2)" (*Zeitschrift für die Neutestamentliche Wissenschaft* 58 [1967], 68–72), the close connection with "my father's house," which almost certainly represents Heaven, favors the traditional interpretation.

¹⁰*Church and Tribulation*, 153. For the pretribulational interpretation, see Walvoord, *The Return of the Lord* (Grand Rapids: Dunham, 1955), 55.

¹¹For this interpretation, see Charles Hodge, *An Exposition of the First Epistle to the Corinthians* (Grand Rapids: Baker, 1980 [= 1857]); 354; Leon Morris, *The First Epistle of Paul to the Corinthians* (Tyndale New Testament Commentary; Grand Rapids: Eerdmans, 1958), 233.

¹²Contra Walvoord, *Rapture Question*, 34–35.

¹³Reese, *Approaching Advent*, 63.

¹⁴G. Kittel and G. Friedrich, eds., *Theological Dictionary of the New Testament*, 10 vols. (Grand Rapids: Eerdmans, 1964–1976), 7:87, s.v. "σάλπιγξ"; C. K. Barrett, *A Commentary on the First Epistle to the Corinthians* (Harper's New Testament Commentary; New York: Harper & Row, 1968), 381; Morris, *Corinthians*, 234.

¹⁵Contra Vos, *Pauline Eschatology*, 247–51.

¹⁶James Everett Frame, *A Critical and Exegetical Commentary on the Epistles of St. Paul to the Thessalonians* (International Critical Commentary; Edinburgh: T. & T. Clark, 1912), 164; also A. L. Moore, *1 and 2 Thessalonians* (New Century Bible; London: Nelson, 1969), 108–9. Gundry's suggestion, that the Thessalonians believed that the dead would not rise until the end of the Millennium (*Church and Tribulation*, 101), goes beyond what can be legitimately inferred from the text.

¹⁷This seems to be assumed by Walvoord, *Blessed Hope*, 96. The notion that the Thessalonians would have rejoiced in the death of loved ones if they knew that they would thereby escape the Tribulation (D. Edmond Hiebert, *The Thessalonian Epistles: A Call to Readiness* [Chicago: Moody, 1971], 205) is self-refuting. Do all today who hold a posttribulational view rejoice when loved ones die?

¹⁸Reese, *Approaching Advent*, 142.

¹⁹This could indicate that Paul thinks of a specific word of Christ found in the Gospels (such as Matt. 24:31 or John 11:25–26 [for the latter, see Gundry, *Church and Tribulation*, 102–3]); of the tradition of Jesus' teaching on the Parousia (David Wenham, "Paul and the Synoptic Apocalypse" [a paper read at the July, 1980, meeting of the Tyndale House Gospels Research Project], 6, n. 1); of an unknown saying of Jesus (Frame, *Thessalonians*, 171; Morris, *Thessalonians*, 141); or of a revelation received by Paul (Milligan, *Thessalonians*, 58; Hiebert, *Thessalonian Epistles*, 195).

²⁰For these parallels, see especially J. B. Orchard, "Thessalonians and the Synoptic Gospels," *Biblica* 19 (1938): 19–42; Lars Hartman, *Prophecy Interpreted: The Formation of Some Jewish Apocalyptic Texts and of the Eschatological Discourse Mark 13 Par.* (Coniectanea Biblica, New Testament Series I; Lund: Gleerup, 1966), 188–89; Wenham, "Synoptic Apocalypse," 4–5.

²¹Hartman, *Prophecy Interpreted*, 188–89.

²²F. F. Bruce, "1 and 2 Thessalonians," *The New Bible Commentary: Revised*, ed. D. Guthrie and J. A. Motyer (Grand Rapids: Eerdmans, 1970), 1159.

[23]Henry C. Thiessen, *Will the Church Pass Through the Tribulation?* (2nd ed.; New York: Loizeaux Brothers, 1941), 42; Hiebert, *Thessalonian Epistles,* 202.

[24]BAG, 170; cf. also Margaret E. Thrall, *Greek Particles in the New Testament: Linguistic and Exegetical Studies* (New Testament Tools and Studies III; Grand Rapids: Eerdmans, 1962), 51–52.

[25]Cf. H. H. Rowley, *The Faith of Israel: Aspects of Old Testament Thought* (London: SCM, 1956), 178–200.

[26]It is probable that at least eighteen different expressions refer to this concept:

1. "The day": Rom. 13:12, 13 (?); 1 Thess. 5:4; Heb. 11:24
2. "The great day": Jude 6
3. "That day": Matt. 7:22; 24:36; 25:13; Luke 17:31; 21:34; 2 Thess. 1:10; 2 Tim. 1:12, 18; 4:8
4. "The last day": John 6:39, 40, 44, 54; 11:24; 12:48
5. "The day of judgment": Matt. 10:15; 11:22, 24; 12:36; 2 Peter 2:9; 3:7; 1 John 4:17
6. "The day of visitation": 1 Peter 2:12 (?)
7. "The day of wrath": Rom. 2:5
8. "The day when God judges": Rom. 2:16
9. "The evil day": Eph. 6:13
10. "The day of redemption": Eph. 4:30
11. "The day of God": 2 Peter 3:12
12. "The day of God almighty": Rev. 16:14
13. "The day of the Lord": Acts 2:20; 1 Cor. 5:5; 1 Thess. 5:2; 2 Thess. 2:2; 2 Peter 3:10
14. "The day of Christ": Phil. 1:10; 2:16
15. "The day of our Lord Jesus": 2 Cor. 1:14
16. "The day of Jesus Christ": Phil. 1:6
17. "The day of our Lord Jesus Christ": 1 Cor. 1:8
18. "The day of the Son of Man": Luke 17:30

[27]Note particularly the way Paul, when referring to the Day, can combine "Lord" and "Christ" in one expression (1 Cor. 1:8); similarly "Lord" and "Jesus" (2 Cor. 1:14). Surely this suggests that since for Paul Jesus Christ *is* the Lord, he uses terms such as "Day of the Lord" and "Day of Christ" interchangeably. Walvoord makes an interesting admission in his argument for distinguishing "Day of Christ" from "Day of the Lord": "If the pretribulational rapture is established on other grounds, these references seem to refer specifically to the rapture rather than to the time of judgment on the world" (*Blessed Hope,* 119). In other words, the terms by themselves offer no basis for such a distinction.

[28]Herman Ridderbos, *Paul: An Outline of His Theology* (Grand Rapids: Eerdmans, 1975), 530–31. Cf. also George Eldon Ladd, *A Theology of the New Testament* (Grand Rapids: Eerdmans, 1974), 555.

[29]For these points, see E. Michael Rusten, "A Critical Evaluation of Dispensational Interpretation of the Book of Revelation" (New York University Ph.D., 1977), 488–89; Norman F. Douty, *Has Christ's Return Two Stages?* (New York: Pageant, 1956), 76–77.

[30]W. J. Grier, *The Momentous Event: A Discussion of Scripture Teaching on the Second Advent* (London: Banner of Truth Trust, 1941), 71; Payne, *Imminent Appearing,* 68–69.

[31]For these parallels, see especially Wenham, "Synoptic Apocalypse," 10, and Hartman, *Prophecy Interpreted,* 192.

³²*Things to Come,* 161–62; *Rapture Question,* 111–13.

³³On this meaning of the terms *grēgoreō* ("watch") and *nēphō* ("be sober"), see especially Evald Lövestam, *Spiritual Wakefulness in the New Testament* (Lunds Universitets Årsskrift, n.s., 55; Lund: Gleerup, 1963).

The phrase "sons of the day" (v. 5) also probably associates believers with the "Day of the Lord," since the eschatological dimensions of the term are to be included here (Lövestam, *Spiritual Wakefulness,* 49–51; Best, *Thessalonians,* 210; Morris, *Thessalonians,* 156). D. E. H. Whiteley, however (*Thessalonians in the Revised Standard Version* [New Clarendon Bible; Oxford: Oxford University Press, 1969], 78) takes the view that no such eschatological overtones are to be seen in the term.

³⁴Cf., e.g., Frame, *Thessalonians,* 188; Best, *Thessalonians,* 216.

³⁵Johannes Munck, "I Thess. I. 9–10 and the Missionary Preaching of Paul. Textual Exegesis and Hermeneutical Reflexions," *New Testament Studies* 9 (1962/1963): 100.

³⁶Walvoord, *Blessed Hope,* 123–24.

³⁷Allen Beechick, *The Pre-Tribulation Rapture* (Denver: Accent, 1980), 122.

³⁸*Saleuō* ("to be unsettled") ". . . suggests that the readers were driven from their sober sense like a ship from its moorings" (Frame, *Thessalonians,* 248). *Throeō* ("to be troubled"), in the present tense, connotes ". . . a continuous state of nervous excitement and anxiety" (Best, *Thessalonians,* 275).

³⁹John F. Walvoord, *The Thessalonian Epistles* (Findlay, Ohio: Dunham, n.d.), 115; Hiebert, *Thessalonian Epistles,* 304.

⁴⁰It is possible that *enestēken* ("has come") could be translated, "is in the process of coming" (A. Oepke, *Theological Dictionary,* 2:544, n. 2; Ridderbos, *Paul,* 511, n. 68; cf. also Morris, *Thessalonians,* 216–17). The verb cannot mean "is imminent" (Frame, *Thessalonians,* 248–49).

⁴¹Paul never furnishes an *apodosis* (a "then" clause) to complete his protasis ("If first the apostasy does not come and the man of lawlessness is not revealed") in v. 3. But there is general agreement that something like "then that Day has not come" must be supplied (cf. KJV, RSV, NASB, NIV and especially the excellent discussion of Best [*Thessalonians,* 280–81]. Best offers a penetrating critique of the novel theory put forth by Charles H. Giblin [*The Threat to Faith: An Exegetical and Theological Re-examination of 2 Thessalonians 2* (Analecta Biblica 31; Rome: Pontifical Biblical Institute, 1967), 122–35]).

⁴²Desmond Ford (*The Abomination of Desolation in Biblical Eschatology* [Washington, D.C.: University Press of America, 1979], 199–200, 207) provides a good discussion of the parallels between Daniel and the portrayal of Antichrist in the New Testament.

⁴³This interpretation of *apostasia* is based on the usage of the term in biblical Greek and on the observation that a religious rebellion was frequently associated with the time of the end (as in Mark 13:6ff.). Cf., e.g., Gundry, *Church and Tribulation,* 115–16; Ford, *Abomination,* 201–3.

⁴⁴E. Schuyler English, *Re-thinking the Rapture* (Traveler's Rest, S. C.: Southern Bible Book House, 1954), 67–71; Kenneth S. Wuest, "The Rapture: Precisely When?" *Bibliotheca Sacra* 114 (1957): 64–66; Gordon Lewis, "Biblical Evidence for Pretribulationism," *Bibliotheca Sacra* 125 (1968): 217–18; L. J. Wood, *The Bible and Future Events* (Grand Rapids: Zondervan, 1973), 87–88; James Montgomery Boice, *The Last and Future World* (Grand Rapids: Zondervan, 1974), 42–43.

⁴⁵See the full discussion in Gundry, *Church and Tribulation,* 114–18. The impossibility of finding a reference to the Rapture in this word is admitted by the pretribulationists Hiebert (*Thessalonian Epistles,* 305–6) and Walvoord (*Blessed Hope,* 135).

[46]Although Walvoord (*Blessed Hope,* 118) gives this as essentially Paul's answer here, there is simply no evidence in the text for such a reference.

[47]Morris, *Thessalonians,* 228–29. We are assuming, with most commentators, that the subject of the *heōs* clause in v. 7 is the restrainer. It is interesting to note that some of the church fathers already were refuting the view that the restrainer is the Spirit (Rigaux, *Thessaloniciens,* 261).

[48]Gundry, *Church and Tribulation,* 125–26.

[49]Frame, *Thessalonians,* 259–61; Best, *Thessalonians,* 301; D. W. B. Robinson, "II Thess. 2:6: 'That which restrains' or 'That which holds sway'?" *Studia Evangelica* II (Texte und Untersuchungen 87; Berlin: Akademie, 1964), 635–38.

[50]Tertullian, *Apolog.* 32, and many other church fathers; Otto Betz, "Der Katechon," *New Testament Studies* 9 (1962/1963): 283–85.

[51]Milligan, *Thessalonians,* 101; William Hendriksen, *New Testament Commentary: Exposition of I and II Thessalonians* (Grand Rapids: Baker, 1955), 181–82.

[52]Ladd, *Blessed Hope,* 95; Ridderbos, *Paul,* 524–25.

[53]Orchard, "Thessalonians," 40–41; Rusten, "Revelation," 449–57; F. Prat. *The Theology of Saint Paul* (Westminster, Md.: Newman, 1952), 1:80–83.

[54]In the early church Theodoret and Theodore of Mopsuestia; Oscar Cullmann, *Christ and Time: The Primitive Christian Conception of Time and History* (Philadelphia: Westminster, 1950), 164–66; Johannes Munck, *Paul and the Salvation of Mankind* (Richmond, Va.: John Knox, 1959) 36–43; A. L. Moore, *The Parousia in the New Testament* (Supplements to Novum Testamentum, 13; Leiden: Brill, 1966), 112–13; J. Christian Beker, *Paul the Apostle: The Triumph of God in Life and Thought* (Philadelphia: Fortress, 1980), 161.

[55]The view of J. Coppens, according to Giblin (*Threat to Faith,* 14).

[56]Leas Sirard, "La Parousie de l'Antéchrist, 2 Thess 2, 3–9," *Studiorum Paulinorum Congressus Internationalis Catholicus 1961* (Analecta Biblica 17–18; Rome: Pontifical Biblical Institute, 1963) 2:94–99; Giblin, *Threat to Faith,* 164–246.

[57]Ford, *Abomination,* 216–22.

[58]B. B. Warfield, "The Prophecies of St. Paul," *Biblical and Theological Studies* (Grand Rapids: Baker, 1968), 473–74.

[59]C. E. B. Cranfield, "St. Mark 13," *Scottish Journal of Theology* 6 and 7 (1953 and 1954), 6, 195–96; Lloyd Gaston, *No Stone on Another: Studies in the Significance of the Fall of Jerusalem in the Synoptic Gospels* (Supplements to Novum Testamentum 23; Leiden: Brill, 1970), 12.

[60]This phrase undoubtedly is taken from Daniel, where a similar expression occurs in 8:13; 9:27; 11:31; 12:11. Of these, Jesus' use of the term has most in common with 9:27 (Beda Rigaux, "ΒΔΕΛΥΓΜΑ ΤΗΣ ΕΡΗΜΩΣ ΕΩΣ Mc. 13, 14; Matt. 24, 15," *Biblica* 40 (1959), 678–79; Ford, *Abomination,* 153–54). The phrase is usually taken to indicate a detestable idol that causes religious desecration (Cranfield, "Mark 13," 298–99; G. R. Beasley-Murray, *A Commentary on Mark 13* [London: Macmillan, 1957], 55), but it may be that connotations of physical destruction should not be eliminated (Rudolf Pesch, *Naherwartungen: Tradition und Redaktion in Mk 13* [Kommentare und Beiträge zum Alten und Neuen Testament; Düsseldorf: Patmos, 1968], 142; Ford, *Abomination,* 167–68).

[61]John F. Walvoord, "Christ's Olivet Discourse on the End of the Age," *Bibliotheca Sacra* 128 (1971), 208. It is sometimes argued that this phraseology is proverbial and need not be taken in its literal force (Beasley-Murray, *Commentary,* 78).

[62]Contra Alfred Plummer (*An Exegetical Commentary on the Gospel According to S. Matthew* [London: Robert Scott, 1915], 335), Matthew's *eutheōs* ("immediately") cannot be deprived of its temporal force in light of Matthean usage. Nor can "in these days" in Mark 13:27 be taken as a general expression for eschatological time

(contra Henry Barclay Swete, *Commentary on Mark* [Grand Rapids: Kregel, 1977 (= 1913)], 310–11; William Lane, *The Gospel According to Mark,* New International Commentary [Grand Rapids: Eerdmans, 1974], 474).

[63]Marcellus J. Kik, *The Eschatology of Victory* (Nutley, N.J.: Presbyterian and Reformed, 1971), 60–144; R. V. G. Tasker, *The Gospel According to St. Matthew* (Tyndale New Testament Commentary; Grand Rapids: Eerdmans, 1961), 223–27; A. Feuillet, "Le discours de Jésus sur la ruine du temple d'après Marc XIII et Luc XXI:5–36," *Revue Biblique* 55 (1948), 481–502; 56 (1949), 61–92; R. T. France, *Jesus and the Old Testament* (London: Tyndale, 1971), 228–39.

[64]Luke seems to distinguish more carefully between A.D. 70 and the time of the end; many would attribute vv. 8–24 to the destruction of Jerusalem in A.D. 70 and vv. 25ff. to the end (cf. M. J. Lagrange, *L'Evangile selon Saint Luc* [6th ed.; Paris: Gabalda, 1941], 521; William Hendriksen, *New Testament Commentary: Exposition of the Gospel According to Luke* [Grand Rapids: Baker, 1978], 937).

[65]However, David Wenham has made a good case for taking Mark 13:14–23 and parallels as a description of the tribulation that will characterize the entire church age. (His material will appear in published form shortly in a monograph on the Olivet Discourse.) There is much to be said for this view. If adopted, it would mean that the abomination of desolation would have reference to A.D. 70 only. My argument about the church's relationship to this event would therefore lose its force. But my argument about the church's presence during the Tribulation and the witnesses of the Parousia would still stand.

[66]*Blessed Hope,* 86–87. Cf. also W. K. Price, *Jesus' Prophetic Sermon: The Olivet Key to Israel, the Church and the Nations* (Chicago: Moody, 1972), 40–41.

[67]Beechick, recognizing the impact of these parallels with Paul, suggests that Jesus describes both the pretribulational *and* posttribulational Parousia in the Olivet Discourse (*Rapture,* 233–63). But this explanation does not do justice to the clear temporal indicators in the discourse—the Parousia occurs only *after* the Tribulation.

[68]Payne, *Imminent Appearing,* 55. Douty (*Christ's Return,* 33) points out that as early as c. A.D. 100 the elect were understood as the church (in the *Didachē*).

[69]Beasley-Murray, *Commentary,* 93. Walvoord's view, that this text refers to the gathering of peoples into the millennial kingdom ("Olivet Discourse," 326) is adequate as far as it goes, but fails to account for the parallels with Paul's depiction of the Rapture.

[70]Feuillet, "Le discours de Jesus," 75–78; Hartman, *Prophecy Interpreted,* 158; Lane, *Mark,* 476–77.

[71]Walvoord, *Blessed Hope,* 89–90. Walvoord's attempt to bolster his case by appealing to Luke 17:37 is not successful—although this is a very obscure verse, it is improbable that it implies that the body was thrown to the vultures.

[72]James Oliver Buswell, *A Systematic Theology of the Christian Religion* (2 vols. in one; Grand Rapids: Zondervan, 1962) 2:386; I. Howard Marshall, *The Gospel of Luke* (New International Greek Testament Commentary, Grand Rapids: Eerdmans, 1978), 668; Alan Hugh McNeile, *The Gospel According to St. Matthew* (London: MacMillan, 1928), 357; Gundry, *Church and Tribulation,* 137–38.

[73]Cf. Rusten, "Revelation," 204–5. Walvoord gives no reason for his assertion that this language should not here be applied to the Parousia (*The Revelation of Jesus Christ* [Chicago: Moody, 1966], 81). Nor is it legitimate to confine the warning to unbelievers only (contra Beechick, *Rapture,* 172–73).

[74]Although Rusten ("Revelation," 216–19) thinks of the period following the Parousia and Payne of a historical period of suffering (*Imminent Appearing,* 78–79).

[75]In light of Jesus' explicit assertion in the same verse that the disciples will remain in the world, it is difficult to see how John 17:15 could indicate noncontact

NOTES

with the "Evil One." And there is no indication that the spiritual realm of Satan is intended (contra Jeffrey L. Townsend, "The Rapture in Revelation 3:10," *Bibliotheca Sacra* 137 [1980]: 258–59).

⁷⁶For example, the combination *airō ek,* used in John 17:15, would have plainly indicated "take out of."

⁷⁷G. R. Beasley-Murray, *The Book of Revelation* (New Century Bible; London: Marshall, Morgan and Scott, 1974), 101; Robert H. Mounce, *The Book of Revelation,* New International Commentary (Grand Rapids: Eerdmans, 1977), 119; Schuyler Brown, " 'The Hour of Trial' (Rev. 3:10)," *Journal of Biblical Literature* 85 (1966): 310.

⁷⁸*Revelation,* 103.

⁷⁹*Revelation,* 30–31.

⁸⁰Buswell (*Systematic Theology* 2:389–90) and Norman B. Harrison (*The End: Re-thinking the Revelation* [Minneapolis: The Harrison Services, 1941], 116–21) argue that the Rapture of the church is indicated here and that the time is the middle of Daniel's seventieth week.

⁸¹G. B. Caird, *A Commentary on the Revelation of St. John the Divine* (Harper's New Testament Commentary; New York: Harper & Row, 1966), 190; Beasley-Murray, *Revelation,* 228; Gundry, *Church and Tribulation,* 83–84.

⁸²Henry Barclay Swete, *Commentary on Revelation* (Grand Rapids: Kregel, 1977 [= 1913]), 189–90; Gundry, *Church and Tribulation,* 83–88; Rusten, "Revelation," 516–21.

⁸³So, apparently, Walvoord, *Revelation,* 221–22.

⁸⁴Beasley-Murray, *Revelation,* 228; Mounce, *Revelation,* 279–80; Isbon T. Beckwith, *The Apocalypse of John* (Grand Rapids: Baker, 1967 [= 1919]), 662.

⁸⁵Walvoord, *Revelation,* 296–97; Mounce, *Revelation,* 355–56.

⁸⁶Since *tas psuchas* ("the souls") is accusative, it is best taken as a second object after *eidon* (Swete, *Revelation,* 262).

⁸⁷Contra Roy L. Aldrich, "Divisions of the First Resurrection," *Bibliotheca Sacra* 128 (1971): 117–19.

⁸⁸This is probably why John in Rev. 13:9 omits "to the churches" from the familiar refrain, "He who has ears let him hear . . ." (in response to Walvoord, *Revelation,* 103; and Beechick, *Rapture,* 179–79).

⁸⁹Gundry, *Church and Tribulation,* 78.

⁹⁰Caird, *Revelation,* 63; Leon Morris, *The Revelation of St. John,* Tyndale New Testament Commentary (Grand Rapids: Eerdmans, 1969), 88; George Eldon Ladd, *A Commentary on the Revelation of John* (Grand Rapids: Eerdmans, 1972), 75; Beasley-Murray, *Revelation,* 114; Mounce, *Revelation,* 135.

⁹¹Cf. especially André Feuillet, "The Twenty-four Elders of the Apocalypse," *Johannine Studies* (Staten Island: Alba House, 1965), 185–94; J. Massyngberde Ford, *Revelation,* Anchor Bible (Garden City, N. Y.: Doubleday, 1975), 72.

⁹²This reading is certainly preferred over the weakly attested variants.

⁹³See Rusten, "Revelation," 231–53.

⁹⁴Rusten, "Revelation," 133–34.

⁹⁵Most of the differences held out as requiring a distinction between the pretribulational Rapture and the posttribulation coming (cf. Pentecost, *Things to Come,* 206–7; Walvoord, *Rapture Question,* 101–2) are to be explained on the basis of this selectivity. Unless clear contradictions are involved, such differences do not establish a need to separate in time the Parousia events.

⁹⁶Pentecost, *Things to Come,* 168; Walvoord, *Rapture Question,* 82.

⁹⁷*Imminent Appearing.*

⁹⁸See the excellent refutation by Gundry (*Church and Tribulation,* 193–200).

[99]*Church and Tribulation,* 29–43.

[100]See particularly Gundry (*Church and Tribulation,* 30–32) for studies of these words. On *grēgoreō, nēphō* and *agrupneō,* see the excellent treatment of Lövestam, *Spiritual Wakefulness.*

[101]Evidence from Qumran indicates that "generation" could be used to denote the last generation before the end (E. Earle Ellis, *The Gospel of Luke,* New Century Bible, rev. ed. [London: Marshall, Morgan & Scott, 1974], 246–47).

[102]Cf. Frost, *Matthew Twenty-four,* 34–36; Gundry, *Church and Tribulation,* 42–43.

[103]Contra Payne, *Imminent Appearing,* 89–91; Walvoord, *Rapture Question,* 150–51.

[104]Millard J. Erickson, *Contemporary Options in Eschatology: A Study of the Millennium* (Grand Rapids: Baker, 1977), 142; Gundry, *Church and Tribulation,* 37.

[105]See, for instance, *Ep. Barn.* 4; Justin, *Dial. with Trypho,* 110; *Shep. of Hermas,* 1:4, 1–3. I cannot agree with Payne (*Imminent Appearing,* 12–14), who seeks to establish the doctrine of the any-moment Parousia in the Fathers.

Response: Paul D. Feinberg

[1]Daniel B. Wallace, "A Critique of the Posttribulational Understanding of 1 Thessalonians 4:13–18" (paper given at Grace Theological Seminary, 1982), 5–6.

[2]Robert H. Gundry, *The Church and the Tribulation* (Grand Rapids: Zondervan, 1973), 100–102.

[3]Wallace, "A Critique," 4–5.

[4]Zane C. Hodges, "The Rapture in 1 Thessalonians 5:1–11," in *Walvoord: A Tribute,* ed. by Donald K. Campbell (Chicago: Moody, 1982), 68–70; Robert L. Thomas, "1 Thessalonians" in *The Expositor's Bible Commentary* (Grand Rapids: Zondervan, 1978), 11:280–81.

PERSON INDEX

SUBJECT INDEX

Abomination (of desolation), 151, 190–92, 229, 245, 246, 250

American Bible and prophetic conference: resolutions of the 1878 conference, 12–13

Amillennialism, 77

Annual Conference on the Lord's Coming (Los Angeles), 32

Antichrist: judgment on, 16, 107; mentioned, 54, 61, 62, 63, 73, 79, 89, 105–6, 108, 126, 127, 140–42, 165–66, 175, 188–89, 192, 205–6, 209, 218, 220, 228, 249; Parousia, 21

"Any-moment" Rapture view: attacked by Cameron, 23; comfort of, 133–35; and the Danielic image, 19; and Paul the apostle, 117, 126; mentioned, 234, 235; and signs, 130–32. *See also* Niagara Bible Conference; Imminency.

Apantēsis (meeting), 181, 224, 226

Apokalypsis (revelation), 30, 176–77, 227, 238

Apostasia (apostasy), 32, 61, 125, 188–89, 206, 228, 249

Argumentation, nature of, 85

Armageddon, 56–58, 61, 81, 87, 103–5, 112, 115–16, 118, 121–22, 124, 143, 149, 163, 165–66, 173, 213, 215–16, 223

Beast, 79, 84, 104–5, 108–9, 121, 126–27, 140–41, 175, 184, 216

Babylon, 56, 110

Bowls, diagram of, 204, 206; the first, 175; mentioned 56–59, 88, 103, 105, 175, 199, 221, 223; the seventh, 203

Church. *See* Ecclesiology.

Day of the Lord, 57, 60–61, 76, 81, 107, 116–18, 126, 153–54, 156, 160, 173, 179, 182, 183–84, 185–86, 188, 216, 218, 226–28, 241, 245–46, 248–49

Dispensationalism: ecclesiology, 48; initial stage of development in North America, 13; mentioned, 12, 233; posttribulational, 21, 27–28; pretribulational, 39, 48–49

Ecclesia (church), 201–3

Ecclesiology: 35, 35–36, 37, 39, 48, 51, 82–83, 98–99, 135–36, 171–72, 192–96, 201–3, 205–7

Elders (the twenty-four), 201–2, 244

Elect, 194, 229–30, 231

Epiphaneia (manifestation), 30, 176, 177, 238

Episynagō, 195, 230–31

Eternal state, 77–78

Evangelical Free Church of America, 33, 37, 41–42

Exodus, 56–57

Ezēsan, 200–201

Fundamentals, The, 24, 26, 29

Futurism: adopted by premillennialists, 12, 14, 233; and Daniel 9:24–27, 49, 54–55

Gregoreō (watch): 195, 197, 206, 208, 210, 248, 253

Harvest, first, 200

SCRIPTURE INDEX